DOVER · THRIFT · EDITIONS

Great English Essays
From Bacon to Chesterton

Edited by
BOB BLAISDELL

DOVER PUBLICATIONS, INC.
Mineola, New York

DOVER THRIFT EDITIONS

GENERAL EDITOR: MARY CAROLYN WALDREP
EDITOR OF THIS VOLUME: BOB BLAISDELL

Dedication

To my friends, colleagues, and students.
—B.B.

Acknowledgments

"On Pleasure Bent" by George Bernard Shaw is reprinted by permission of The Society of Authors, on behalf of the Bernard Shaw Estate.

"Hours in a Library" by Virginia Woolf is reprinted by permission of The Society of Authors as the Literary Representatives of the Estate of Virginia Woolf.

Copyright

Bibliographical Note

This Dover edition, first published in 2005, is a new anthology of essays reprinted from standard sources. An introductory Note and explanatory footnotes have been specially prepared for the present edition.

Library of Congress Cataloging-in-Publication Data

Great English essays : from Bacon to Chesterton / edited by Bob Blaisdell.
    p. cm. — (Dover thrift editions)
  Includes bibliographical references.
  ISBN 0-486-44082-6 (pbk.)
   1. English essays. I. Blaisdell, Robert. II. Series.

PR1363.G74 2005
824.008—dc22

2005040288

Manufactured in the United States of America
Dover Publications, Inc., 31 East 2nd Street, Mineola, N.Y. 11501

Note

THE PERSONAL ESSAY is perhaps the most attractive of all literary genres. The writer takes for granted our friendship, and we are happy to let him, as he (or she) has no greater desire than to amuse us and himself. The essay is the monologue of conversational writing, but the speaker never forgets we are there, and he rarely tries our patience. He has our attention for as long as we enjoy his company, as long as he keeps us entertained. If he lectures us or sermonizes, he knows, unlike the professor or preacher, that we may, if bored or annoyed, get up and walk off. Because the tension of piquing our interest is not the tension of conversation, but of imagined conversation, he tends to be better behaved, yet wittier, quirkier, more eager to please, than he might be if he really were at our side. "Though naturally pensive," writes Oliver Goldsmith, inviting us along with him on a stroll, "yet I am fond of gay company, and take every opportunity of thus dismissing the mind from duty. From this motive I am often found in the centre of a crowd; and wherever pleasure is to be sold, am always a purchaser. . . .

"Attracted by the serenity of the evening, a friend and I lately went to gaze upon the company in one of the public walks near the city. Here we sauntered together for some time, either praising the beauty of such as were handsome, or the dresses of such as had nothing else to recommend them." ("The Character of an Important Trifler . . .")

It is true, also, that sometimes our essayist is so imposing and authoritative—Samuel Johnson, for instance—that, though he speaks to us, we don't dare squawk. We humbly listen because he expects that we understand that what he has to say is more important and compelling than anything we pipsqueaks could say: "It may be laid down as a position which will seldom deceive, that when a man cannot bear his own company, there is something wrong. He must fly from himself, either because he feels a tediousness in life from the equipoise of an empty mind, which, having no tendency to one motion more than another but as it is impelled by some external power, must always have recourse to foreign objects; or he must be afraid of the intrusion of some unpleasing ideas, and, perhaps, is struggling to escape from the remembrance of a loss, the fear of a calamity, or some other thought of greater horror." ("Spring")

Just as when we are with our friends, essays promise the excitement of our never knowing what the next topic will be. William Hazlitt's favorite essay of his contemporary Charles Lamb is one where the delightful eccentricities of Lamb are less prominent than usual and Lamb turns over the show to an equally eccentric Mrs. Battle: "To those puny objectors against cards, as nurturing the bad passions, [Sarah Battle] would retort, that man is a gaming animal. He must be always trying to get the better in something or other—that this passion can scarcely be more safely expended than upon a game of cards: that cards are a temporary illusion; in truth, a mere drama; for we do but *play* at being mightily concerned, where a few idle shillings are at stake, yet, during the illusion, we *are* as mightily concerned as those whose stake is crowns and kingdoms."

What distinct, wonderful voices our essayists have! First there is Francis Bacon, reputed to be the English author who imported the literary genre of "essaies" from the French originator, Michel de Montaigne. Bacon, a favored courtier of Queen Elizabeth I, drew on his political expertise to make suggestions on the use and abuse of "cunning": "There is a cunning, which we in England call 'the turning of the cat in the pan'; which is, when that which a man says to another, he lays it as if another had said it to him; and, to say truth, it is not easy, when such a matter passed between two, to make it appear from which of them it first moved and began."

There is the voice of Joseph Addison, musing on the character of his creation, Sir Roger de Coverley: "I do not remember I have anywhere mentioned in Sir Roger's character, his custom of saluting every body that passes by him with a good-morrow or a good-night. This the old man does out of the overflowings of his humanity, though at the same time it renders him so popular among all his country neighbours, that it is thought to have gone a good way in making him once or twice knight of the shire. He cannot forbear this exercise of benevolence even in town, when he meets with any one in his morning or evening walk. It broke from him to several boats that passed by us upon the water; but, to the knight's great surprise, as he gave the good-night to two or three young fellows a little before our landing, one of them, instead of returning the civility, asked us what queer old put we had in the boat, and whether he was not ashamed to go a wenching at his years; with a great deal of like Thames-ribaldry." ("Sir Roger de Coverley at Spring-Garden")

There is John Ruskin, the greatest Victorian art critic, who is never not himself, never not emphatically personal: "But not only is there a *partial* and variable mystery thus caused by clouds and vapors throughout great spaces of landscape; there is a continual mystery caused throughout *all* spaces, caused by the absolute infinity of things. WE NEVER SEE ANY-THING CLEARLY. . . . The fact is, that everything we look at, be it large or small, near or distant, has an equal quantity of mystery in it; and the only question is, not how much mystery there is, but at what part of the object mystification begins." ("The Clouds *Are There*")

There is Virginia Woolf, young and up to her ears in books: "For the first time, perhaps, all restrictions have been removed, we can read what we like; libraries are at our command, and, best of all, friends who find themselves in the same position. For days upon end we do nothing but read. It is a time of extraordinary excitement and exaltation. We seem to rush about recognizing heroes. There is a sort of wonderment in our minds that we ourselves are really doing this, and mixed with it the absurd arrogance and desire to show our familiarity with the greatest human beings who have ever lived in the world." ("Hours in a Library")

There is, finally, D. H. Lawrence, as confident, as spirited, as immediate as any of the great writers before him, evoking his memories of (of all wonderful things) the family rabbit: "He had cultivated the bad habit of pensively nibbling certain bits of cloth in the hearth-rug. When chased from this pasture, he would retreat under the sofa. There he would twinkle in Buddhist meditation until suddenly, no one knew why, he would go off like an alarm clock. With a sudden bumping scuffle he would whirl out of the room, going through the doorway with his little ears flying. Then we would hear his thunderbolt hurtling round in the parlour, but before we could follow, the wild streak of Adolph would flash past us, on an electric wind that swept him round the scullery and carried him back, a little mad thing, flying possessed like a ball round the parlour." ("Adolf")

Unlike, for example, an anthology of poetry, where we become aware of an awesome, no longer (seemingly) achievable technical proficiency or a literary chasm between our age and the poet's, these essayists, many of them working on deadline for periodicals, continually suggest a timeless familiarity. There are surprises and tricks, put-ons and depthless revelations. What the writer gives us is himself, at his most casual best, a friend who has come to dinner and is pleased by and responsive to but not awed by the company. Yet, as Hazlitt reminds us: "To write a genuine familiar or truly English style, is to write as any one would speak in common conversation, who had a thorough command and choice of words, or who could discourse with ease, force, and perspicuity, setting aside all pedantic and oratorical flourishes. Or, to give another illustration, to write naturally is the same thing in regard to common conversation, as to read naturally is in regard to common speech. It does not follow that it is an easy thing to give the true accent and inflection to the words you utter, because you do not attempt to rise above the level of ordinary life and colloquial speaking. You do not assume indeed the solemnity of the pulpit, or the tone of stage-declamation: neither are you at liberty to gabble on at a venture, without emphasis or discretion, or to resort to vulgar dialect or clownish pronunciation. You must steer a middle course." ("On Familiar Style")

The awesome Dr. Johnson, musing on the personal essay in one of his hundreds of personal essays, noted, deprecatingly, "A careless glance upon a favourite author, or transient survey of the varieties of life, is sufficient to supply the first hint or seminal idea, which enlarged by the gradual accretion of matter stored in the mind, is by the warmth of fancy easily expanded into flowers, and sometimes ripened into fruit."[1] Among the ripe fruits in this volume are musings on walking, writing, travelling, sleeping, dreaming, pets, friends, food, fires, love, children, and childhood.

Our friends in this volume are the renowned masters of the English essay: Bacon, Addison, Richard Steele, Johnson, Lamb, Hazlitt; the overlooked or forgotten: Thomas Fuller, Abraham Cowley, Alice Meynell, W. H. Hudson, Richard Jefferies; as well as the most famous of British authors who made their reputations in other genres: Swift, Dickens, Thackeray, Trollope, Ruskin, Stevenson, Shaw, Chesterton, Woolf, and Lawrence. And they are all wonderfully entertaining friends.

I have dated the essays whenever the publication dates have been indicated by the authors or previous editors. (For better or worse, the authors are presented chronologically by birth rather than by publication.) Please see the bibliography for the particular editions used, most of which were found in the dark and deep stacks of Columbia University's Butler Library. Due to copyright restrictions, the selections end with 1922. The best anthology covering a similar span and authors is Ernest Rhys's Everyman's Library edition, *A Century of English Essays.* Philip Lopate's excellent *The Art of the Personal Essay* (1994) features international authors from the classical era through the end of the twentieth century.

---

[1] *The Rambler,* No. 184. December 21, 1751.

Contents

*Note: The lettered code in italics following some of the essay titles
is keyed to the list of sources on page xi.*

Sources

Addison, Joseph. *The Works of the Right Honourable Joseph Addison*. Volume 4. London: Bell and Daldy, 1866.

Bacon, Francis. *Bacon's Essays.* Introduction by Sir Henry Newbolt. London: T. Nelson & Sons, ca. 1906.

Birrell, Augustine. *Obiter Dicta.* New York: Charles Scribner's Sons, 1894.

Chalmers, Alexander, ed. *The British Essayists.* Volume 16 [Samuel Johnson]. Boston: Little, Brown and Co., 1856.

Chalmers, Alexander, ed. *The Spectator.* Volumes 1 and 4. New York: D. Appleton and Co., 1864.

Chapman, R. W. *The Portrait of a Scholar and Other Essays Written in Macedonia 1916–1918.* London: Oxford University Press, 1922.

Cowley, Abraham. *Cowley's Prose Works.* Cambridge: Cambridge University Press, 1887.

The Dial. Chicago, 1920.

Goldsmith, Oliver. *The Works of Oliver Goldsmith.* Volume 3. London: George Bell and Sons, 1908.

Hazlitt, William. *Table-Talk, or Original Essays.* London, 1822.

Hudson, W. H. *A Traveller in Little Things.* New York: Dutton, 1921.

The London Magazine, or Gentlemen's Monthly Intelligencer. London, 1778, 1781.

Makower, Stanley V. and Basil H. Blackwell, eds. *A Book of English Essays (1600–1900)*. Oxford: Oxford University Press, 1913. [*EE*]

Meynell, Alice. *Essays*. New York: Charles Scribner's Sons, 1916.

Peacock, William, ed. *English Prose*. Volume 1. Oxford: Oxford University Press, 1921. [*EP*]

Peacock, William, ed. *English Prose from Mandeville to Ruskin*. Oxford: Oxford University Press, 1903. [*EPMR*]

Peacock, William, ed. *Selected English Essays*. Oxford: Oxford University Press, 1912. [*SEE*]

Rhys, Ernest, ed. *A Century of English Essays: An Anthology Ranging from Caxton to R. L. Stevenson*. London: J. M. Dent, 1915. [*CEE*]

Roscoe, Thomas, ed. *The Works of Jonathan Swift*. London: Henry G. Bohn, 1851.

Ruskin, John. *Modern Painters*. Volume 4. New York: John W. Lovell, ca. 1890.

Shaw, George Bernard. *Dramatic Opinions and Essays with an Apology by Bernard Shaw*. New York: Brentano's, 1906.

Steele, Richard. *Steele: Selections from The Tatler, Spectator and Guardian*. Introduction and notes by Austin Dobson. Oxford: Clarendon Press, 1896.

Stevenson, Robert Louis. *Letters and Miscellanies of Robert Louis Stevenson: Sketches, Criticisms, Etc.* New York: Charles Scribner's Sons, 1898.

Thackeray, William Makepeace. *The Complete Works of William Makepeace Thackeray: Roundabout Papers, Etc.* New York: Fred DeFau and Company, 1889.

The Times Literary Supplement. London, 1916.

OF LOVE
Francis Bacon

THE STAGE is more beholding to love, than the life of man. For as to the stage, love is ever matter of comedies, and now and then of tragedies; but in life it doth much mischief; sometimes like a siren, sometimes like a fury. You may observe, that amongst all the great and worthy persons (whereof the memory remaineth, either ancient or recent) there is not one, that hath been transported to the mad degree of love: which shows that great spirits, and great business, do keep out this weak passion. You must except, nevertheless, Marcus Antonius, the half partner of the empire of Rome, and Appius Claudius, the decemvir and lawgiver; whereof the former was indeed a voluptuous man, and inordinate; but the latter was an austere and wise man: and therefore it seems (though rarely) that love can find entrance, not only into an open heart, but also into a heart well fortified, if watch be not well kept. It is a poor saying of Epicurus, *Satis magnum alter alteri theatrum sumus;* as if man, made for the contemplation of heaven, and all noble objects, should do nothing but kneel before a little idol and make himself a subject, though not of the mouth (as beasts are), yet of the eye; which was given him for higher purposes. It is a strange thing, to note the excess of this passion, and how it braves the nature, and value of things, by this; that the speaking in a perpetual hyperbole, is comely in nothing but in love. Neither is it merely in the phrase; for whereas it hath been well said, that the arch-flatterer, with whom all the petty flatterers have intelligence, is a man's self; certainly the lover is more. For there was never proud man thought so absurdly well of himself, as the lover doth of the person loved; and therefore it was well said, That it is impossible to love, and to be wise. Neither doth this weakness appear to others only, and not to the party loved; but to the loved most of all, except the love be reciproque. For it is a true rule, that love is ever rewarded, either with the reciproque, or with an inward and secret contempt. By how much the more, men ought to beware of this passion, which loseth not only other things, but itself! As for the other losses, the poet's relation doth well figure them: that he that preferred Helena, quitted the gifts of Juno and Pallas. For whosoever esteemeth too much of amorous affection, quitteth both riches and wisdom. This passion hath his floods, in very times of weakness; which are great prosperity, and great adversity; though this latter hath been less observed: both which times kindle love, and make it more fervent, and therefore show it to be the child of folly. They do best, who if they cannot but admit love, yet make it keep quarters; and sever it wholly from their serious affairs, and actions, of life; for if it check once with business, it troubleth men's fortunes, and maketh men, that they can no ways be true to their own ends. I know not how, but martial men are given to love: I think, it is but as they are given to wine; for perils commonly ask to be paid in pleasures. There is in man's nature, a secret inclination and motion, towards love of others, which if it be not spent upon some one or a few, doth naturally spread itself towards many, and maketh men become humane and charitable; as it is seen sometime in friars. Nuptial love maketh mankind; friendly love perfecteth it; but wanton love corrupteth, and embaseth it.

OF CUNNING

Francis Bacon

WE TAKE cunning for a sinister, or crooked wisdom; and certainly there is a great difference between a cunning man and a wise man, not only in point of honesty, but in point of ability. There be that can pack the cards, and yet cannot play well; so there are some that are good in canvasses and factions, that are otherwise weak men. Again, it is one thing to understand persons and another thing to understand matters; for many are perfect in men's humours that are not greatly capable of the real part of business, which is the constitution of one that hath studied men more than books. Such men are fitter for practice than for counsel, and they are good but in their own alley: turn them to new men, and they have lost their aim; so as the old rule, to know a fool from a wise man, "Mitte ambos nudos ad ignotos, et videbis,"[1] doth scarce hold for them. And because these cunning men are like haberdashers of small wares, it is not amiss to set forth their shop.

It is a point of cunning to wait upon him with whom you speak, with your eye, as the Jesuits give it in precept—for there be many wise men that have secret hearts and transparent countenances; yet this would be done with a demure abasing of your eye sometimes, as the Jesuits also do use.

Another is, that when you have anything to obtain of present dispatch, you entertain and amuse the party with whom you deal with some other discourse, that he be not too much awake to make objections. I knew a counsellor and secretary that never came to Queen Elizabeth of England with bills to sign but he would always first put her into some discourse of state, that she might the less mind the bills.

The like surprise may be made by moving things when the party is in haste, and cannot stay to consider advisedly of that is moved.

If a man would cross a business that he doubts some other would

---

[1]"Send them naked to strangers, and see."

handsomely and effectually move, let him pretend to wish it well, and move it himself, in such sort as may foil it.

The breaking off in the midst of that one was about to say, as if he took himself up, breeds a greater appetite in him with whom you confer to know more.

And because it works better when anything seemeth to be gotten from you by question, than if you offer it of yourself, you may lay a bait for a question by showing another visage and countenance than you are wont; to the end, to give occasion for the party to ask what the matter is of the change, as Nehemiah did,—"And I had not before that time been sad before the king."

In things that are tender and unpleasing, it is good to break the ice by some whose words are of less weight, and to reserve the more weighty voice to come in as by chance, so that he may be asked the question upon the other's speech; as Narcissus did, in relating to Claudius the marriage of Messalina and Silius.

In things that a man would not be seen in himself, it is a point of cunning to borrow the name of the world; as to say, "The world says," or, "There is a speech abroad."

I knew one that, when he wrote a letter, he would put that which was most material in the postscript, as if it had been a bye matter.

I knew another that, when he came to have speech, he would pass over that he intended most, and go forth, and come back again, and speak of it as a thing he had almost forgot.

Some procure themselves to be surprised at such times as it is like the party, that they work upon, will suddenly come upon them, and be found with a letter in their hand, or doing somewhat which they are not accustomed, to the end they may be apposed of those things which of themselves they are desirous to utter.

It is a point of cunning to let fall those words in a man's own name which he would have another man learn and use, and thereupon take advantage. I knew two that were competitors for the secretary's place in Queen Elizabeth's time, and yet kept good quarter between themselves, and would confer one with another upon the business; and the one of them said that to be a secretary in the declination of a monarchy was a ticklish thing, and that he did not affect it; the other straight caught up those words, and discoursed with divers of his friends, that he had no reason to desire to be secretary in the declining of a monarchy. The first man took hold of it, and found means it was told the queen; who, hearing of a declination of monarchy, took it so ill, as she would never after hear of the other's suit.

There is a cunning, which we in England call "the turning of the cat in the pan"; which is, when that which a man says to another, he lays it as if another had said it to him; and, to say truth, it is not easy, when such a matter passed between two, to make it appear from which of them it first moved and began.

It is a way that some men have, to glance and dart at others by justifying themselves by negatives; as to say, "This I do not"; as Tigellinus did towards Burrhus, saying, "Se non diversas spes, sed incolumitatem imperatoris simpliciter spectare."[2]

Some have in readiness so many tales and stories, as there is nothing they would insinuate but they can wrap it into a tale; which serveth both to keep themselves more in guard, and to make others carry it with more pleasure.

It is a good point of cunning for a man to shape the answer he would have in his own words and propositions, for it makes the other party stick the less.

It is strange how long some men will lie in wait to speak somewhat they desire to say, and how far about they will fetch, and how many other matters they will beat over to come near it; it is a thing of great patience, but yet of much use.

A sudden, bold, and unexpected question doth many times surprise a man, and lay him open. Like to him that, having changed his name, and walking in Paul's, another suddenly came behind him, and called him by his true name, whereat straightways he looked back.

But these small wares and petty points of cunning are infinite, and it were a good deed to make a list of them; for that nothing doth more hurt in a State than that cunning men pass for wise.

But certainly some there are that know the resorts and falls of business, that cannot sink into the main of it; like a house that hath convenient stairs and entries, but never a fair room: therefore you shall see them find out pretty looses in the conclusion, but are no ways able to examine or debate matters; and yet commonly they take advantage of their inability, and would be thought wits of direction. Some build rather upon the abusing of others, and (as we now say) putting tricks upon them, than upon soundness of their own proceedings; but Solomon saith, "Prudens advertit ad gressus suos; stultus divertit ad dolos."[3]

---

[2]"He did not have varying aims; he only cared about the emperor's safety."
[3]"The wise man watches his step; the fool gets distracted."

OF AMBITION
Francis Bacon

AMBITION IS like choler; which is an humor that maketh men active, earnest, full of alacrity, and stirring, if it be not stopped. But if it be stopped, and cannot have his way, it becometh adust, and thereby malign and venomous. So ambitious men, if they find the way open for their rising, and still get forward, they are rather busy than dangerous; but if they be checked in their desires, they become secretly discontent, and look upon men and matters with an evil eye, and are best pleased, when things go backward; which is the worst property in a servant of a prince, or state. Therefore it is good for princes, if they use ambitious men, to handle it, so as they be still progressive and not retrograde; which, because it cannot be without inconvenience, it is good not to use such natures at all. For if they rise not with their service, they will take order, to make their service fall with them. But since we have said, it were good not to use men of ambitious natures, except it be upon necessity, it is fit we speak, in what cases they are of necessity. Good commanders in the wars must be taken, be they never so ambitious; for the use of their service, dispenseth with the rest; and to take a soldier without ambition, is to pull off his spurs. There is also great use of ambitious men, in being screens to princes in matters of danger and envy; for no man will take that part, except he be like a seeled dove, that mounts and mounts, because he cannot see about him. There is use also of ambitious men, in pulling down the greatness of any subject that over-tops; as Tiberius used Marco, in the pulling down of Sejanus. Since, therefore, they must be used in such cases, there resteth to speak, how they are to be bridled, that they may be less dangerous. There is less danger of them, if they be of mean birth, than if they be noble; and if they be rather harsh of nature, than gracious and popular: and if they be rather new raised, than grown cunning, and fortified, in their greatness. It is counted by some, a weakness in princes, to have favorites; but it is, of all others, the best remedy against ambitious great-ones. For when the way of pleasuring, and displeasuring, lieth by the favorite, it is impossible any other should be overgreat. Another means to curb them, is to balance them by others, as proud as they. But then there must be some middle counsellors, to keep things steady; for without that ballast, the ship will roll too much. At the least, a prince may animate and inure some meaner persons, to be as it were scourges, to ambitious men. As for the having of them obnoxious to ruin; if they be of fearful natures, it may do well; but if they be stout and daring, it may precipitate their designs, and prove dangerous. As for the pulling of them down, if the affairs require it, and that it may not be done with safety suddenly, the only way is the interchange, continually, of favors and disgraces; whereby they may not know what to expect, and be, as it were, in a wood. Of ambitions, it is less harmful, the ambition to prevail in great things, than that other, to appear in every thing; for that breeds confusion, and mars business. But yet it is less danger, to have an ambitious man stirring in business, than great in dependences. He that seeketh to be eminent amongst able men, hath a great task; but that is ever good for the public. But he, that plots to be the only figure amongst ciphers, is the decay of a whole age. Honor hath three things in it: the vantage ground to do good; the approach to kings and principal persons; and the raising of a man's own fortunes. He that hath the best of these intentions, when he aspireth, is an honest man; and that prince, that can discern of these intentions in another that aspireth, is a wise prince. Generally, let princes and states choose such ministers, as are more sensible of duty than of rising; and such as love business rather upon conscience, than upon bravery, and let them discern a busy nature, from a willing mind.

OF GARDENS
Francis Bacon

GOD ALMIGHTY first planted a garden, and, indeed, it is the purest of human pleasures; it is the greatest refreshment to the spirits of man, without which buildings and palaces are but gross handyworks: and a man shall ever see, that when ages grow to civility and elegancy, men come to build stately, sooner than to garden finely; as if gardening were the greater perfection. I do hold it, in the royal ordering of gardens, there ought to be gardens for all the months in the year, in which, severally, things of beauty may be then in season. For December and January, and the latter part of November, you must take such things as are green all winter; holly, ivy, bays, juniper, cypress-trees, yew, pines, fir-trees, rosemary, lavender; periwinkle, the white, the purple, and the blue; germander, flag, orange-trees, lemon-trees, and myrtles, if they be stoved; and sweet marjoram, warm set. There followeth, for the latter part of January and February, the mezereon tree, which then blossoms; crocus vernus, both the yellow and the grey; primroses, anemones, the early tulip, hyacinthus orientalis, chamaïris, fritellaria. For March, there come violets, especially the single blue, which are the earliest; the early daffodil, the daisy, the almond-tree in blossom, the peach-tree in blossom, the cornelian-tree in blossom, sweetbriar. In April, follow the double white violet, the wall-flower, the stock-gilliflower, the cowslip, flower-de-luces, and lilies of all natures; rosemary-flowers, the tulip, the double peony, the pale daffodil, the French honeysuckle, the cherry-tree in blossom, the damascene and plum-trees in blossom, the white thorn in leaf, the lilac-tree. In May and June come pinks of all sorts, especially the blush pink; roses of all kinds, except the musk, which comes later; honeysuckles, strawberries, bugloss, columbine, the French marigold, flos Africanus, cherry-tree in fruit, ribes, figs in fruit, rasps, vine flowers, lavender in flowers, the sweet satyrian, with the white flower: herba muscaria, lilium convallium, and apple-tree in blossom. In July come gilliflowers of all varieties, musk roses, the lime-tree in blossom, early pears, and plums in fruit, gennitings, quodlins.

8

In August come plums of all sorts in fruit, pears, apricocks, barberries, filberds, musk melons, monks-hoods, of all colours. In September come grapes, apples, poppies of all colours, peaches, melocotones, nectarines, cornelians, wardens, quinces. In October and the beginning of November come services, medlars, bullaces, roses cut or removed to come late, hollyoaks, and suchlike. These particulars are for the climate of London; but my meaning is perceived, that you may have *ver perpetuum,*[1] as the place affords.

And because the breath of flowers is far sweeter in the air (where it comes and goes, like the warbling of music) than in the hand, therefore nothing is more fit for that delight, than to know what be the flowers and plants that do best perfume the air. Roses, damask and red, are fast flowers of their smells; so that you may walk by a whole row of them, and find nothing of their sweetness; yea, though it be in a morning's dew. Bays, likewise, yield no smell as they grow, rosemary little, nor sweet marjoram; that which, above all others, yields the sweetest smell in the air is the violet; especially the white double violet, which comes twice a-year—about the middle of April, and about Bartholomew-tide. Next to that is the musk rose; then the strawberry leaves dying, with a most excellent cordial smell; then the flower of the vines—it is a little dust like the dust of a bent, which grows upon the cluster in the first coming forth—then sweetbriar, then wallflowers, which are very delightful to be set under a parlour or lower chamber window; then pinks and gilliflowers, especially the matted pink and clove gilliflowers; then the flowers of the lime-tree; then the honeysuckles, so they be somewhat afar off. Of bean-flowers I speak not, because they are field flowers; but those which perfume the air most delightfully, not passed by as the rest, but being trodden upon and crushed, are three, that is, burnet, wild thyme, and water-mints; therefore, you are to set whole alleys of them, to have the pleasure when you walk or tread.

For gardens (speaking of those which are, indeed, prince-like, as we have done of buildings), the contents ought not well to be under thirty acres of ground, and to be divided into three parts; a green in the entrance, a heath or desert in the going forth, and the main garden in the midst, besides alleys on both sides; and I like well that four acres of ground be assigned to the green, six to the heath, four and four to either side, and twelve to the main garden. The green hath two pleasures: the one, because nothing is more pleasant to the eye than green grass kept finely shorn; the other, because it will give you a fair alley in the midst, by which you may go in front upon a stately hedge, which is to enclose

---

[1] Eternal spring.

the garden: but because the alley will be long, and, in great heat of the
year, or day, you ought not to buy the shade in the garden by going in
the sun through the green, therefore you are, of either side the green, to
plant a covert alley, upon carpenters' work, about twelve feet in height,
by which you may go in shade into the garden. As for the making of
knots, or figures, with divers-coloured earths, that they may lie under the
windows of the house on that side on which the garden stands, they be
but toys: you may see as good sights many times in tarts. The garden is
best to be square, encompassed on all the four sides with a stately arched
hedge; the arches to be upon pillars of carpenters' work, of some ten feet
high, and six feet broad, and the spaces between of the same dimensions
with the breadth of the arch. Over the arches let there be an entire hedge
of some four feet high, framed also upon carpenters' work; and upon the
upper hedge, over every arch, a little turret, with a belly enough to
receive a cage of birds: and over every space between the arches some
other little figure, with broad plates of round coloured glass gilt, for the
sun to play upon: but this hedge I intend to be raised upon a bank, not
steep, but gently slope, of some six feet, set all with flowers. Also, I understand that this square of the garden, should not be the whole breadth of
the ground, but to leave on either side ground enough for diversity of
side alleys, unto which the two covert alleys of the green may deliver
you; but there must be no alleys with hedges at either end of this great
enclosure—not at the hither end, for letting your prospect upon this fair
hedge from the green—nor at the farther end, for letting your prospect
from the hedge through the arches upon the heath.

For the ordering of the ground within the great hedge, I leave it to
variety of device, advising, nevertheless, that whatsoever form you cast it
into first, it be not too busy, or full of work; wherein I, for my part, do
not like images cut out in juniper or other garden stuff—they be for children. Little low hedges, round like welts, with some pretty pyramids, I
like well; and in some places, fair columns, upon frames of carpenters'
work. I would also have the alleys spacious and fair. You may have closer
alleys upon the side grounds, but none in the main garden. I wish, also,
in the very middle, a fair mount, with three ascents and alleys, enough
for four to walk abreast; which I would have to be perfect circles, without any bulwarks or embossments; and the whole mount to be thirty feet
high, and some fine banqueting-house, with some chimneys neatly cast,
and without too much glass.

For fountains, they are a great beauty and refreshment; but pools mar
all, and make the garden unwholesome, and full of flies and frogs.
Fountains I intend to be of two natures, the one that sprinkleth or
spouteth water; the other a fair receipt of water, of some thirty or forty
feet square, but without any fish, or slime, or mud. For the first, the orna-

ments of images, gilt, or of marble, which are in use, do well; but the main matter is so to convey the water as it never stay, either in the bowls or in the cistern—that the water be never by rest discoloured, green or red, or the like, or gather any mossiness or putrefaction; besides that, it is to be cleansed every day by the hand—also some steps up to it, and some fine pavement about it do well. As for the other kind of fountain, which we may call a bathing pool, it may admit much curiosity and beauty, wherewith we will not trouble ourselves: as, that the bottom be finely paved, and with images; the sides likewise; and withal embellished with coloured glass, and such things of lustre, encompassed also with fine rails of low statues; but the main point is the same which we mentioned in the former kind of fountain, which is, that the water be in perpetual motion, fed by a water higher than the pool, and delivered into it by fair spouts, and then discharged away under ground, by some equality of bores, that it stay little: and for fine devices of arching water without spilling, and making it rise in several forms (of feathers, drinking glasses, canopies, and the like), they be pretty things to look on, but nothing to health and sweetness.

For the heath, which was the third part of our plot, I wished it to be framed as much as may be to a natural wildness. Trees I would have none in it, but some thickets made only of sweetbriar and honeysuckle, and some wild vines amongst, and the ground set with violets, strawberries, and primroses; for these are sweet, and prosper in the shade, and these are to be in the heath here and there, not in any order. I like also little heaps, in the nature of mole-hills (such as are in wild heaths), to be set, some with wild thyme, some with pinks, some with germander, that gives a good flower to the eye; some with periwinkle, some with violets, some with strawberries, some with cowslips, some with daisies, some with red roses, some with lilium convallium, some with sweetwilliams red, some with bear's-foot, and the like low flowers, being withal sweet and sightly—part of which heaps to be with standards of little bushes pricked upon their top, and part without—the standards to be roses, juniper, holly, berberries (but here and there, because of the smell of their blossom), red currents, gooseberries, rosemary, bays, sweetbriar, and suchlike; but these standards to be kept with cutting, that they grow not out of course.

For the side grounds, you are to fill them with variety of alleys, private to give a full shade; some of them wheresoever the sun be. You are to frame some of them likewise for shelter, that, when the wind blows sharp, you may walk as in a gallery; and those alleys must be likewise hedged at both ends, to keep out the wind, and these closer alleys must be ever finely gravelled, and no grass, because of going wet. In many of these alleys, likewise, you are to set fruit-trees of all sorts, as well upon the walls as in ranges; and this should be generally observed, that the borders wherein you plant your fruit-trees be fair, and large, and low, and not steep, and set with fine flowers, but thin and sparingly, lest they deceive the trees. At the end of both the side grounds I would have a mount of some pretty height, leaving the wall of the enclosure breast-high, to look abroad into the fields.

For the main garden, I do not deny but there should be some fair alleys ranged on both sides, with fruit-trees, and some pretty tufts of fruit-trees and arbours with seats, set in some decent order; but these to be by no means set too thick, but to leave the main garden so as it be not close, but the air open and free. For as for shade, I would have you rest upon the alleys of the side grounds, there to walk, if you be disposed, in the heat of the year or day; but to make account, that the main garden is for the more temperate parts of the year, and, in the heat of summer, for the morning and the evening, or overcast days.

For aviaries, I like them not, except they be of that largeness as they may be turfed, and have living plants and bushes set in them, that the birds may have more scope and natural nestling, and that no foulness appear on the floor of the aviary. So I have made a platform of a princely garden, partly by precept, partly by drawing—not a model, but some general lines of it—and in this I have spared for no cost; but it is nothing for great princes, that, for the most part, taking advice with workmen, with no less cost, set their things together, and sometimes add statues, and such things, for state and magnificence, but nothing to the true pleasure of a garden.

THE GOOD SCHOOLMASTER

Thomas Fuller

THERE IS scarce any profession in the commonwealth more necessary, which is so slightly performed. The reasons whereof I conceive to be these: First, young scholars make this calling their refuge; yea, perchance, before they have taken any degree in the university, commence schoolmasters in the country, as if nothing else were required to set up this profession but only a rod and a ferula. Secondly, others who are able, use it only as a passage to better preferment, to patch the rents in their present fortune, till they can provide a new one, and betake themselves to some more gainful calling. Thirdly, they are disheartened from doing their best with the miserable reward which in some places they receive, being masters to their children and slaves to their parents. Fourthly, being grown rich, they grow negligent, and scorn to touch the school but by the proxy of the usher. But see how well our schoolmaster behaves himself.

His genius inclines him with delight to his profession. Some men had as well be schoolboys as schoolmasters, to be tied to the school, as Cooper's Dictionary and Scapula's Lexicon are chained to the desk therein; and though great scholars, and skilful in other arts, are bunglers in this. But God, of His goodness, hath fitted several men for several callings, that the necessity of Church and State, in all conditions, may be provided for. So that he who beholds the fabric thereof, may say, God hewed out the stone, and appointed it to lie in this very place, for it would fit none other so well, and here it doth most excellent. And thus God mouldeth some for a schoolmaster's life, undertaking it with desire and delight, and discharging it with dexterity and happy success.

He studieth his scholars' natures as carefully as they their books; and ranks their dispositions into several forms. And though it may seem difficult for him in a great school to descend to all particulars, yet experienced schoolmasters may quickly make a grammar of boys' natures, and reduce them all—saving some few exceptions—to these general rules:

1. Those that are ingenious and industrious. The conjunction of two such planets in a youth presage much good unto him. To such a lad a frown may be a whipping, and a whipping a death; yea, where their master whips them once, shame whips them all the week after. Such natures he useth with all gentleness.

2. Those that are ingenious and idle. These think with the hare in the fable, that running with snails—so they count the rest of their schoolfellows—they shall come soon enough to the post, though sleeping a good while before their starting. Oh, a good rod would finely take them napping.

3. Those that are dull and diligent. Wines, the stronger they be, the more lees they have when they are new. Many boys are muddy-headed till they be clarified with age, and such afterwards prove the best. Bristol diamonds are both bright, and squared, and pointed by nature, and yet are soft and worthless; whereas orient ones in India are rough and rugged naturally. Hard, rugged, and dull natures of youth, acquit themselves afterwards the jewels of the country, and therefore their dulness at first is to be borne with, if they be diligent. That schoolmaster deserves to be beaten himself who beats nature in a boy for a fault. And I question whether all the whipping in the world can make their parts which are naturally sluggish rise one minute before the hour nature hath appointed.

4. Those that are invincibly dull, and negligent also. Correction may reform the latter, not amend the former. All the whetting in the world can never set a razor's edge on that which hath no steel in it. Such boys he consigneth over to other professions. Shipwrights and boat-makers will choose those crooked pieces of timber which other carpenters refuse. Those may make excellent merchants and mechanics which will not serve for scholars.

He is able, diligent, and methodical in his teaching; not leading them rather in a circle than forwards. He minces his precepts for children to swallow, hanging clogs on the nimbleness of his own soul, that his scholars may go along with him.

He is and will be known to be an absolute monarch in his school. If cockering mothers proffer him money to purchase their sons' exemption from his rod—to live, as it were, in a peculiar, out of their master's jurisdiction—with disdain he refuseth it, and scorns the late custom in some places of commuting whipping into money, and ransoming boys from the rod at a set price. If he hath a stubborn youth, correction-proof, he debaseth not his authority by contesting with him, but fairly, if he can, puts him away before his obstinacy hath infected others.

He is moderate in inflicting deserved correction. Many a schoolmaster better answereth the name *paidotribes* than *paidagogos*,[1] rather tearing his scholars' flesh with whipping than giving them good education. No wonder if his scholars hate the muses, being presented unto them in the shape of fiends and furies.

Such an Orbilius mars more scholars than he makes. Their tyranny hath caused many tongues to stammer which spake plain by nature, and whose stuttering at first was nothing else but fears quavering on their speech at their master's presence; and whose mauling them about their heads hath dulled those who in quickness exceeded their master.

He makes his school free to him who sues to him *in formâ pauperis*. And surely learning is the greatest alms that can be given. But he is a beast who, because the poor scholar cannot pay him his wages, pays the scholar in his whipping; rather are diligent lads to be encouraged with all excitements to learning. This minds me of what I have heard concerning Mr. Bust, that worthy late schoolmaster of Eton, who would never suffer any wandering begging scholar—such as justly the statute hath ranked in the fore-front of rogues—to come into his school, but would thrust him out with earnestness—however privately charitable unto him—lest his schoolboys should be disheartened from their books, by seeing some scholars after their studying in the university preferred to beggary.

He spoils not a good school to make thereof a bad college, therein to teach his scholars logic. For, besides that logic may have an action of trespass against grammar for encroaching on her liberties, syllogisms are solecisms taught in the school, and oftentimes they are forced afterwards in the university to unlearn the fumbling skill they had before.

Out of his school he is no way pedantical in carriage or discourse; contenting himself to be rich in Latin, though he doth not gingle with it in every company wherein he comes.

To conclude, let this, amongst other motives, make schoolmasters careful in their place—that the eminences of their scholars have commended the memories of their schoolmasters to posterity, who, otherwise in obscurity, had altogether been forgotten. Who had ever heard of R. Bond, in Lancashire, but for the breeding of learned Ascham, his scholar? or of Hartgrave, in Brundly School, in the same county, but because he was the first did teach worthy Dr. Whitaker? Nor do I honour the memory of Mulcaster for anything so much as his scholar, that gulf of learning, Bishop Andrews. This made the Athenians, the day before the great feast of Theseus, their founder, to sacrifice a ram to the memory of Conidas, his schoolmaster, that first instructed him.

---

[1] Wrestling coach.

OF DREAMS

Owen Feltham

DREAMS ARE notable means of discovering our own inclinations. The wise man learns to know himself as well by the night's black mantle, as the searching beams of day. In sleep, we have the naked and natural thoughts of our souls: outward objects interpose not, either to shuffle in occasional cogitations, or hale out the included fancy. The mind is then shut up in the Borough of the body; none of the Cinque Ports of the Isle of Man are then open, to in-let any strange disturbers. Surely, how we fall to vice, or rise to virtue, we may by observation find in our dreams. It was the wise Zeno that said, he could collect a man by his dreams. For then the soul, stated in a deep repose, bewrayed her true affections: which, in the busy day, she would either not show, or not note. It was a custom among the Indians, when their kings went to their sleep, to pray with piping acclamations, that they might have happy dreams; and withal consult well for their subjects' benefit: as if the night had been a time, wherein they might grow good and wise. And certainly, the wise man is the wiser for his sleeping, if he can order well in the day, what the eyeless night presenteth him. Every dream is not to be counted of: nor yet are all to be cast away with contempt. I would neither be a Stoic, superstitious in all; nor yet an Epicure, considerate of none. If the physician may by them judge of the disease of the body, I see not but the divine may do so, concerning the soul. I doubt not but the genius of the soul is waking, and motive even in the fastest closures of the imprisoning eyelids. But to presage from these thoughts of sleep, is a wisdom that I would not reach to. The best use we can make of dreams, is observation: and by that, our own correction, or encouragement. For 'tis not doubtable, but that the mind is working, in the dullest depth of sleep. I am confirmed by Claudian,

> Day thoughts, transwinged from th' industrious breast,
> All seem re-acted in the night's dumb rest.
> When the tired Huntsman his repose begins,

Then flies his mind to woods, and wild beasts' dens.
Judges dream cases: Champions seem to run,
With their night Coursers, the vain bounds to shun.
Love hugs his rapes, the Merchant traffic minds.
The miser thinks he some lost treasure finds.
And to the thirsty sick some potion cold
Stiff flattering sleep inanely seems to hold.
Yea, and in th' age of silent rest, even I,
Troubled with Art's deep musings, nightly lie.

Dreams do sometimes call us to a recognition of our inclinations, which print the deeper, in so undisturbed times. I could wish men to give them their consideration, but not to allow them their trust, though sometimes 'tis easy to pick out a profitable moral. Antiquity had them in much more reverence, and did oft account them prophecies, as is easily found in the sacred volume: and among the Heathen, nothing was more frequent. Astyages had two, of his daughter Mandana, the vine and the flood. Calphurnia of her Caesar; Hecuba of Paris; and almost every prince among them, had his fate showed in interpreted dreams. Galen tells of one, that dreamed his thigh was turned to stone, and soon after, it was struck with a dead palsy. The aptness of the humours to the like effects might suggest something to the mind, then apt to receive. So that I doubt not but either to preserve health or amend the life, dreams may, to a wise observer, be of special benefit. I would neither depend upon any, to incur a prejudice, nor yet cast them all away in a prodigal neglect and scorn. I find it of one that having long been troubled with the paining spleen: that he dreamt, if he opened a certain vein, between two of his fingers, he should be cured: which he awaked, did, and mended. But indeed I would rather believe this, than be drawn to practise after it. These plain predictions are more rare foretellings, used to be lapped in more obscure folds: and now, that art lost, Christianity hath settled us to less inquisition; it is for a Roman soothsayer to read those darker spirits of the night, and tell that still Dictator, his dream of his mother signified his subjecting the world to himself. 'Tis now so out of use, that I think it not to be recovered. And were it not for the power of the Gospel, in crying down the vanity of men, it would appear a wonder, how a science so pleasing to humanity, should fall so quite to ruin.

OF MYSELF
Abraham Cowley

IT IS a hard and nice subject for a man to write of himself; it grates his own heart to say any thing of disparagement, and the reader's ears to hear any thing of praise from him. There is no danger from me of offending him in this kind; neither my mind, nor my body, nor my fortune, allow me any materials for that vanity. It is sufficient for my own contentment, that they have preserved me from being scandalous, or remarkable on the defective side. But, besides that, I shall here speak of myself, only in relation to the subject of these precedent discourses, and shall be likelier thereby to fall into the contempt, than rise up to the estimation, of most people.

As far as my memory can return back into my past life, before I knew, or was capable of guessing, what the world, or the glories or business of it, were, the natural affections of my soul gave me a secret bent of aversion from them, as some plants are said to turn away from others, by an antipathy imperceptible to themselves, and inscrutable to man's understanding. Even when I was a very young boy at school, instead of running about on holydays and playing with my fellows, I was wont to steal from them, and walk into the fields, either alone with a book, or with some one companion, if I could find any of the same temper. I was then, too, so much an enemy to all constraint, that my masters could never prevail on me, by any persuasions or encouragements, to learn without book the common rules of grammar; in which they dispenced with me alone, because they found I made a shift to do the usual exercise out of my own reading and observation. That I was then of the same mind as I am now (which, I confess, I wonder at, myself) may appear by the latter end of an ode, which I made when I was but thirteen years old, and which was then printed with many other verses. The beginning of it is boyish; but of this part, which I here set down (if a very little were corrected), I should hardly now be much ashamed.

18

9.

This only grant me, that my means may lye
Too low for envy, for contempt too high.
   Some honour I would have,
Not from great deeds, but good alone;
The unknown are better, than ill known:
   Rumour can ope the grave.
Acquaintance I would have, but when 't depends
Not on the number, but the choice of friends.

10.

Books should, not business, entertain the light,
And sleep, as undisturb'd as death, the night.
   My house a cottage more
Than palace; and should fitting be
For all my use, no luxurie.
My garden painted o'er
With nature's hand, nor art's; and pleasures yield,
Horace might envy in his Sabine field.

11.

Thus would I double my life's fading space;
For he, that runs it well, twice runs his race.
   And in this true delight,
These unbought sports, that happy state,
I would not fear, nor wish, my fate;
   But boldly say each night,
To-morrow let my sun his beams display,
Or, in clouds hide them; I have liv'd, to-day.

You may see by it, I was even then acquainted with the poets (for the conclusion is taken out of Horace); and perhaps it was the immature and immoderate love of them, which stampt first, or rather engraved, the characters in me: they were like letters cut into the bark of a young tree, which with the tree still grow proportionably. But, how this love came to be produced in me so early, is a hard question: I believe, I can tell the particular little chance that filled my head first with such chimes of verse, as have never since left ringing there: for I remember, when I began to read, and take some pleasure in it, there was wont to lye in my mother's parlour (I know not by what accident, for she herself never in her life read any book but of devotion) but there was wont to lye Spenser's works: this I happened to fall upon, and was infinitely delighted with the stories of the knights, and gyants, and monsters, and brave houses, which I found every where there (though my understanding had little to do with all this); and, by degrees, with the tinkling of the rhyme and dance of the numbers; so that, I think, I had read him all over before I was twelve years old.

With these affections of mind, and my heart wholly set upon letters, I went to the university; but was soon torn from thence by that violent public storm, which would suffer nothing to stand where it did, but rooted up every plant, even from the princely cedars to me the hyssop. Yet, I had as good fortune as could have befallen me in such a tempest; for I was cast by it into the family of one of the best persons, and into the court of one of the best princesses, of the world. Now, though I was here engaged in ways most contrary to the original design of my life, that is, into much company, and no small business, and into a daily sight of greatness, both militant and triumphant (for that was the state then of the English and French courts); yet all this was so far from altering my opinion, that it only added the confirmation of reason to that which was before but natural inclination. I saw plainly all the paint of that kind of life, the nearer I came to it; and that beauty, which I did not fall in love with, when, for aught I knew, it was real, was not like to bewitch or intice me, when I saw that it was adulterate. I met with several great persons, whom I liked very well; but could not perceive that any part of their greatness was to be liked or desired, no more than I would be glad or content to be in a storm, though I saw many ships which rid safely and bravely in it: a storm would not agree with my stomach, if it did with my courage. Though I was in a crowd of as good company as could be found any where, though I was in business of great and honourable trust, though I ate at the best table, and enjoyed the best conveniences for present subsistence that ought to be desired by a man of my condition in banishment and publick distresses; yet I could not abstain from renewing my old school-boy's wish, in a copy of verses to the same effect:

1.

Well then; I now do plainly see
This busie world and I shall ne'er agree.
The very Honey of all earthly joy
 Does of all meats the soonest cloy,
 And they (methinks) deserve my pity,
Who for it can endure the stings,
The crowd, and buzz, and murmurings
 Of this great hive, the city.

2.

Ah, yet, ere I descend to th' grave,
May I a small house and large garden have!
And a few friends, and many books, both true,
 Both wise, and both delightful too!
 And since love ne'er will from me flee,
A Mistress moderately fair,
And good as guardian-angels are,
 Only beloved, and loving me!

3.

   O Fountains, when in you shall I
Myself, eas'd of unpeaceful thoughts espy?
Oh fields! Oh woods! when, when shall I be made,
   The happy tenant of your shade?
   Here's the spring-head of pleasure's flood;
Where all the riches lye, that she
   Has coyn'd and stampt for good.

4.

   Pride and Ambition here
Only in far fetcht metaphors appear;
Here nought but winds can hurtful murmurs scatter,
   And nought but Echo flatter,
   The gods when they descended hither
From heaven, did always chuse their way;
And therefore we may boldly say,
   That 'tis the way to thither.

5.

   How happy here should I
And one dear she live, and embracing dye!
She who is all the world, and can exclude
   In desarts solitude
   I should have then this only fear,
Lest men, when they my pleasures see,
Should hither throng to live like me,
   And so make a city here.

And I never then proposed to myself any other advantage from his majesty's happy restauration, but the getting into some moderately convenient retreat in the country; which I thought, in that case, I might easily have compassed, as well as some others, with no greater probabilities or pretences, have arrived to extraordinary fortunes: but I had before written a shrewd prophesie against myself; and I think Apollo inspired me in the truth, though not in the elegance, of it:

   Thou neither great at court, nor in the war,
   Nor at th' exchange shalt be, nor at the wrangling bar.
   Content thyself with the small barren praise,
      That neglected verse does raise.
     She spake; and all my years to come
      Took their unlucky doom.
   Their several ways of life let others chuse,
     Their several pleasures let them use;
   But I was born for Love, and for a Muse.

4.

With Fate what boots it to contend?
Such I began, such am, and so must end.
　The Star, that did my being frame,
　Was but a lambent flame,
　And some small light it did dispence,
　But neither heat nor influence.
No matter, Cowley; let proud Fortune see,
That thou canst her despise no less than she does thee.
　Let all her gifts the portion be
　Of folly, lust, and flatterie,
　Fraud, extortion, calumnie,
　Murder, infidelitie,
　Rebellion and hypocrisie.
　Do thou not grieve nor blush to be,
　As all th' inspired tuneful men,
And all thy great forefathers were, from Homer down to Ben.

However, by the failing of the forces which I had expected, I did not acquit the design which I had resolved on; I cast myself into it a *corps perdu,* without making capitulations, or taking counsel of fortune. But God laughs at a man, who says to his soul, *Take thy ease:* I met presently not only with many little incumbrances and impediments, but with so much sickness (a new misfortune to me) as would have spoiled the happiness of an emperor as well as mine: yet I do neither repent, nor alter my course. "Non ego perfidum dixi sacramentum"; nothing shall separate me from a mistress, which I have loved so long, and have now at last married; though she neither has brought me a rich portion, nor lived yet so quietly with me as I hoped from her:

　　　　———"Nec vos, dulcissima mundi
　　Nomina, vos Musæ, libertas, otia, libri,
　　Hortique sylvæque, anima remanente, relinquam."
　　　　　　　Nor by me e'er shall you,
　　You, of all names the sweetest, and the best,
　　You, Muses, books, and liberty, and rest;
　　You, gardens, fields, and woods, forsaken be,
　　As long as life itself forsakes not me.

A MEDITATION UPON A BROOMSTICK,

ACCORDING TO THE STYLE AND MANNER OF THE HON. ROBERT BOYLE'S MEDITATIONS

Jonathan Swift

THIS SINGLE stick, which you now behold ingloriously lying in that neglected corner, I once knew in a flourishing state in a forest; it was full of sap, full of leaves, and full of boughs; but now in vain does the busy art of man pretend to vie with nature, by tying that withered bundle of twigs to its sapless trunk; it is now at best but the reverse of what it was, a tree turned upside down, the branches on the earth, and the root in the air; it is now handled by every dirty wench, condemned to do her drudgery, and, by a capricious kind of fate, destined to make her things clean, and be nasty itself; at length, worn out to the stumps in the service of the maids, it is either thrown out of doors, or condemned to the last use of kindling a fire. When I beheld this, I sighed, and said within myself: Surely mortal man is a broomstick! nature sent him into the world strong and lusty, in a thriving condition, wearing his own hair on his head, the proper branches of this reasoning vegetable, until the axe of intemperance has lopped off his green boughs, and left him a withered trunk; he then flies to art, and puts on a periwig, valuing himself upon an unnatural bundle of hairs, all covered with powder, that never grew on his head; but now should this our broomstick pretend to enter the scene, proud of those birchen spoils it never bore, and all covered with dust, though the sweepings of the finest lady's chamber, we should be apt to ridicule and despise its vanity. Partial judges that we are of our own excellences, and other men's defaults!

But a broomstick, perhaps you will say, is an emblem of a tree standing on its head: and pray, what is man but a topsy-turvy creature, his animal faculties perpetually mounted on his rational, his head where his heels should be—grovelling on the earth! and yet, with all his faults, he sets up to be a universal reformer and corrector of abuses, a remover of grievances; rakes into every slut's corner of nature, bringing hidden corruptions to the light, and raises a mighty dust where there was none before, sharing deeply all the while in the very same pollutions he pretends to sweep away. His last days are spent in slavery to women, and generally the least deserving; till, worn to the stumps, like his brother-besom, he is either kicked out of doors, or made use of to kindle flames for others to warm themselves by.

A MODEST PROPOSAL

FOR PREVENTING THE CHILDREN OF POOR PEOPLE IN IRELAND FROM BEING A BURTHEN TO THEIR PARENTS OR COUNTRY, AND FOR MAKING THEM BENEFICIAL TO THE PUBLIC.

Jonathan Swift

IT IS a melancholy object to those who walk through this great town or travel in the country, when they see the streets, the roads, and cabin doors, crowded with beggars of the female sex, followed by three, four, or six children, all in rags and importuning every passenger for an alms. These mothers, instead of being able to work for their honest livelihood, are forced to employ all their time in strolling to beg sustenance for their helpless infants: who as they grow up either turn thieves for want of work, or leave their dear native country to fight for the pretender in Spain,[1] or sell themselves to the Barbadoes.

I think it is agreed by all parties that this prodigious number of children in the arms, or on the backs, or at the heels of their mothers, and frequently of their fathers, is in the present deplorable state of the kingdom a very great additional grievance; and therefore whoever could find out a fair, cheap, and easy method of making these children sound useful members of the commonwealth, would deserve so well of the public as to have his statue set up for a preserver of the nation.

But my intention is very far from being confined to provide only for the children of professed beggars; it is of a much greater extent, and shall take in the whole number of infants at a certain age who are born of parents in effect as little able to support them as those who demand our charity in the streets.

---

[1] *pretender in Spain*] James Francis Edward Stuart (1688–1766), son of the deposed James II of England and claimant to the British throne. During his exile, he distinguished himself fighting for the French in the War of the Spanish Succession (1701–1714).

As to my own part, having turned my thoughts for many years upon this important subject, and maturely weighed the several schemes of our projectors, I have always found them grossly mistaken in their computation. It is true, a child just dropped from its dam, may be supported by her milk for a solar year, with little other nourishment; at most not above the value of 2*s*., which the mother may certainly get, or the value in scraps by her lawful occupation of begging; and it is exactly at one year old that I propose to provide for them in such a manner as instead of being a charge upon their parents or the parish, or wanting food and raiment for the rest of their lives, they shall on the contrary contribute to the feeding, and partly to the clothing, of many thousands.

There is likewise another great advantage in my scheme, that it will prevent those voluntary abortions, and that horrid practice of women murdering their bastard children, alas, too frequent among us! sacrificing the poor innocent babes I doubt more to avoid the expense than the shame, which would move tears and pity in the most savage and inhuman breast.

The number of souls in this kingdom being usually reckoned one million and a half, of these I calculate there may be about 200,000 couple whose wives are breeders; from which number I subtract 30,000 couple who are able to maintain their own children, (although I apprehend there cannot be so many, under the present distresses of the kingdom;) but this being granted, there will remain 170,000 breeders. I again subtract 50,000 for those women who miscarry, or whose children die by accident or disease within the year. There only remain 120,000 children of poor parents annually born. The question therefore is, how this number shall be reared and provided for? which as I have already said under the present situation of affairs is utterly impossible by all the methods hitherto proposed. For we can neither employ them in handicraft or agriculture; we neither build houses (I mean in the country) nor cultivate land; they can very seldom pick up a livelihood by stealing, till they arrive at six years old, except where they are of towardly parts; although I confess they learn the rudiments much earlier, during which time, they can however be properly looked upon only as probationers; as I have been informed by a principal gentleman in the county of Cavan, who protested to me that he never knew above one or two instances under the age of six, even in a part of the kingdom so renowned for the quickest proficiency in that art.

I am assured by our merchants, that a boy or a girl before twelve years old is no saleable commodity; and even when they come to this age they will not yield above 3*l*. or 3*l*. 2*s*. 6*d*. at most on the exchange; which cannot turn to account either to the parents or kingdom, the charge of nutriment and rags having been at least four times that value.

I shall now therefore humbly propose my own thoughts, which I hope will not be liable to the least objection.

I have been assured by a very knowing American of my acquaintance in London, that a young healthy child well nursed is at a year old a most delicious, nourishing, and wholesome food, whether stewed, roasted, baked, or boiled; and I make no doubt that it will equally serve in a fricassee or a ragout.

I do therefore humbly offer it to public consideration that of the 120,000 children already computed, 20,000 may be reserved for breed, whereof only one-fourth part to be males; which is more than we allow to sheep, black cattle or swine; and my reason is, that these children are seldom the fruits of marriage, a circumstance not much regarded by our savages, therefore one male will be sufficient to serve four females. That the remaining 100,000 may at a year old, be offered in sale to the persons of quality and fortune through the kingdom; always advising the mother to let them suck plentifully in the last month, so as to render them plump and fat for a good table. A child will make two dishes at an entertainment for friends; and when the family dines alone, the fore or hind quarter will make a reasonable dish, and seasoned with a little pepper or salt will be very good boiled on the fourth day, especially in winter.

I have reckoned upon a medium that a child just born will weigh 12 pounds, and in a solar year, if tolerably nursed, will increase to 28 pounds.

I grant this food will be somewhat dear, and therefore very proper for landlords, who, as they have already devoured most of the parents, seem to have the best title to the children.

Infant's flesh will be in season throughout the year, but more plentifully in March, and a little before and after: for we are told by a grave author, an eminent French physician, that fish being a prolific diet, there are more children born in Roman catholic countries about nine months after Lent than at any other season; therefore, reckoning a year after Lent, the markets will be more glutted than usual, because the number of popish infants is at least three to one in this kingdom: and therefore it will have one other collateral advantage, by lessening the number of papists among us.

I have already computed the charge of nursing a beggar's child (in which list I reckon all cottagers, labourers, and four-fifths of the farmers) to be about 2s. per annum, rags included; and I believe no gentleman would repine to give 10s. for the carcass of a good fat child, which as I have said will make four dishes of excellent nutritive meat, when he has only some particular friend or his own family to dine with him. Thus the squire will learn to be a good landlord, and grow popular among his tenants; the mother will have 8s. net profit, and be fit for work till she produces another child.

Those who are more thrifty (as I must confess the times require) may flay the carcass; the skin of which artificially dressed will make admirable gloves for ladies, and summer boots for fine gentlemen.

As to our city of Dublin, shambles may be appointed for this purpose in the most convenient parts of it, and butchers we may be assured will not be wanting; although I rather recommend buying the children alive than dressing them hot from the knife as we do roasting pigs.

A very worthy person, a true lover of his country and whose virtues I highly esteem, was lately pleased in discoursing on this matter to offer a refinement upon my scheme. He said that many gentlemen of this kingdom, having of late destroyed their deer, he conceived that the want of venison might be well supplied by the bodies of young lads and maidens, not exceeding 14 years of age nor under 12; so great a number of both sexes in every country being now ready to starve for want of work and service; and these to be disposed of by their parents if alive, or otherwise by their nearest relations. But with due deference to so excellent a friend and so deserving a patriot, I cannot be altogether in his sentiments; for as to the males, my American acquaintance assured me, from frequent experience, that their flesh was generally tough and lean, like that of our schoolboys by continual exercise, and their taste disagreeable; and to fatten them would not answer the charge. Then as to the females, it would I think with humble submission be a loss to the public, because they soon would become breeders themselves: and besides, it is not improbable that some scrupulous people might be apt to censure such a practice, (although indeed very unjustly,) as a little bordering upon cruelty; which, I confess, has always been with me the strongest objection against any project, how well soever intended.

But in order to justify my friend, he confessed that this expedient was put into his head by the famous Psalmanazar,[2] a native of the island Formosa, who came from thence to London above twenty years ago; and in conversation told my friend, that in his country when any young person happened to be put to death, the executioner sold the carcass to persons of quality as a prime dainty; and that in his time the body of a plump girl of 15, who was crucified for an attempt to poison the emperor, was sold to his imperial majesty's prime minister of state, and other great mandarins of the court, in joints from the gibbet, at 400 crowns. Neither indeed can I deny, that if the same use were made of several plump young girls in this town, who without one single groat to their fortunes cannot stir abroad without a

---

[2] *Psalmanazar*] George Psalmanazar (c. 1679–1763), French literary imposter who "translated" the Church of England catechism and a book about Formosa (Taiwan) into "Formosan," a language he invented.

chair, and appear at playhouse and assemblies in foreign fineries which they never will pay for, the kingdom would not be the worse.

Some persons of a desponding spirit are in great concern about that vast number of poor people, who are aged, diseased, or maimed, and I have been desired to employ my thoughts what course may be taken to ease the nation of so grievous an encumbrance. But I am not in the least pain upon that matter, because it is very well known that they are every day dying and rotting by cold and famine, and filth and vermin, as fast as can be reasonably expected. And as to the young labourers they are now in almost as hopeful a condition; they cannot get work, and consequently pine away for want of nourishment, to a degree that if at any time they are accidentally hired to common labour, they have not strength to perform it; and thus the country and themselves are happily delivered from the evils to come.

I have too long digressed and therefore shall return to my subject. I think the advantages by the proposal which I have made, are obvious and many as well as of the highest importance.

For first, as I have already observed, it would greatly lessen the number of papists, with whom we are yearly over-run, being the principal breeders of the nation as well as our most dangerous enemies; and who stay at home on purpose to deliver the kingdom to the pretender, hoping to take their advantage by the absence of so many good protestants, who have chosen rather to leave their country than stay at home and pay tithes against their conscience to an episcopal curate.

Secondly, The poorer tenants will have something valuable of their own, which by law may be made liable to distress and help to pay their landlord's rent, their corn and cattle being already seized, and money a thing unknown.

Thirdly, Whereas the maintenance of an 100,000 children, from two years old and upward, cannot be computed at less than 10s. a-piece per annum, the nation's stock will be thereby increased 50,000l. per annum, beside the profit of a new dish introduced to the tables of all gentlemen of fortune in the kingdom who have any refinement in taste. And the money will circulate among ourselves, the goods being entirely of our own growth and manufacture.

Fourthly, The constant breeders, beside the gain of 8s. sterling per annum by the sale of their children, will be rid of the charge of maintaining them after the first year.

Fifthly, This food would likewise bring great custom to taverns; where the vintners will certainly be so prudent as to procure the best receipts for dressing it to perfection, and consequently have their houses frequented by all the fine gentlemen, who justly value themselves upon their knowledge in good eating: and a skilful cook, who understands how to oblige his guests, will contrive to make it as expensive as they please.

Sixthly, This would be a great inducement to marriage, which all wise nations have either encouraged by rewards or enforced by laws and penalties. It would increase the care and tenderness of mothers toward their children, when they were sure of a settlement for life to the poor babes, provided in some sort by the public, to their annual profit or expense. We should see an honest emulation among the married women, which of them could bring the fattest child to the market. Men would become as fond of their wives during the time of their pregnancy as they are now of their mares in foal, their cows in calf, their sows when they are ready to farrow; nor offer to beat or kick them (as is too frequent a practice) for fear of a miscarriage.

Many other advantages might be enumerated. For instance, the addition of some thousand carcasses in our exportation of barreled beef, the propagation of swine's flesh, and improvement in the art of making good bacon, so much wanted among us by the great destruction of pigs, too frequent at our table; which are no way comparable in taste or magnificence to a well-grown, fat, yearling child, which roasted whole will make a considerable figure at a lord mayor's feast or any other public entertainment. But this and many others I omit, being studious of brevity.

Supposing that 1000 families in this city would be constant customers for infants' flesh, beside others who might have it at merry-meetings, particularly at weddings and christenings, I compute that Dublin would take off annually about 20,000 carcasses; and the rest of the kingdom (where probably they will be sold somewhat cheaper) the remaining 80,000.

I can think of no one objection that will possibly be raised against this proposal, unless it should be urged that the number of people will be thereby much lessened in the kingdom. This I freely own, and it was indeed one principal design in offering it to the world. I desire the reader will observe, that I calculate my remedy for this one individual kingdom of Ireland and for no other that ever was, is, or I think ever can be upon earth. Therefore let no man talk to me of other expedients: of taxing our absentees at 5s. a pound: of using neither clothes nor household furniture except what is of our own growth and manufacture: of utterly rejecting the materials and instruments that promote foreign luxury: of curing the expensiveness of pride, vanity, idleness, and gaming in our women: of introducing a vein of parsimony, prudence, and temperance: of learning to love our country, in the want of which we differ even from LAPLANDERS and the inhabitants of TOPINAMBOO: of quitting our animosities and factions, nor acting any longer like the Jews, who were murdering one another at the very moment their city was taken: of being a little cautious not to sell our country and conscience for nothing: of teaching landlords to have at least one degree of mercy toward their tenants: lastly, of putting a spirit of honesty, industry, and skill into our shopkeepers, who, if a resolution could now be taken to buy only our negative goods, would immediately unite to cheat and exact upon us in the price, the measure, and the goodness, nor could ever yet be brought to make one fair proposal of just dealing though often and earnestly invited to it.

Therefore I repeat, let no man talk to me of these and the like expedients, till he has at least some glimpse of hope that there will be ever some hearty and sincere attempt to put them in practice.

But as to myself, having been wearied out for many years with offering vain, idle, visionary thoughts, and at length utterly despairing of success I fortunately fell upon this proposal; which, as it is wholly new, so it has something solid and real, of no expense and little trouble, full in our own power and whereby we can incur no danger in disobliging ENGLAND. For this kind of commodity will not bear exportation, the flesh being of too tender a consistence to admit a long continuance in salt, although perhaps I could name a country which would be glad to eat up our whole nation without it.

After all, I am not so violently bent upon my own opinion as to reject any offer proposed by wise men, which shall be found equally innocent, cheap, easy, and effectual. But before something of that kind shall be advanced in contradiction to my scheme, and offering a better, I desire the author or authors will be pleased maturely to consider two points. First, as things now stand, how they will be able to find food and raiment for 100,000 useless mouths and backs. And secondly, there being a round million of creatures in human figure throughout this kingdom, whose whole subsistence put into a common stock would leave them in debt 2,000,000*l.* sterling, adding those who are beggars by profession to the bulk of farmers, cottagers, and labourers, with their wives and children who are beggars in effect; I desire those politicians who dislike my overture, and may perhaps be so bold as to attempt an answer, that they will first ask the parents of these mortals, whether they would not at this day think it a great happiness to have been sold for food at a year old in the manner I prescribe, and thereby have avoided such a perpetual scene of misfortunes as they have since gone through by the oppression of landlords, the impossibility of paying rent without money or trade, the want of common sustenance, with neither house nor clothes to cover them from the inclemencies of the weather, and the most inevitable prospect of entailing the like or greater miseries upon their breed for ever.

I profess, in the sincerity of my heart, that I have not the least personal interest in endeavoring to promote this necessary work, having no other motive than the public good of my country, by advancing our trade, providing for infants, relieving the poor, and giving some pleasure to the rich. I have no children by which I can propose to get a single penny; the youngest being nine years old, and my wife past child-bearing.

SIR ROGER DE COVERLEY
AT SPRING-GARDEN

Joseph Addison

Criminibus debent hortos.—
Juv. Sat. i. 75.
A beauteous garden, but by vice maintain'd.

As I WAS sitting in my chamber, and thinking on a subject for my next
Spectator, I heard two or three irregular bounces at my landlady's door,
and, upon the opening of it, a loud cheerful voice inquiring whether the
philosopher was at home. The child who went to the door answered
very innocently, that he did not lodge there. I immediately recollected
that it was my good friend sir Roger's voice; and that I had promised to
go with him on the water to Spring-Garden, in case it proved a good
evening. The knight put me in mind of my promise from the bottom of
the staircase, but told me that if I was speculating he would stay below
till I had done. Upon my coming down, I found all the children of the
family got about my old friend; and my landlady herself, who is a notable
prating gossip, engaged in a conference with him; being mightily pleased
with his stroking her little boy upon the head, and bidding him to be a
good child and mind his book.

We were no sooner come to the Temple-stairs, but we were surrounded with a crowd of watermen, offering us their respective services.
Sir Roger, after having looked about him very attentively, spied one with
a wooden leg, and immediately gave him orders to get his boat ready. As
we were walking towards it, "You must know," says sir Roger, "I never
make use of any body to row me, that has not either lost a leg or an arm.
I would rather bate him a few strokes of his oar than not employ an honest man, that has been wounded in the queen's service. If I was a lord or
a bishop, and kept a barge, I would not put a fellow in my livery that had
not a wooden leg."

My old friend, after having seated himself, and trimmed the boat with his coachman, who, being a very sober man, always serves for ballast on these occasions, we made the best of our way for Faux-hall. Sir Roger obliged the waterman to give us the history of his right leg; and, hearing that he had left it at La Hogue, with many particulars which passed in that glorious action, the knight, in the triumph of his heart, made several reflections on the greatness of the British nation; as, that one Englishman could beat three Frenchmen; that we could never be in danger of popery so long as we took care of our fleet; that the Thames was the noblest river in Europe; that London bridge was a greater piece of work than any of the seven wonders of the world; with many other honest prejudices which naturally cleave to the heart of a true Englishman.

After some short pause, the old knight, turning about his head twice or thrice, to take a survey of this great metropolis, bid me observe how thick the city was set with churches, and that there was scarce a single steeple on this side Temple-bar. "A most heathenish sight!" says sir Roger: "there is no religion at this end of the town. The fifty new churches will very much mend the prospect; but church-work is slow, church-work is slow."

I do not remember I have anywhere mentioned in sir Roger's character, his custom of saluting every body that passes by him with a good-morrow or a good-night. This the old man does out of the overflowings of his humanity, though at the same time it renders him so popular among all his country neighbours, that it is thought to have gone a good way in making him once or twice knight of the shire. He cannot forbear this exercise of benevolence even in town, when he meets with any one in his morning or evening walk. It broke from him to several boats that passed by us upon the water; but, to the knight's great surprise, as he gave the good-night to two or three young fellows a little before our landing, one of them, instead of returning the civility, asked us what queer old put we had in the boat, and whether he was not ashamed to go a wenching at his years; with a great deal of the like Thames-ribaldry. Sir Roger seemed a little shocked at first, but at length assuming a face of magistracy, told us, that if he were a Middlesex justice, he would make such vagrants know that her majesty's subjects were no more to be abused by water than by land.

We were now arrived at Spring-Garden, which is exquisitely pleasant at this time of the year. When I considered the fragrancy of the walks and bowers, with the choirs of birds that sung upon the trees, and the loose tribe of people that walked under their shades, I could not but look upon the place as a kind of Mahometan paradise. Sir Roger told me, it put him in mind of a little coppice by his house in the country, which his chaplain used to call an aviary of nightingales. "You must understand," says the knight, "there is nothing in the world that pleases a man in love so much as your nightingale. Ah, Mr. Spectator, the many moon-light nights that I have walked by myself, and thought on the widow by the music of the nightingale!" He here fetched a deep sigh, and was falling into a fit of musing, when a mask, who came behind him, gave him a gentle tap upon the shoulder, and asked him if he would drink a bottle of mead with her. But the knight, being startled at so unexpected a familiarity, and displeased to be interrupted in his thoughts of the widow, told her she was a wanton baggage; and bid her go about her business.

We concluded our walk with a glass of Burton ale, and a slice of hung beef. When we had done eating ourselves, the knight called a waiter to him, and bid him carry the remainder to a waterman that had but one leg. I perceived the fellow stared upon him at the oddness of the message, and was going to be saucy; upon which I ratified the knight's command with a peremptory look.

As we were going out of the garden, my old friend thinking himself obliged, as a member of the quorum, to animadvert upon the morals of the place, told the mistress of the house, who sat at the bar, that he should be a better customer to her garden, if there were more nightingales, and fewer strumpets.

THE TORY FOX-HUNTER

Joseph Addison

Studiis rudis, sermone barbarus, impetu strenuus, manu
promptus, cogitatione celer. Vell. Paterc.[1]

FOR THE honour of his Majesty, and the safety of his government, we
cannot but observe that those who have appeared the greatest enemies to
both are of that rank of men, who are commonly distinguished by the
title of Fox-hunters. As several of these have had no part of their education in cities, camps, or courts, it is doubtful whether they are of greater
ornament or use to the nation in which they live. It would be an everlasting reproach to politics, should such men be able to overturn an
establishment which has been formed by the wisest laws, and is supported by the ablest heads. The wrong notions and prejudices which
cleave to many of these country gentlemen, who have always lived out
of the way of being better informed, are not easy to be conceived by a
person who has never conversed with them.

That I may give my readers an image of these rural statesmen, I shall,
without further preface, set down an account of a discourse I chanced to
have with one of them some time ago. I was travelling towards one of the
remote parts of England, when about three o'clock in the afternoon, seeing a country gentleman trotting before me with a spaniel by his horse's
side, I made up to him. Our conversation opened, as usual, upon the
weather; in which we were very unanimous; having both agreed that it
was too dry for the season of the year. My fellow-traveller, upon this,
observed to me that there had been no good weather since the
Revolution. I was a little startled at so extraordinary a remark, but would
not interrupt him till he proceeded to tell me of the fine weather they
used to have in King Charles the Second's reign. I only answered that I

---

[1] "He was uneducated, a rude speaker, bold in action, quick in plans."

did not see how the badness of the weather could be the king's fault; and, without waiting for his reply, asked him whose house it was we saw upon the rising ground at a little distance from us. He told me it belonged to an old fanatical cur, Mr. Such-a-one. "You must have heard of him," says he "he's one of the Rump." I knew the gentleman's character upon hearing his name, but assured him, that to my knowledge he was a good churchman: "Ay!" says he, with a kind of surprise, "We were told in the country, that he spoke twice, in the queen's time, against taking off the duties upon French claret." This naturally led us into the proceedings of late parliaments, upon which occasion he affirmed roundly, that there had not been one good law passed since King William's accession to the throne, except the act for preserving the game. I had a mind to see him out, and therefore did not care for contradicting him. "Is it not hard," says he, "that honest gentlemen should be taken into custody of messengers to prevent them from acting according to their consciences? But," says he, "what can we expect when a parcel of factious sons of whores——" He was going on in great passion, but chanced to miss his dog, who was amusing himself about a bush, that grew at some distance behind us. We stood still till he had whistled him up; when he fell into a long panegyric upon his spaniel, who seemed, indeed, excellent in his kind: but I found the most remarkable adventure of his life was, that he had once like to have worried a dissenting teacher. The master could hardly sit on his horse for laughing all the while he was giving me the particulars of his story, which I found had mightily endeared his dog to him, and as he himself told me, had made him a great favourite among all the honest gentlemen of the country. We were at length diverted from this piece of mirth by a post-boy, who winding his horn at us, my companion gave him two or three curses, and left the way clear for him. "I fancy," said I, "that post brings news from Scotland. I shall long to see the next Gazette." "Sir," says he, "I make it a rule never to believe any of your printed news. We never see, sir, how things go, except now and then in Dyer's Letter, and I read that more for the style than the news. The man has a clever pen, it must be owned. But is it not strange that we should be making war upon Church of England men with Dutch and Swiss soldiers, men of anti-monarchical principles? these foreigners will never be loved in England, sir; they have not that wit and good-breeding that we have." I must confess I did not expect to hear my new acquaintance value himself upon these qualifications, but finding him such a critic upon foreigners, I asked him if he had ever travelled; he told me, he did not know what travelling was good for, but to teach a man to ride the great horse, to jabber French, and to talk against passive obedience; to which he added, that he scarce ever knew a traveller in his life who had not forsaken his principles, and lost his hunting-seat. "For my part," says he, "I and my father before me have always been for passive obedience, and shall be always for opposing a prince who makes use of ministers that are of another opinion. But where do you intend to inn to-night? (for we were now come in sight of the next town;) I can help you to a very good landlord if you will go along with me. He is a lusty, jolly fellow, that lives well, at least three yards in the girth, and the best Church of England man upon the road." I had a curiosity to see this high-church inn-keeper, as well as to enjoy more of the conversation of my fellow-traveller, and therefore readily consented to set our horses together for that night. As we rode side by side through the town, I was let into the characters of all the principal inhabitants whom we met in our way. One was a dog, another a whelp, another a cur, and another the son of a bitch, under which several denominations were comprehended all that voted on the Whig side, in the last election of burgesses. As for those of his own party, he distinguished them by a nod of his head, and asking them how they did by their Christian names. Upon our arrival at the inn, my companion fetched out the jolly landlord, who knew him by his whistle. Many endearments and private whispers passed between them; though it was easy to see by the landlord's scratching his head that things did not go to their wishes. The landlord had swelled his body to a prodigious size, and worked up his complexion to a standing crimson by his zeal for the prosperity of the church, which he expressed every hour of the day, as his customers dropped in, by repeated bumpers. He had not time to go to church himself, but, as my friend told me in my ear, had headed a mob at the pulling down of two or three meeting-houses. While supper was preparing, he enlarged upon the happiness of the neighbouring shire; "For," says he, "there is scarce a Presbyterian in the whole county, except the bishop." In short, I found by his discourse that he had learned a great deal of politics, but not one word of religion, from the parson of his parish; and, indeed, that he had scarce any other notion of religion, but that it consisted in hating Presbyterians. I had a remarkable instance of his notions in this particular. Upon seeing a poor decrepit old woman pass under the window where we sat, he desired me to take notice of her; and afterwards informed me, that she was generally reputed a witch by the country people, but that, for his part, he was apt to believe she was a Presbyterian.

Supper was no sooner served in, than he took occasion from a shoulder of mutton that lay before us, to cry up the plenty of England, which would be the happiest country in the world, provided we would live within ourselves. Upon which, he expatiated on the inconveniences of trade, that carried from us the commodities of our country, and made a parcel of upstarts as rich as men of the most ancient families of England. He then declared frankly, that he had always been against all treaties and alliances with foreigners: "Our wooden walls," says he, "are our security, and we may bid defiance to the whole world, especially if they should attack us when the militia is out." I ventured to reply, that I had as great an opinion of the English fleet as he had; but I could not see how they could be paid, and manned, and fitted out, unless we encouraged trade and navigation. He replied, with some vehemence, that he would undertake to prove trade would be the ruin of the English nation. I would fain have put him upon it; but he contented himself with affirming it more eagerly, to which he added two or three curses upon the London merchants, not forgetting the directors of the bank. After supper he asked me if I was an admirer of punch; and immediately called for a sneaker. I took this occasion to insinuate the advantages of trade, by observing to him, that water was the only native of England that could be made use of on this occasion: but that the lemons, the brandy, the sugar, and the nutmeg were all foreigners. This put him into some confusion; but the landlord, who overheard me, brought him off, by affirming, that for constant use, there was no liquor like a cup of English water, provided it had malt enough in it. My squire laughed heartily at the conceit, and made the landlord sit down with us. We sat pretty late over our punch; and, amidst a great deal of improving discourse, drank the healths of several persons in the country, whom I had never heard of, that, they both assured me, were the ablest statesmen in the nation; and of some Londoners, whom they extolled to the skies for their wit, and who, I knew, passed in town for silly fellows. It being now midnight, and my friend perceiving by his almanac that the moon was up, he called for his horse, and took a sudden resolution to go to his house, which was at three miles' distance from the town, after having bethought himself that he never slept well out of his own bed. He shook me very heartily by the hand at parting, and discovered a great air of satisfaction in his looks, that he had met with an opportunity of showing his parts, and left me a much wiser man than he found me.

MEDITATIONS IN WESTMINSTER ABBEY

Joseph Addison

Pallida mors æquo pulsat pede pauperum tabernas
   Regumque turres O beate Sexti.
Vitæ summa brevis spem nos vetat inchoare longam,
   Jam te premet nox, fubulæque manes,
Et domus exilis Plutonia.—
HOR. 1 Od. iv. 13.

With equal foot, rich friend, impartial fate
Knocks at the cottage, and the palace gate:
Life's span forbids thee to extend thy cares,
And stretch thy hopes beyond thy years:
Night soon will seize, and you must quickly go
To story'd ghosts, and Pluto's house below.
CREECH.

WHEN I am in a serious humour, I very often walk by myself in Westminster Abbey; where the gloominess of the place, and the use to which it is applied, with the solemnity of the building, and the condition of the people who lie in it, are apt to fill the mind with a kind of melancholy, or rather thoughtfulness, that is not disagreeable. I yesterday passed a whole afternoon in the church-yard, the cloisters, and the church, amusing myself with the tomb-stones and inscriptions that I met with in those several regions of the dead. Most of them recorded nothing else of the buried person, but that he was born upon one day, and died upon another: the whole history of his life being comprehended in those two circumstances that are common to all mankind. I could not but look upon these registers of existence, whether of brass or marble, as a kind of satire upon the departed persons; who left no other memorial of them, but that they were born, and that they died. They put me in mind of several persons mentioned in the battles of heroic poems, who have sounding names given them, for no other reason but that they may be killed, and are celebrated for nothing but being knocked on the head.

Γλαύκόν τε Μεδόντα τε Θερσιλοχόν τε.
HOM.

Glaucumque, Medontaque, Thersilochumque.
VIRG.

Glaucus, and Medon, and Thersilochus.

The life of these men is finely described in holy writ by "the path of an arrow," which is immediately closed up and lost.

Upon my going into the church, I entertained myself with the digging of a grave; and saw in every shovel-full of it that was thrown up, the fragment of a bone or skull intermixt with a kind of fresh mouldering earth, that some time or other had a place in the composition of an human body. Upon this I began to consider with myself, what innumerable multitudes of people lay confused together under the pavement of that ancient cathedral; how men and women, friends and enemies, priests and soldiers, monks and prebendaries, were crumbled amongst one another, and blended together in the same common mass; how beauty, strength, and youth, with old age, weakness, and deformity, lay undistinguished in the same promiscuous heap of matter.

After having thus surveyed this great magazine of mortality, as it were in the lump, I examined it more particularly by the accounts which I found on several of the monuments which are raised in every quarter of that ancient fabric. Some of them were covered with such extravagant epitaphs, that if it were possible for the dead person to be acquainted with them, he would blush at the praises which his friends have bestowed on him. There are others so excessively modest, that they deliver the character of the person departed in Greek or Hebrew, and by that means are not understood once in a twelvemonth. In the poetical quarter, I found there were poets who had no monuments, and monuments which had no poets. I observed, indeed, that the present war had filled the church with many of these uninhabited monuments, which had been erected to the memory of persons whose bodies were perhaps buried in the plains of Blenheim, or in the bosom of the ocean.

I could not but be very much delighted with several modern epitaphs, which are written with great elegance of expression and justness of thought, and therefore do honour to the living as well as to the dead. As a foreigner is very apt to conceive an idea of the ignorance or politeness of a nation from the turn of their public monuments and inscriptions, they should be submitted to the perusal of men of learning and genius before they are put in execution. Sir Cloudesly Shovel's monument has very often given me great offence. Instead of the brave rough English admiral, which was the distinguishing character of that plain gallant man, he is represented on his tomb by the figure of a beau, dressed in a long periwig, and reposing himself upon velvet cushions under a canopy of state. The inscription is answerable to the monument; for, instead of celebrating the many remarkable actions he had performed in the service of his country, it acquaints us only with the manner of his death, in which it was impossible for him to reap any honour. The Dutch, whom we are apt to despise for want of genius, show an infinitely greater taste of antiquity and politeness in their buildings and works of this nature, than what we meet with in those of our own country. The monuments of their admirals, which have been erected at the public expense, represent them like themselves, and are adorned with rostral crowns and naval ornaments, with beautiful festoons of sea-weed, shells, and coral.

But to return to our subject. I have left the repository of our English kings for the contemplation of another day, when I shall find my mind disposed for so serious an amusement. I know that entertainments of this nature are apt to raise dark and dismal thoughts in timorous minds and gloomy imaginations; but for my own part, though I am always serious, I do not know what it is to be melancholy; and can therefore take a view of nature in her deep and solemn scenes, with the same pleasure as in her most gay and delightful ones. By this means I can improve myself with those objects, which others consider with terror. When I look upon the tombs of the great, every emotion of envy dies in me; when I read the epitaphs of the beautiful, every inordinate desire goes out; when I meet with the grief of parents upon a tomb-stone, my heart melts with compassion; when I see the tomb of the parents themselves, I consider the vanity of grieving for those whom we must quickly follow. When I see kings lying by those who deposed them, when I consider rival wits placed side by side, or the holy men that divided the world with their contests and disputes, I reflect with sorrow and astonishment on the little competitions, factions, and debates of mankind. When I read the several dates of the tombs, of some that died yesterday, and some six hundred years ago, I consider that great day when we shall all of us be contemporaries, and make our appearance together.

JACK LIZARD

Richard Steele

JACK LIZARD was about fifteen when he was first entered in the university, and being a youth of a great deal of fire, and a more than ordinary application to his studies, it gave his conversation a very particular turn. He had too much spirit to hold his tongue in company; but at the same time so little acquaintance with the world, that he did not know how to talk like other people.

After a year and half's stay at the university, he came down among us to pass away a month or two in the country. The first night after his arrival, as we were at supper, we were all of us very much improved by Jack's table-talk. He told us, upon the appearance of a dish of wild-fowl, that according to the opinion of some natural philosophers they might be lately come from the moon. Upon which the Sparkler bursting out into a laugh, he insulted her with several questions relating to the bigness and distance of the moon and stars; and after interrogatory would be winking upon me, and smiling at his sister's ignorance. Jack gained his point; for the mother was pleased, and all the servants stared at the learning of their young master. Jack was so encouraged at this success, that for the first week he dealt wholly in paradoxes. It was a common jest with him to pinch one of his sister's lap-dogs, and afterwards prove he could not feel it. When the girls were sorting a set of knots, he would demonstrate to them that all the ribbands were of the same colour; or rather, says Jack, of no colour at all. My Lady Lizard her self, though she was not a little pleas'd with her son's improvements, was one day almost angry with him; for having accidentally burnt her fingers as she was lighting the lamp for her tea-pot; in the midst of her anguish, Jack laid hold of the opportunity to instruct her that there was no such thing as heat in fire. In short, no day pass'd over our heads, in which Jack did not imagine he made the whole family wiser than they were before.

That part of his conversation which gave me the most pain, was what pass'd among those country gentlemen that came to visit us. On such occasions Jack usually took upon him to be the mouth of the company; and thinking himself obliged to be very merry, would entertain us with a great many odd sayings and absurdities of their college-cook. I found this fellow had made a very strong impression upon Jack's imagination; which he never considered was not the case of the rest of the company, 'till after many repeated tryals he found that his stories seldom made any body laugh but himself.

I all this while looked upon Jack as a young tree shooting out into blossoms before its time; the redundancy of which, though it was a little unseasonable, seemed to foretel an uncommon fruitfulness.

In order to wear out the vein of pedantry which ran through his conversation, I took him out with me one evening, and first of all insinuated to him this rule, which I had my self learned from a very great author, *To think with the wise, but talk with the vulgar.* Jack's good sense soon made him reflect that he had often exposed himself to the laughter of the ignorant by a contrary behaviour; upon which he told me, that he would take care for the future to keep his notions to himself, and converse in the common received sentiments of mankind. He at the same time desired me to give him any other rules of conversation which I thought might be for his improvement. I told him I would think of it; and accordingly, as I have a particular affection for the young man, I gave him next morning the following rules in writing, which may perhaps have contributed to make him the agreeable man he now is.

The faculty of interchanging our thoughts with one another, or what we express by the word *conversation,* has always been represented by moral writers as one of the noblest privileges of reason, and which more particularly sets mankind above the brute part of the creation.

Though nothing so much gains upon the affections as this *extempore eloquence,* which we have constantly occasion for, and are obliged to practice every day, we very rarely meet with any who excel in it.

The conversation of most men is disagreeable, not so much for want of wit and learning, as of good-breeding and discretion.

If you resolve to please, never speak to gratifie any particular vanity or passion of your own, but always with a design either to divert or inform the company. A man who only aims at one of these, is always easie in his discourse. He is never out of humour at being interrupted, because he considers that those who hear him are the best judges whether what he was saying could either divert or inform them.

A modest person seldom fails to gain the good-will of those he converses with, because no body envies a man who does not appear to be pleased with himself.

We should talk extreamly little of our selves. Indeed what can we say? It would be as imprudent to discover our faults, as ridiculous to count over our fancied virtues. Our private and domestick affairs are no less improper to be introduced in conversation. What does it concern the company how many horses you keep in your stables? Or whether your servant is most knave or fool?

A man may equally affront the company he is in, by engrossing all the talk, or observing a contemptuous silence.

Before you tell a story it may be generally not amiss to draw a short character, and give the company a true idea of the principal persons concerned in it. The beauty of most things consisting not so much in their being said or done, as in their being said or done by such a particular person, or on such a particular occasion.

Notwithstanding all the advantages of youth, few young people please in conversation; the reason is, that want of experience makes them positive, and what they say is rather with a design to please themselves than any one else.

It is certain that age it self shall make many things pass well enough, which would have been laughed at in the mouth of one much younger.

Nothing, however, is more insupportable to men of sense, than an empty formal man who speaks in proverbs, and decides all controversies with a short sentence. This piece of stupidity is the more insufferable, as it puts on the air of wisdom.

A prudent man will avoid talking much of any particular science for which he is remarkably famous. There is not methinks an handsomer thing said of Mr. Cowley in his whole life, than that none of his intimate friends ever discovered he was a great poet by his discourse: Besides the decency of this rule, it is certainly founded in good policy. A man who talks of any thing he is already famous for, has little to get, but a great deal to lose. I might add, that he who is sometimes silent on a subject where every one is satisfied he could speak well, will often be thought no less knowing in other matters, where perhaps he is wholly ignorant.

Women are frightened at the name of argument, and are sooner convinced by an happy turn, or witty expression, than by demonstration.

Whenever you commend, add your reasons for doing so; it is this which distinguishes the approbation of a man of sense from the flattery of sycophants, and admiration of fools.

Raillery is no longer agreeable than while the whole company is pleased with it. I would least of all be understood to except the person rallied.

Though good-humour, sense and discretion can seldom fail to make a man agreeable, it may be no ill policy sometimes to prepare your self in a particular manner for conversation, by looking a little farther than your neighbours into whatever is become a reigning subject. If our armies are besieging a place of importance abroad, or our House of Commons debating a bill of consequence at home, you can hardly fail of being heard with pleasure, if you have nicely informed your self of the strength, situation, and history of the first, or of the reasons for and against the latter. It will have the same effect if when any single person begins to make a noise in the world, you can learn some of the smallest accidents in his life or conversation, which though they are too fine for the observation of the vulgar, give more satisfaction to men of sense, (as they are the best openings to a real character) than the recital of his most glaring actions. I know but one ill consequence to be feared from this method, namely, that coming full charged into company, you should resolve to unload whether an handsome opportunity offers it self or no.

Though the asking of questions may plead for it self the specious names of modesty, and a desire of information, it affords little pleasure to the rest of the company who are not troubled with the same doubts; besides which, he who asks a question would do well to consider that he lies wholly at the mercy of another before he receives an answer.

Nothing is more silly than the pleasure some people take in what they call *speaking their minds*. A man of this make will say a rude thing for the meer pleasure of saying it, when an opposite behaviour, full as innocent, might have preserved his friend, or made his fortune.

It is not impossible for a man to form to himself as exquisite a pleasure in complying with the humour and sentiments of others, as of bringing others over to his own; since 'tis the certain sign of a superior genius, that can take and become whatever dress it pleases.

I shall only add, that besides what I have here said, there is something which can never be learnt but in the company of the polite. The virtues of men are catching as well as their vices, and your own observations added to these, will soon discover what it is that commands attention in one man and makes you tired and displeased with the discourse of another.

RECOLLECTIONS OF CHILDHOOD
Richard Steele

Dies, ni fallor, adest, quem semper acerbum,
Semper honoratum, sic dii voluistis, habebo.[1]
VIRGIL, *The Aeneid,* Book V, line 49.

THERE ARE those among mankind, who can enjoy no relish of their being, except the world is made acquainted with all that relates to them, and think every thing lost that passes unobserved; but others find a solid delight in stealing by the crowd, and modelling their life after such a manner, as is as much above the approbation as the practice of the vulgar. Life being too short to give instances great enough of true friendship or good will, some sages have thought it pious to preserve a certain reverence for the manes of their deceased friends; and have withdrawn themselves from the rest of the world at certain seasons, to commemorate in their own thoughts such of their acquaintance who have gone before them out of this life. And indeed, when we are advanced in years, there is not a more pleasing entertainment, than to recollect in a gloomy moment the many we have parted with, that have been dear and agreeable to us, and to cast a melancholy thought or two after those, with whom, perhaps, we have indulged ourselves in whole nights of mirth and jollity. With such inclinations in my heart I went to my closet yesterday in the evening, and resolved to be sorrowful; upon which occasion I could not but look with disdain upon myself, that though all the reasons which I had to lament the loss of many of my friends are now as forcible as at the moment of their departure, yet did not my heart swell with the same sorrow which I felt at the time; but I could, without tears, reflect upon many pleasing adventures I have had with some, who have long been blended with common earth. Though it

---

[1] "That day I shall always consider grievous, but also honored, for the gods wanted it that way."

is by the benefit of nature, that length of time thus blots out the violence of afflictions; yet, with tempers too much given to pleasure, it is almost necessary to revive the old places of grief in our memory; and ponder step by step on past life, to lead the mind into that sobriety of thought which poises the heart, and makes it beat with due time, without being quickened with desire, or retarded with despair, from its proper and equal motion. When we wind up a clock that is out of order, to make it go well for the future, we do not immediately set the hand to the present instant, but we make it strike the round of all its hours, before it can recover the regularity of its time. Such, thought I, shall be my method this evening; and since it is that day of the year which I dedicate to the memory of such in another life as I much delighted in when living, an hour or two shall be sacred to sorrow and their memory, while I run over all the melancholy circumstances of this kind which have occurred to me in my whole life.

The first sense of sorrow I ever knew was upon the death of my father, at which time I was not quite five years of age; but was rather amazed at what all the house meant, than possessed with a real understanding why nobody was willing to play with me. I remember I went into the room where his body lay, and my mother sat weeping alone by it. I had my battledore in my hand, and fell a beating the coffin, and calling Papa; for, I know not how, I had some slight idea that he was locked up there. My mother catched me in her arms, and, transported beyond all patience of the silent grief she was before in, she almost smothered me in her embraces; and told me in a flood of tears, "Papa could not hear me, and would play with me no more, for they were going to put him under ground, whence he could never come to us again." She was a very beautiful woman, of a noble spirit, and there was a dignity in her grief amidst all the wildness of her transport; which, methought, struck me with an instinct of sorrow, that, before I was sensible of what it was to grieve, seized my very soul, and has made pity the weakness of my heart ever since. The mind in infancy is, methinks, like the body in embryo; and receives impressions so forcible, that they are as hard to be removed by reason, as any mark with which a child is born is to be taken away by any future application. Hence it is, that good-nature in me is no merit; but having been so frequently overwhelmed with her tears before I knew the cause of any affliction, or could draw defences from my own judgment, I imbibed commiseration, remorse, and an unmanly gentleness of mind, which has since insnared me into ten thousand calamities; and from whence I can reap no advantage, except it be, that, in such a humour as I am now in, I can the better indulge myself in the softnesses of humanity, and enjoy the sweet anxiety which arises from the memory of past afflictions.

We, that are very old, are better able to remember things which befell us in our distant youth, than the passages of later days. For this reason it

is, that the companions of my strong and vigorous years present themselves more immediately to me in this office of sorrow. Untimely and
unhappy deaths are what we are most apt to lament; so little are we able
to make it indifferent when a thing happens, though we know it must
happen. Thus we groan under life, and bewail those who are relieved
from it. Every object that returns to our imagination raises different passions, according to the circumstance of their departure. Who can have
lived in an army, and in a serious hour reflect upon the many gay and
agreeable men that might long have flourished in the arts of peace, and
not join with the imprecations of the fatherless and widow on the tyrant
to whose ambition they fell sacrifices? But gallant men, who are cut off
by the sword, move rather our veneration than our pity; and we gather
relief enough from their own contempt of death, to make that no evil,
which was approached with so much cheerfulness, and attended with so
much honour. But when we turn our thoughts from the great parts of
life on such occasions, and instead of lamenting those who stood ready
to give death to those from whom they had the fortune to receive it; I
say, when we let our thoughts wander from such noble objects, and consider the havock which is made among the tender and the innocent, pity
enters with an unmixed softness, and possesses all our souls at once.

Here (were there words to express such sentiments with proper tenderness) I should record the beauty, innocence, and untimely death, of
the first object my eyes ever beheld with love. The beauteous virgin!
how ignorantly did she charm, how carelessly excel? Oh death! thou hast
right to the bold, to the ambitious, to the high, and to the haughty; but
why this cruelty to the humble, to the meek, to the undiscerning, to the
thoughtless? Nor age, nor business, nor distress, can erase the dear image
from my imagination. In the same week, I saw her dressed for a ball, and
in a shroud. How ill did the habit of death become the pretty trifler? I
still behold the smiling earth—A large train of disasters were coming on
to my memory, when my servant knocked at my closet-door, and interrupted me with a letter, attended with a hamper of wine, of the same sort
with that which is to be put to sale on Thursday next, at Garraway's
coffee-house. Upon the receipt of it, I sent for three of my friends. We
are so intimate, that we can be company in whatever state of mind we
meet, and can entertain each other without expecting always to rejoice.
The wine we found to be generous and warming, but with such a heat
as moved us rather to be cheerful than frolicksome. It revived the spirits,
without firing the blood. We commended it until two of the clock this
morning; and having to-day met a little before dinner, we found, that
though we drank two bottles a man, we had much more reason to recollect than forget what had passed the night before.

[*Tatler*, No. 181. June 6, 1710.]

DICK MINIM THE CRITIC
PART 1

Samuel Johnson

CRITICISM IS a study by which men grow important and formidable at very small expense. The power of invention has been conferred by nature upon few, and the labour of learning those sciences which may, by mere labour, be obtained is too great to be willingly endured; but every man can exert such judgement as he has upon the works of others; and he whom nature has made weak, and idleness keeps ignorant, may yet support his vanity by the name of a Critic.

I hope it will give comfort to great numbers who are passing through the world in obscurity, when I inform them how easily distinction may be obtained. All the other powers of literature are coy and haughty, they must be long courted, and at last are not always gained; but Criticism is a goddess easy of access, and forward of advance, who will meet the slow, and encourage the timorous; the want of meaning she supplies with words, and the want of spirit she recompenses with malignity.

This profession has one recommendation peculiar to itself, that it gives vent to malignity without real mischief. No genius was ever blasted by the breath of critics. The poison which, if confined, would have burst the heart, fumes away in empty hisses, and malice is set at ease with very little danger to merit. The Critic is the only man whose triumph is without another's pain, and whose greatness does not rise upon another's ruin.

To a study at once so easy and so reputable, so malicious and so harmless, it cannot be necessary to invite my readers by a long or laboured exhortation; it is sufficient, since all would be critics if they could, to show by one eminent example that all can be critics if they will.

Dick Minim, after the common course of puerile studies, in which he was no great proficient, was put an apprentice to a brewer, with whom he had lived two years, when his uncle died in the city, and left him a large fortune in the stocks. Dick had for six months before used the company of the lower players, of whom he had learned to scorn a trade, and, being now at liberty to follow his genius, he resolved to be a man of wit and humour. That he might be properly initiated in his new character, he frequented the coffee-houses near the theatres, where he listened very diligently, day after day, to those who talked of language and sentiments, and unities and catastrophes, till, by slow degrees, he began to think that he understood something of the stage, and hoped in time to talk himself.

But he did not trust so much to natural sagacity as wholly to neglect the help of books. When the theatres were shut, he retired to Richmond with a few select writers whose opinions he impressed upon his memory by unwearied diligence; and, when he returned with other wits to the town, was able to tell, in very proper phrases, that the chief business of art is to copy nature; that a perfect writer is not to be expected, because genius decays as judgement increases; that the great art is the art of blotting; and that, according to the rule of Horace, every piece should be kept nine years.

Of the great authors he now began to display the characters, laying down as a universal position, that all had beauties and defects. His opinion was, that Shakespeare, committing himself wholly to the impulse of nature, wanted that correctness which learning would have given him; and that Jonson, trusting to learning, did not sufficiently cast his eye on nature. He blamed the stanzas of Spenser, and could not bear the hexameters of Sidney. Denham and Waller he held the first reformers of English numbers; and thought that if Waller could have obtained the strength of Denham, or Denham the sweetness of Waller, there had been nothing wanting to complete a poet. He often expressed his commiseration of Dryden's poverty, and his indignation at the age which suffered him to write for bread; he repeated with rapture the first lines of *All for Love,* but wondered at the corruption of taste which could bear anything so unnatural as rhyming tragedies. In Otway he found uncommon powers of moving the passions, but was disgusted by his general negligence, and blamed him for making a conspirator his hero; and never concluded his disquisition, without remarking how happily the sound of the clock is made to alarm the audience. Southern would have been his favourite, but that he mixes comic with tragic scenes, intercepts the natural course of the passions, and fills the mind with a wild confusion of mirth and melancholy. The versification of Rowe he thought too melodious for the stage, and too little varied in different passions. He made it the great fault of Congreve, that all his persons were wits, and that he always wrote with more art than nature. He considered *Cato* rather as a poem than a play, and allowed Addison to be the complete master of allegory and grave humour, but paid no great deference to him as a critic. He thought the chief merit of Prior was in his easy tales and lighter poems, though he allowed that his *Solomon* had many noble sentiments elegantly expressed. In Swift he discovered an inimitable vein of irony, and an easiness which all would hope and few would attain. Pope he was inclined to degrade from a poet to a versifier, and thought his numbers rather luscious than sweet. He often lamented the neglect of *Phaedra and Hippolitus,* and wished to see the stage under better regulations.

These assertions passed commonly uncontradicted; and if now and then an opponent started up, he was quickly repressed by the suffrages of the company, and Minim went away from every dispute with elation of heart and increase of confidence.

He now grew conscious of his abilities, and began to talk of the present state of dramatic poetry; wondered what had become of the comic genius which supplied our ancestors with wit and pleasantry, and why no writer could be found that durst now venture beyond a farce. He saw no reason for thinking that the vein of humour was exhausted, since we live in a country where liberty suffers every character to spread itself to its utmost bulk, and which therefore produces more originals than all the rest of the world together. Of tragedy he concluded business to be the soul, and yet often hinted that love predominates too much upon the modern stage.

He was now an acknowledged critic, and had his own seat in a coffee-house, and headed a party in the pit. Minim has more vanity than ill-nature, and seldom desires to do much mischief; he will perhaps murmur a little in the ear of him that sits next to him, but endeavours to influence the audience to favour, by clapping when an actor exclaims, "Ye gods!" or laments the misery of his country.

By degrees he was admitted to rehearsals; and many of his friends are of opinion, that our present poets are indebted to him for their happiest thoughts; by his contrivance the bell was rung twice in *Barbarossa,* and by his persuasion the author of *Cleone* concluded his play without a couplet; for what can be more absurd, said Minim, than that part of a play should be rhymed, and part written in blank verse? and by what acquisition of faculties is the speaker, who never could find rhymes before, enabled to rhyme at the conclusion of an act?

He is the great investigator of hidden beauties, and is particularly delighted when he finds "the sound of an echo to the sense." He has read all our poets with particular attention to this delicacy of versification, and wonders at the supineness with which their works have been hitherto perused, so that no man has found the sound of a drum in this distich:

> When pulpit, drum ecclesiastic,
> Was beat with fist instead of a stick;

and that the wonderful lines upon honour and a bubble have hitherto passed without notice:

> Honour is like the glassy bubble,
> Which cost philosophers such trouble;
> Where, one part crack'd, the whole does fly,
> And wits are crack'd to find out why.

In these verses, says Minim, we have two striking accommodations of
the sound to the sense. It is impossible to utter the first two lines emphatically without an act like that which they describe; *bubble* and *trouble* caus-
ing a momentary inflation of the cheeks by the retention of the breath,
which is afterwards forcibly emitted, as in the practice of *blowing bubbles*.
But the greatest excellence is in the third line, which is *crack'd* in the middle to express a crack, and then shivers into monosyllables. Yet has this
diamond lain neglected with common stones, and among the innumerable admirers of Hudibras, the observation of this superlative passage has
been reserved for the sagacity of Minim.

PART 2[1]

Mr. Minim had now advanced himself to the zenith of critical reputation; when he was in the pit, every eye in the boxes was fixed upon
him: when he entered his coffee-house, he was surrounded by circles of
candidates, who passed their novitiate of literature under his tuition: his
opinion was asked by all who had no opinion of their own, and yet loved
to debate and decide; and no composition was supposed to pass in safety
to posterity, till it had been secured by Minim's approbation.

Minim professes great admiration of the wisdom and munificence by
which the academies of the continent were raised; and often wishes for
some standard of taste, for some tribunal, to which merit may appeal
from caprice, prejudice, and malignity. He has formed a plan for an academy of criticism, where every work of imagination may be read before
it is printed, and which shall authoritatively direct the theatres what
pieces to receive or reject, to exclude or revive.

Such an institution would, in Dick's opinion, spread the fame of
English literature over Europe, and make London the metropolis of elegance and politeness, the place to which the learned and ingenious of all
countries would repair for instruction and improvement, and where
nothing would any longer be applauded or endured that was not con-
formed to the nicest rules, and finished with the highest elegance.

Till some happy conjunction of the planets shall dispose our princes
or ministers to make themselves immortal by such an academy, Minim

---

[1] Dr. Johnson continued his essay on Dick Minim the following week in *The Idler*.

contents himself to preside four nights in a week in a critical society selected by himself, where he is heard without contradiction, and whence his judgment is disseminated through "the great vulgar and the small."

When he is placed in the chair of criticism, he declares loudly for the noble simplicity of our ancestors, in opposition to the petty refinements and ornamental luxuriance. Sometimes he is sunk in despair, and perceives false delicacy daily gaining ground, and sometimes brightens his countenance with a gleam of hope, and predicts the revival of the true sublime. He then fulminates his loudest censures against the monkish barbarity of rhyme; wonders how beings that pretend to reason can be pleased with one line always ending like another; tells how unjustly and unnaturally sense is sacrificed to sound; how often the best thoughts are mangled by the necessity of confining or extending them to the dimensions of a couplet; and rejoices that genius has, in our days, shaken off the shackles which had encumbered it so long. Yet he allows that rhyme may sometimes be borne, if the lines be often broken, and the pauses judiciously diversified.

From blank verse he makes an easy transition to Milton, whom he produces as an example of the slow advance of lasting reputation. Milton is the only writer in whose books Minim can read for ever without weariness. What cause it is that exempts this pleasure from satiety he has long and diligently inquired, and believes it to consist in the perpetual variation of the numbers, by which the ear is gratified and the attention awakened. The lines that are commonly thought rugged and unmusical, he conceives to have been written to temper the melodious luxury of the rest, or to express things by a proper cadence: for he scarcely finds a verse that has not this favourite beauty; he declares that he could shiver in a hot-house when he reads that

> the ground
> Burns frore, and cold performs th' effect of fire;

and that, when Milton bewails his blindness, the verse,

> So thick a drop serene has quenched these orbs,

has, he knows not how, something that strikes him with an obscure sensation like that which he fancies would be felt from the sound of darkness.

Minim is not so confident of his rules of judgement as not very eagerly to catch new light from the name of the author. He is commonly so prudent as to spare those whom he cannot resist, unless, as will sometimes happen, he finds the public combined against them. But a fresh pretender to fame he is strongly inclined to censure, till his own honour requires that he commend him. Till he knows the success of a composition, he entrenches himself in general terms; there are some new thoughts and beautiful passages, but there is likewise much which he would have advised the author to expunge. He has several favourite epithets, of which he never settled the meaning, but which are very commodiously applied to books which he has not read, or cannot understand. One is *manly,* another is *dry,* another *stiff,* and another *flimsy*; sometimes he discovers delicacy of style, and sometimes meets with *strange expressions.*

He is never so great, or so happy, as when a youth of promising parts is brought to receive his directions for the prosecution of his studies. He then puts on a very serious air; he advises the pupil to read none but the best authors, and, when he finds one congenial to his own mind, to study his beauties, but avoid his faults; and, when he sits down to write, to consider how his favourite author would think at the present time on the present occasion. He exhorts him to catch those moments when he finds his thoughts expanded and his genius exalted, but to take care lest imagination hurry him beyond the bounds of nature. He holds diligence the mother of success; yet enjoins him, with great earnestness, not to read more than he can digest, and not to confuse his mind by pursuing studies of contrary tendencies. He tells him, that every man has his genius, and that Cicero could never be a poet. The boy retires illuminated, resolves to follow his genius, and to think how Milton would have thought: and Minim feasts upon his own beneficence till another day brings another pupil.

SPRING

Samuel Johnson

Et nunc omnis ager, nunc omnis parturit arbos,
Nunc frondent silvœ, nunc formosissimus annus.

VIRGIL ECL. iii. 56.

Now every field, now every tree is green;
Now genial nature's fairest face is seen.

ELPHINSTON.

EVERY MAN is sufficiently discontented with some circumstances of his present state, to suffer his imagination to range more or less in quest of future happiness, and to fix upon some point of time, in which, by the removal of the inconvenience which now perplexes him, or acquisition of the advantage which he at present wants, he shall find the condition of his life very much improved.

When this time, which is too often expected with great impatience, at last arrives, it generally comes without the blessing for which it was desired; but we solace ourselves with some new prospect, and press forward again with equal eagerness.

It is lucky for a man, in whom this temper prevails, when he turns his hopes upon things wholly out of his own power; since he forbears then to precipitate his affairs, for the sake of the great event that is to complete his felicity, and waits for the blissful hour with less neglect of the measures necessary to be taken in the mean time.

I have long known a person of this temper, who indulged his dream of happiness with less hurt to himself than such chimerical wishes commonly produce, and adjusted his scheme with such address, that his hopes were in full bloom three parts of the year, and in the other part never wholly blasted. Many, perhaps, would be desirous of learning by what means he procured to himself such a cheap and lasting satisfaction. It was gained by a constant practice of referring the removal of all his uneasiness to the coming of the next spring; if his health was impaired, the spring would restore it; if what he wanted was at a high price, it would fall its value in the spring.

The spring, indeed, did often come without any of these effects, but he was always certain that the next would be more propitious; nor was ever convinced, that the present spring would fail him before the middle of summer; for he always talked of the spring as coming till it was past, and when it was once past, every one agreed with him that it was coming.

By long converse with this man, I am, perhaps, brought to feel immoderate pleasure in the contemplation of this delightful season; but I have the satisfaction of finding many, whom it can be no shame to resemble, infected with the same enthusiasm; for there is, I believe, scarce any poet of eminence, who has not left some testimony of his fondness for the flowers, the zephyrs, and the warblers of the spring. Nor has the most luxuriant imagination been able to describe the serenity and happiness of the golden age, otherwise than by giving a perpetual spring as the highest reward of uncorrupted innocence.

There is, indeed, something inexpressibly pleasing in the annual renovation of the world, and the new display of the treasures of nature. The cold and darkness of winter, with the naked deformity of every object on which we turn our eyes, make us rejoice at the succeeding season, as well for what we have escaped, as for what we may enjoy; and every budding flower, which a warm situation brings early to our view, is considered by us as a messenger to notify the approach of more joyous days.

The spring affords to a mind, so free from the disturbance of cares or passions as to be vacant to calm amusements, almost every thing that our present state makes us capable of enjoying. The variegated verdure of the fields and woods, the succession of grateful odours, the voice of pleasure pouring out its notes on every side, with the gladness apparently conceived by every animal, from the growth of his food, and the clemency of the weather, throw over the whole earth an air of gayety, significantly expressed by the smile of nature.

Yet there are men to whom these scenes are able to give no delight, and who hurry away from all the varieties of rural beauty, to lose their hours and divert their thoughts by cards, or assemblies, a tavern dinner, or the prattle of the day.

It may be laid down as a position which will seldom deceive, that when a man cannot bear his own company, there is something wrong. He must fly from himself, either because he feels a tediousness in life from the equipoise of an empty mind, which, having no tendency to one motion more than another but as it is impelled by some external power, must always have recourse to foreign objects; or he must be afraid of the intrusion of some unpleasing ideas, and, perhaps, is struggling to escape

from the remembrance of a loss, the fear of a calamity, or some other
thought of greater horror.

Those whom sorrow incapacitates to enjoy the pleasures of contemplation, may properly apply to such diversions, provided they are innocent, as lay strong hold on the attention; and those, whom fear of any
future affliction chains down to misery, must endeavour to obviate the
danger.

My considerations shall, on this occasion, be turned on such as are
burdensome to themselves merely because they want subjects for reflection, and to whom the volume of nature is thrown open, without affording them pleasure or instruction, because they never learned to read the
characters.

A French author has advanced this seeming paradox, that "very few
men know how to take a walk"; and, indeed, it is true, that few know
how to take a walk with a prospect of any other pleasure, than the same
company would have afforded them at home.

There are animals that borrow their colour from the neighbouring
body, and consequently vary their hue as they happen to change their
place. In like manner it ought to be the endeavour of every man to derive
his reflections from the objects about him; for it is to no purpose that he
alters his position, if his attention continues fixed to the same point. The
mind should be kept open to the access of every new idea, and so far
disengaged from the predominance of particular thoughts as easily to
accommodate itself to occasional entertainment.

A man that has formed this habit of turning every new object to his
entertainment, finds in the productions of nature an inexhaustible stock
of materials upon which he can employ himself, without any temptations
to envy or malevolence; faults, perhaps, seldom totally avoided by those,
whose judgment is much exercised upon the works of art. He has always
a certain prospect of discovering new reasons for adoring the sovereign
Author of the universe, and probable hopes of making some discovery of
benefit to others, or of profit to himself. There is no doubt but many
vegetables and animals have qualities that might be of great use, to the
knowledge of which there is not required much force of penetration or
fatigue of study, but only frequent experiments and close attention. What
is said by the chemists of their darling mercury, is, perhaps, true of every
body through the whole creation, that, if a thousand lives should be spent
upon it, all its properties would not be found out.

Mankind must necessarily be diversified by various tastes, since life
affords and requires such multiplicity of employments, and a nation of
naturalists is neither to be hoped nor desired; but it is surely not improper
to point out a fresh amusement to those who languish in health, and
repine in plenty, for want of some source of diversion that may be less

easily exhausted, and to inform the multitudes of both sexes, who are burdened with every new day, that there are many shows which they have not seen.

He that enlarges his curiosity after the works of nature, demonstrably multiplies the inlets to happiness; and, therefore, the younger part of my readers, to whom I dedicate this vernal speculation, must excuse me for calling upon them, to make use at once of the spring of the year, and the spring of life; to acquire, while their minds may be yet impressed with new images, a love of innocent pleasures, and an ardour for useful knowledge; and to remember that a blighted spring makes a barren year, and that the vernal flowers, however beautiful and gay, are only intended by nature as preparatives to autumnal fruits.

ART CONNOISSEURS
Sir Joshua Reynolds

SIR,

I was much pleased with your ridicule of those shallow Critics, whose judgment, though often right as far as it goes, yet reaches only to inferior beauties, and who, unable to comprehend the whole, judge only by parts, and from thence determine the merit of extensive works. But there is another kind of Critic still worse, who judges by narrow rules, and those too often false, and which, though they should be true, and founded on nature, will lead him but a very little way towards the just estimation of the sublime beauties in works of genius; for whatever part of an art can be executed or criticised by rules, that part is no longer the work of genius, which implies excellence out of the reach of rules. For my own part, I profess myself an Idler, and love to give my judgment, such as it is, from my immediate perceptions, without much fatigue of thinking; and I am of opinion, that if a man has not those perceptions right, it will be in vain for him to endeavour to supply their place by rules, which may enable him to talk more learnedly, but not to distinguish more acutely. Another reason which has lessened my affection for the study of criticism is, that Critics, so far as I have observed, debar themselves from receiving any pleasure from the polite arts, at the same time that they profess to love and admire them: for these rules, being always uppermost, give them such a propensity to criticise, that, instead of giving up the reins of their imagination into their author's hands, their frigid minds are employed in examining whether the performance be according to the rules of art.

To those who are resolved to be Critics in spite of nature, and, at the same time, have no great disposition to make much reading and study, I would recommend to them to assume the character of Connoisseur, which may be purchased at a much cheaper rate than that of a Critic in poetry. The remembrance of a few names of painters, with their general characters, with a few rules of the Academy, which they may pick up among the painters, will go a great way towards making a very notable Connoisseur.

With a gentleman of this cast I visited last week the Cartoons at Hampton Court: he was just returned from Italy, a Connoisseur of course, and of course his mouth full of nothing but the grace of Raffaelle, the purity of Domenichino, the learning of Poussin, the air of Guido, the greatness of taste of the Caraches, and the sublimity and grand *contorno* of Michael Angelo; with all the rest of the cant of criticism, which he emitted with that volubility which generally those orators have who annex no idea to their words.

As we were passing through the rooms, in our way to the gallery, I made him observe a whole length of Charles the First, by Vandyke, as a perfect representation of the character as well as the figure of the man. He agreed it was very fine, but it wanted spirit and contrast, and had not the flowing line, without which a figure could not possibly be graceful. When we entered the Gallery, I thought I could perceive him recollecting his rules by which he was to criticise Raffaelle. I shall pass over his observation of the boats being too little, and other criticisms of that kind, till we arrived at *St. Paul preaching.* "This, (says he) is esteemed the most excellent of all the Cartoons; what nobleness, what dignity there is in that figure of St. Paul! and yet what an addition to the nobleness could Raffaelle have given, had the art of contrast been known in his time! but, above all, the flowing line, which constitutes grace and beauty. You would not then have seen an upright figure standing equally on both legs, and both hands stretched forward in the same direction, and his drapery, to all appearance, without the least art of disposition." The following picture is the *Charge to Peter.* "Here (says he) are twelve upright figures; what a pity it is that Raffaelle was not acquainted with the pyramidal principle! He would then have contrived the figures in the middle to have been on higher ground, or the figures at the extremities stooping or lying, which would not only have formed the group into the shape of a pyramid, but likewise have contrasted the standing figures. Indeed," added he, "I have often lamented that so great a genius as Raffaelle had not lived in this enlightened age, since the art has been reduced to principles, and had had his education in one of the modern academies; what glorious works might we then have expected from his divine pencil!"

I shall trouble you no longer with my friend's observations, which, I suppose, you are now able to continue by yourself. It is curious to observe, that, at the same time that great admiration is pretended for a name of fixed reputation, objections are raised against those very qualities by which that great name was acquired.

Those critics are continually lamenting that Raffaelle had not the colouring and harmony of Rubens, or the light and shadow of Rembrandt, without considering how much the gay harmony of the former, and affection of the latter, would take from the dignity of Raffaelle; and yet Rubens had great harmony, and Rembrandt understood light and shadow; but what may be an excellence in a lower class of painting, becomes a blemish in a higher; as the quick sprightly turn which is the life and beauty of epigrammatic compositions, would but ill suit with the majesty of heroic poetry.

To conclude: I would not be thought to infer from anything that has been said that rules are absolutely unnecessary; but to censure scrupulosity, a servile attention to minute exactness, which is some times inconsistent with higher excellency, and is lost in the blaze of expanded genius.

I do not know whether you will think painting a general subject. By inserting this letter, perhaps you will incur the censure a man would deserve, whose business being to entertain a whole room, should turn his back to the company, and talk to a particular person.

I am, Sir, &c.

The Idler.

THE CHARACTER OF AN IMPORTANT
TRIFLER, BEAU TIBBS
Oliver Goldsmith

THOUGH NATURALLY pensive, yet I am fond of gay company, and take every opportunity of thus dismissing the mind from duty. From this motive, I am often found in the centre of a crowd; and wherever pleasure is to be sold, am always a purchaser. In those places, without being remarked by any, I join in whatever goes forward; work my passions into a similitude of frivolous earnestness, shout as they shout, and condemn as they happen to disapprove. A mind thus sunk for a while below its natural standard, is qualified for stronger flights, as those first retire who would spring forward with great vigour.

Attracted by the serenity of the evening, my friend and I lately went to gaze upon the company in one of the public walks near the city. Here we sauntered together for some time, either praising the beauty of such as were handsome, or the dresses of such as had nothing else to recommend them. We had gone thus deliberately forward for some time, when, stopping on a sudden, my friend caught me by the elbow, and led me out of the public walk. I could perceive by the quickness of his pace, and by his frequently looking behind, that he was attempting to avoid somebody who followed: we now turned to the right, then to the left: as we went forward, he still went faster, but in vain: the person whom he attempted to escape hunted us through every doubling, and gained upon us each moment, so that at last we fairly stood still, resolving to face what we could not avoid.

Our pursuer soon came up, and joined us with all the familiarity of an old acquaintance. "My dear Drybone," cries he, shaking my friend's hand, "where have you been hiding this half a century? Positively I had fancied you were gone down to cultivate matrimony and your estate in the country." During the reply, I had an opportunity of surveying the appearance of our new companion: his hat was pinched up with peculiar smartness; his looks were pale, thin, and sharp; round his neck he wore a broad black riband, and in his bosom a buckle studded with glass; his coat was trimmed with tarnished twist; he wore by his side a sword with a black hilt; and his stockings of silk, though newly washed, were grown yellow by long service. I was so much engaged with the peculiarity of his dress, that I attended only to the latter part of my friend's reply, in which he complimented Mr. Tibbs on the taste of his clothes, and the bloom in his countenance. "Pshaw, pshaw! Will," cried the figure, "no more of that, if you love me: you know I hate flattery,—on my soul I do; and yet, to be sure, an intimacy with the great will improve one's appearance, and a course of venison will fatten; and yet, faith, I despise the great as much as you do; but there are a great many damn'd honest fellows among them, and we must not quarrel with one half, because the other wants weeding. If they were all such as my Lord Mudler, one of the most good-natured creatures that ever squeezed a lemon, I should myself be among the number of their admirers. I was yesterday to dine at the Duchess of Piccadilly's. My lord was there. 'Ned,' says he to me, 'Ned,' says he, 'I'll hold gold to silver I can tell where you were poaching last night.' 'Poaching, my lord?' says I, 'faith you have missed already; for I staid at home, and let the girls poach for me. That's my way: I take a fine woman as some animals do their prey—stand still, and swoop, they fall into my mouth.'"

"Ah, Tibbs, thou art a happy fellow," cried my companion, with looks of infinite pity; "I hope your fortune is as much improved as our understanding in such company."—"Improved," replied the other; "You shall know,—but let it go no further—a great secret—five hundred a-year to begin with.—My lord's word of honour for it. His lordship took me down in his own chariot yesterday, and we had a tête-a-tête dinner in the country, where we talked of nothing else."—"I fancy you forget, Sir," cried I, "you told us but this moment of your dining yesterday in town."—"Did I say so?" replied he coolly; "to be sure if I said so, it was so—Dined in town; egad, now I do remember, I did dine in town; but I dined in the country too; for you must know, my boys, I eat two dinners. By the by, I am grown as nice as the devil in my eating. I'll tell you a pleasant affair about that:—We were a select party of us to dine at Lady Grogram's—an affected piece, but let it go no farther—a secret—Well, there happened to be no asafœtida in the sauce to a turkey, upon which, says I, 'I'll hold a thousand guineas, and say done first, that—But, dear Drybone, you are an honest creature; lend me half-a-crown for a minute or two, or so, just till—but hearkee, ask me for it the next time we meet, or it may be twenty to one but I forget to pay you."

When he left us, our conversation naturally turned upon so extraordinary a character. "His very dress," cries my friend, "is not less extraordinary than his conduct. If you meet him this day, you find him in rags; if the next, in embroidery. With those persons of distinction of whom he talks so familiarly, he has scarce a coffeehouse acquaintance. However, both for the interests of society, and perhaps for his own, Heaven has made him poor, and while all the world perceive his wants, he fancies them concealed from every eye. An agreeable companion, because he understands flattery; and all must be pleased with the first part of his conversation, though all are sure of its ending with a demand on their purse. While his youth countenances the levity of his conduct, he may thus earn a precarious subsistence; but when age comes on, the gravity of which is incompatible with buffoonery, then will he find himself forsaken by all; condemned in the decline of life to hang upon some rich family whom he once despised, there to undergo all the ingenuity of studied contempt, to be employed only as a spy upon the servants, or a bugbear to fright the children into obedience." Adieu.

THE CHARACTER OF THE TRIFLER
CONTINUED: WITH THAT OF HIS WIFE,
HIS HOUSE, AND FURNITURE
Oliver Goldsmith

I AM APT to fancy I have contracted a new acquaintance whom it will be no easy matter to shake off. My little Beau yesterday overtook me again in one of the public walks, and slapping me on the shoulder, saluted me with a air of the most perfect familiarity. His dress was the same as usual, except that he had more powder in his hair, wore a dirtier shirt, a pair of temple spectacles, and his hat under his arm.

As I knew him to be a harmless, amusing little thing, I could not return his smiles with any degree of severity: so we walked forward on terms of the utmost intimacy, and in a few minutes discussed all the usual topics preliminary to particular conversation. The oddities that marked his character, however, soon began to appear; he bowed to several well-dressed persons, who, by their manner of returning the compliment, appeared perfect strangers. At intervals he drew out a pocket-book, seeming to take memorandums before all the company, with much importance and assiduity. In this manner he led me through the length of the whole walk, fretting at his absurdities, and fancying myself laughed at not less than him by every spectator.

When we were got to the end of our procession, "Blast me," cries he, with an air of vivacity, "I never saw the Park so thin in my life before! There's no company at all to-day; not a single face to be seen."—"No company!" interrupted I, peevishly; "no company where there is such a crowd? why, man, there's too much. What are the thousands that have been laughing at us but company?"—"Lord, my dear," returned he, with the utmost good humour, "you seem immensely chagrined; but, blast me, when the world laughs at me, I laugh at the world, and so we are even. My Lord Trip, Bill Squash the Creolian, and I, sometimes make a party at being ridiculous; and so we say and do a thousand things for the joke's sake. But

I see you are grave, and if you are for a fine grave sentimental companion, you shall dine with me and my wife to-day; I must insist on't. I'll introduce you to Mrs. Tibbs, a lady of as elegant qualifications as any in nature; she was bred (but that's between ourselves), under the inspection of the Countess of All-night. A charming body of voice; but no more of that,— she will give us a song. You shall see my little girl too, Carolina Wilhelmina Amelia Tibbs, a sweet pretty creature: I design her for my Lord Drumstick's eldest son; but that's in friendship, let it go no further: she's but six years old, and yet she walks a minuet, and plays on the guitar immensely already. I intend she shall be as perfect as possible in every accomplishment. In the first place, I'll make her a scholar: I'll teach her Greek myself, and learn that language purposely to instruct her; but let that be a secret."

Thus saying, without waiting for a reply, he took me by the arm, and hauled me along. We passed through many dark alleys and winding ways; for, from some motives to me unknown, he seemed to have a particular aversion to every frequented street; at last, however, we got to the door of a dismal-looking house in the outlets of the town, where he informed me he chose to reside for the benefit of the air.

We entered the lower door, which ever seemed to lie most hospitably open; and I began to ascend an old and creaking staircase, when, as he mounted to show me the way, he demanded, whether I delighted in prospects; to which answering in the affirmative, "Then," says he, "I shall show you one of the most charming in the world, out of my window; we shall see the ships sailing, and the whole country for twenty miles round, tip top, quite high. My Lord Swamp would give ten thousand guineas for such a one; but, as I sometimes pleasantly tell him, I always love to keep my prospects at home, that my friends may see me the oftener."

By this time we were arrived as high as the stairs would permit us to ascend, till we came to what he was facetiously pleased to call the first floor down the chimney; and knocking at the door, a voice from within demanded, "Who's there?" My conductor answered that it was him. But this not satisfying the querist, the voice again repeated the demand; to which he answered louder than before; and now the door was opened by an old woman with cautious reluctance.

When we were got in, he welcomed me to his house with great cere-mony, and turning to the old woman, asked where was her lady? "Good troth," replied she, in a peculiar dialect, "she's washing your two shirts at the next door, because they have taken an oath against lending out the tub any longer."—"My two shirts!" cried he in a tone that faltered with con-fusion, "what does the idiot mean?"—"I ken what I mean weel enough," replied the other; "she's washing your two shirts at the next door, because—" "Fire and fury, no more of thy stupid explanations!" cried he;

"go and inform her we have got company. Were that Scotch hag," continued he, turning to me, "to be for ever in my family, she would never learn politeness, nor forget that absurd poisonous accent of hers, or testify the smallest specimen of breeding or high life; and yet it is very surprising too, as I had her from a Parliament man, a friend of mine from the Highlands, one of the politest men in the world; but that's a secret."

We waited some time for Mrs. Tibbs's arrival, during which interval I had a full opportunity of surveying the chamber and all its furniture, which consisted of four chairs with old wrought bottoms, that he assured me were his wife's embroidery; a square table that had been once japanned; a cradle in one corner, a lumbering cabinet in the other; a broken shepherdess, and a mandarine without a head, were stuck over the chimney; and round the walls several paltry unframed pictures, which, he observed, were all his own drawing. "What do you think, Sir, of that head in the corner, done in the manner of Grisoni? there's the true keeping in it; it is my own face, and though there happens to be no likeness, a Countess offered me a hundred for its fellow: I refused her, for, hang it, that would be mechanical you know."

The wife at last made her appearance, at once a slattern and a coquette; much emaciated, but still carrying the remains of beauty. She made twenty apologies for being seen in such odious dishabille, but hoped to be excused, as she had stayed out all night at the gardens with the Countess, who was excessively fond of the horns. "And, indeed, my dear," added she, turning to her husband, "his lordship drank your health in a bumper."—"Poor Jack!" cries he, "a dear good-natured creature, I know he loves me. But I hope, my dear, you have given orders for dinner; you need make no great preparations neither, there are but three of us; something elegant, and little will do,—a turbot, an ortolan, a—" "Or what do you think, my dear," interrupts the wife, "of a nice pretty bit of oxcheek, piping hot, and dressed with a little of my own sauce?"—"The very thing!" replies he; "it will eat best with some smart bottled beer: but be sure to let us have the sauce his Grace was so fond of. I hate your immense loads of meat; that is country all over; extremely disgusting to those who are in the least acquainted with high life."

By this time my curiosity began to abate, and my appetite to increase; the company of fools may at first make us smile, but at last never fails of rendering us melancholy: I therefore pretended to recollect a prior engagement, and, after having shown my respect to the house, according to the fashion of the English, by giving the old servant a piece of money at the door, I took my leave; Mr. Tibbs assuring me, that dinner, if I stayed, would be ready at least in less than two hours."

NATIONAL PREJUDICE [1]

Oliver Goldsmith

THE ENGLISH seem as silent as the Japanese, yet vainer than the inhabitants of Siam. Upon my arrival I attributed that reserve to modesty, which I now find has its origin in pride. Condescend to address them first and you are sure of their acquaintance; stoop to flattery and you conciliate their friendship and esteem. They bear hunger, cold, fatigue, and all the miseries of life without shrinking; danger only calls forth their fortitude; they even exult in calamity: but contempt is what they cannot bear. An Englishman fears contempt more than death; he often flies to death as a refuge from its pressure, and dies when he fancies the world has ceased to esteem him.

Pride seems the source not only of their national vices, but of their national virtues also. An Englishman is taught to love the king as his friend, but to acknowledge no other master than the laws which himself has contributed to enact. He despises those nations who, that one may be free, are all content to be slaves; who first lift a tyrant into terror, and then shrink under his power as if delegated from Heaven. Liberty is echoed in all their assemblies; and thousands might be found ready to offer up their lives for the sound, though perhaps not one of all the number understands its meaning. The lowest mechanic, however, looks upon it as his duty to be a watchful guardian of his country's freedom, and often uses a language that might seem haughty even in the mouth of the great emperor who traces his ancestry to the moon.

A few days ago, passing by one of their prisons, I could not avoid stopping, in order to listen to a dialogue which I thought might afford me some entertainment. The conversation was carried on between a debtor through the grate of his prison, a porter who had stopped to rest his burden, and a soldier at the window. The subject was upon a threatened

[1] From a series of letters supposedly written in London by a visitor from China.

invasion from France, and each seemed extremely anxious to rescue his country from the impending danger. "For my part," cries the prisoner, "the greatest of my apprehension is for our freedom; if the French should conquer, what would become of English liberty? My dear friends, liberty is the Englishman's prerogative; we must preserve that at the expense of our lives; of that the French shall never deprive us. It is not to be expected that men who are slaves themselves would preserve our freedom should they happen to conquer." "Ay, slaves," cries the porter, "they are all slaves, fit only to carry burdens, every one of them. Before I would stoop to slavery let this be my poison" (and he held the goblet in his hand), "may this be my poison; but I would sooner list for a soldier."

The soldier, taking the goblet from his friend with much awe, fervently cried out, "It is not so much our liberties as our religion that would suffer by such a change: ay, our religion, my lads. May the devil sink me into flames" (such was the solemnity of his adjuraton) "if the French should come over, but our religion would be utterly undone." So saying, instead of a libation, he applied the goblet to his lips, and confirmed his sentiments with a ceremony of the most persevering devotion.

In short, every man here pretends to be a politician; even the fair sex are sometimes found to mix the severity of national altercation with the blandishments of love, and often become conquerors by more weapons of destruction than their eyes.

This universal passion for politics is gratified by daily gazettes, as with us in China. But as in ours the emperor endeavours to instruct his people, in theirs the people endeavour to instruct the administration. You must not, however, imagine that they who compile these papers have any actual knowledge of the politics or the government of a state; they only collect their materials from the oracle of some coffee-house, which oracle has himself gathered them the night before from a beau at a gaming-table, who has pillaged his knowledge from a great man's porter, who has had his information from the great man's gentleman, who has invented the whole story for his own amusement the night preceding.

The English, in general, seem fonder of gaining the esteem than the love of those they converse with. This gives a formality to their amusements: their gayest conversations have something too wise for innocent relaxation: though in company you are seldom disgusted with the absurdity of a fool, you are seldom lifted into rapture by those strokes of vivacity which give instant though not permanent pleasure.

What they want, however, in gaiety, they make up in politeness. You smile at hearing me praise the English for their politeness—you who have heard very different accounts from the missionaries at Pekin, who have seen such a different behaviour in their merchants and seamen at home. But I must still repeat it, the English seem more polite than any of their neighbours: their great art in this respect lies in endeavouring, while they oblige, to lessen the force of the favour. Other countries are fond of obliging a stranger, but seem desirous that he should be sensible of the obligation. The English confer their kindness with an appearance of indifference, and give away benefits with an air as if they despised them.

Walking, a few days ago, between an English and a French man, into the suburbs of the city, we were overtaken by a heavy shower of rain. I was unprepared; but they had each large coats, which defended them from what seemed to me a perfect inundation. The Englishman, seeing me shrink from the weather, accosted me thus: "Psha, man, what dost shrink at? Here, take this coat; I don't want it; I find it no way useful to me; I had as lief be without it." The Frenchman began to show his politeness in turn. "My dear friend," cries he, "why don't you oblige me by making use of my coat? you see how well it defends me from the rain; I should not choose to part with it to others, but to such a friend as you I could even part with my skin to do him service."

From such minute instances as these, most reverend Fum Hoam, I am sensible your sagacity will collect instruction. The volume of nature is the book of knowledge; and he becomes most wise who makes the most judicious selection.—Farewell.

PASSIONATE LOVE
James Boswell

Semper ut inducar blandos offers mihi vultus,
Post tamen es misero tristis et asper amor.—Tibullus.

Love still invites me with a smiling eye,
Beneath his smiles what pains and anguish lie.—Granger.

It is curious to consider philosophically the nature and effects of that passion, which, while a man is under its influence, deprives him of all philosophy. This description may be thought applicable to every passion. Anger is justly said to be *furor brevis,* "a short frenzy"; and grief has often been known to overpower the reasoning faculties, so as to remind us of a striking passage in the English translation of Voltaire's Tragedy of Mahomet against another foe of rationality.

What a reasonless machine,
Can *superstition* make the reasoner man!

But the passion which I purpose to make the subject of this essay, is the most universal, the most frequently felt of any. I mean the passion of *Love,* in the usual acceptation of the word; in short the ardent fondness which one has for a person of a different sex.

The Almighty Author of our being has created us with appetites necessary for its continuance in this state, and for the multiplication and renewal of our species. But the *desire* which is implanted in us for the enjoyment of sensual pleasure with the other sex, is no more a passion of the *mind* than hunger or thirst is. It is true that the gratification of every appetite is agreeable, because it is at least affording us relief from a painful craving by which we are stimulated, and is often attended with sensations of positive pleasure; and consequently being prevented from it gives us uneasiness in a greater or lesser degree in proportion to the strength of the appetite; so that in a secondary sense the mind may be affected. But

still it is very plain, that the distress occasioned by mere corporeal priva-
tion is very different from the distress of a lover, whose passion for his
mistress meets with no favourable return. The situation of Count
Ugolino and his sons, when starving to death in a dungeon, which is so
strongly described in the original Italian, and which we have lately had
excellently represented in England both in poetry and painting, in the
former by the Earl of Carlisle, and in the latter by Sir Joshua Reynolds,
is a subject of very affecting horror. But the separation of Oroonoko and
Imoinda, of St. Preux and Eloise, or any other scene of such tender affliction, will touch the finer springs of feeling in the heart in a more exquisite manner.

Pope, who from the best information that I have been able to procure,
was, to use his own words, "no philosopher at all," but the disciple of a
noble pretender to philosophy, whose words he set to the finest musick,
is pleased to give us a very indelicate notion of "gentle love and charms,"
representing the amorous passion as nothing else but mere sensuality a
little refined. In my opinion the original impulse may be sensuality; but
the after progress is quite different. The fire may be kindled by the heat
of coarse materials; but the flame burns into a pure brightness. Sensuality
is the fuel by which the imagination is heated; but it will retain the heat
long after the extinction of the fuel.

Perhaps, indeed, there is an insensible combination of the qualities of
body and spirit in the passion of love; for, if we carefully attend to the
wishes of even the most romantic adorer, we shall find that he is never
completely happy without the idea of being in contact with his mistress.
And however he may talk in an elevated styled that it is not a set of features or a complexion that he admires, yet the closest union of affections
will not set his heart fully at rest, unless he folds his charmer in his arms.
He cannot be sure that the jewel is his unless he has possession of the cas-
ket; and although many gay young fellows have sincerely adopted the
lively licentious thought of Congreve,

> I take her body, you her mind,
> Which has the better bargain?

I know not if there has been found in any age a Platonist, grave, cool,
and abstract enough to reverse the proposition, and content himself with
the celestial part, without caring who should take the terrene.
Anacharsis, the Scythian philosopher, when beaten in a mortar by the
command of a tyrant, is reported to have said with astonishing firmness,
"You beat only the shell of Anacharsis." But I doubt if there ever has
been a lover, philosopher enough to be content with the kernel without

the shell; for whether it be founded in truth or not, it is certain we have all a persuasion not to be laid aside, that the body and mind are so intimately connected, that it is impossible to keep quite clear of the latter, if the former be much affected. Hence it was that Lucretia considered herself to be contaminated by the brutal violence of Tarquin, though her mind was filled with abhorrence of the deed; and, therefore, with the courage of a Roman matron, she killed herself.

The general desire of enjoyment of the other sex, like the general appetite for food, is, no doubt, as natural to the human species as to other animals. But the passion of Love, as we know it by experience to be modified, is quite a different thing. For it is an extreme and inexplicable attachment to one particular woman, to account for which, as I have characterised it as inexplicable, I need not be ashamed to acknowledge myself altogether at a loss. When the natural desire is thus modified, the analogy between it and hunger or thirst ceases. A man who is hungry or thirsty satisfies his appetite with any good sort of meat or drink that he can find; and even one who is very nice, or, as the French express it, *friant,* will be heartily glad of the plainest and coarsest food when his appetite is sharpened to keenness, which gives rise to the vulgar proverb, "Hunger is good sauce." In like manner a man, who is actuated only by sensual desire, will indulge it with any female whom he may meet; and like a glutton, who ravenously devours many dishes, will indiscriminately embrace a plurality of wenches; according to Captain Macheath's maxim, "I love the sex; and a man who loves money might as well be content with one guinea as I with one woman." But a man who *is in love* feels himself fixed to one object which appears to his imagination to be peculiarly delightful; and as it absorbs all his fondness, he is quite indifferent about every other woman.

I am now speaking of a man who *is in love indeed;* for I know that there are numerous gradations of the passion, and that the heart may sometimes be divided into many sections, though no doubt there is always a pre-eminent object, as in every seraglio there is a favourite sultana. But as it is a maxim in politicks, "*Divide et impera,* divide and conquer," so I believe that when Love is shared amongst several objects, the passion is no where so strong but that a man has the command of it. Whereas I wish to direct my speculation to All-powerful Love, and to endeavour to raise curious conjectures, and perhaps salutary reflexions, upon the subject.

That the passion of Love is often suddenly formed I do not believe; for although I should acknowledge my faith in *sympathies* of which Sir Kenelm Digby has treated with an enchanting mysticism, and although I do seriously suppose that there are instances of persons who have corresponding qualities that produce instantaneous mutual attraction, I take these instances to be so very rare, that they are to be regarded only as extraordinary phœnomena in the infinite varieties of the universe.

My notion of the formation of Love then is, that there is at first something in the person which pleases; and by *at first* I mean the point of time when the passion commences; for previous to that it frequently happens that the object of violent love is beheld not only without any favourable emotion but with aversion. When the pleasing sensation is frequently reiterated, the imagination grows heated, and partly by habitually meditating on agreeable qualities really belonging to the person, partly by fancying others, the mind becomes so attached to that particular object that it cannot be separated from it without great pain; as branches of trees will grow so close together as not to be put asunder without tearing and destroying part of their substance. This similitude applies exactly where Love is reciprocal. But even when it is only upon one side it affords a very just image of what is suffered by a separation; and it may be remarked that the usual metaphorical expression upon such an occasion is "being *torn* away."

Love for a beautiful and worthy object can excite no wonder; because the mind entirely approves of it as fit and reasonable. But there is no doubt that the most violent passion may be felt for an object destitute of every agreeable and good quality; nay, not only shall this be the case when a man is under a temporary delusion, as love is feigned to be blind, but a man who is distractedly enamoured of such an object shall be fully sensible of this; and yet shall be unable to free himself from the power of the passion. There is a very good song in one of the collections of smaller pieces of poetry, in which a lover *analyzes his mistress,* if that phrase may be used, and after examining her title to different perfections one by one, and still being obliged to acknowledge her deficiency, he accounts for his preference by saying, in short, "'Tis Celia all together." Thus it is that I account for so strange a passion as that which I have just now mentioned. By habitual intercourse a general impression of a particular woman is formed in the imagination so as to excite pleasure; and it is in vain for reason to endeavour to get the better of it: for in many instances reason with all its strength cannot master the weaker but more subtile faculties of the mind. Thus when the imagination is once strongly impressed with the idea that ghosts will more readily appear in darkness than in light, a thorough conviction of the groundlessness of the fancy will not prevent a certain degree of apprehension, as Mr. Locke has observed, when treating of the association of ideas. I am indeed not quite clear that this is a just instance, because those who believe the appearance of ghosts upon the credit of testimony must also believe that darkness has ever been a concomitant circumstance in their appearance; so that it is reasonable to conclude that another appearance of the same kind will be attended with an usual circumstance. My readers however will be at no loss for instances where imagination bids defiance to reason.

It is one of the great arts of wisdom to govern, or, to speak more properly, to manage the imagination; and as no disorder of the imagination has produced more evils than the passion of Love, it behooves us to guard ourselves with caution against its first appearance; for, as Thomson observes, it is too late when the heart is overwhelmed by a torrent of softness. That admirable poet's description of the feverish wretchedness of a violent lover should be frequently perused by all who feel that they have a propensity to amorous inflammation. It has been well said, "Choose the best way of life; and custom will make it easy." Upon this principle of the influence of repeated impressions of the same object, let my readers calmly consider the consequences of being in love with any particular person before they allow their minds to catch fire, by which means they will avoid the torments of criminal or improper attachments. But, if they have unwarily cherished the spark till the fire is too powerful, let them fly from the cause of their sorrow, and sooner or later the fire which is not fed will die away; unless indeed, which has sometimes happened, its force be such as to ravage the mind itself. Tibullus, in the lines which I have prefixed to this paper, has very poetically represented the pleasing approach, but terrible influence of the passion of love when it has attained full possession. His translator Granger, though he has imitated the lines beautifully, has not given the antithesis in the original between *Vultus* and *post*. But in one of the learned notes with which his book is enriched, he observes that the description probably alludes to the masks worn by Love on the stage, viz. an infant's face, with the head and claws of a lion behind. Though in danger from the lion we may get into safety by flight. But horrible is his situation whom the lion holds in his claws till he has mangled him irrecoverably.

PARENTS AND THEIR CHILDREN
James Boswell

Mortales sumus imo nec diuturni sumus: Una ratione diu supersumus si prosemi namus qui supersint. Vivimus in posteris.—JUSTUS LIPSIUS

"We are mortal. Nay we are not long lived. There is one way by which we may last a considerable time, which is, propagating children to survive us. We live in our posterity."

INSTINCT IN other animals, and instinct in the human species differ very much in many instances, and in none more than with respect to the continuation of the species. Instinct in other animals only prompts to the means of having offspring, and to take care of their young. In the human species it prompts to the end, man being formed not only cœlum tueri to look erect as Ovid finely distinguishes him from the beasts who look prone, as Sallust also observes—but to look forward into futurity; and hence he has a strong desire for descendants. In savage life he thinks of preserving his memorable brave deeds, his affections, his resentments from age to age by means of his sons, and his sons sons in succession; so that "I am the last of my race," is a grievous lamentation in that state of society. In civilized life he thinks of preserving his name, his titles, his possessions; and the pleasure which he has in that imagination is perhaps as strong and as permanent as any one enjoyment of which he is capable.

It is indeed wonderful how very strong the desire of continuing ourselves, as we fancy, by a series of offspring, is in all the human race, when we consider that a child begins to exist and comes into the world, we know not how, and most certainly without our being conscious of any ingenuity or art. There is a good story of a simple gentleman who on being asked how he had contrived to have so many pretty daughters, declared "upon his honour, it was all by chance." I am afraid that in general parents may make a more extensive declaration; and allow that the formation of the tempers and principles of their children has been all by chance.

76

But though education does properly speaking make the character, we find that parents claim, and are allowed, a greater connection with their children than masters; nay, they are vainer of their children's attainments. There is something in the notion of *property*, of whatever kind, of what we consider is *ours*, that is the cause of this. A man is vain of improvements upon his estate in which he and all the world know he had no share but paying for them; and that children should be looked upon in some sense as the property of their parents is no peculiar fancy, but has been received in many nations. Even amongst ourselves it is so consonant with the feelings of parents, that it is not easy for them to give up their delusive pretensions.

The *patria potestas* of the ancient Romans appears to have been a very rigorous institution, and not very compatible with the bold freedom for which that people is so highly celebrated. For, if young men be accustomed to the most abject dependence on unlimited authority in an individual, it would seem their spirits must be broke, so as that they never can attain to that manly resolution without which we never enjoy liberty. In our own country we see fathers who very injudiciously, and in my opinion very unjustly, attempt to keep their sons even when well advanced in life, in such a state of subjection as must either reduce them to unfeeling stupidity, or keep them in perpetual uneasiness and vexation. At what period parental power of compulsion should cease, and be succeeded by voluntary filial reverence, cannot be exactly ascertained, but must be left to settle itself according to various circumstances attending the parties. One thing however is certainly right—that the change should be gradual, that a son may imperceptibly arrive at the dignity of personal independence, so as not to be intoxicated and abuse it. If a father has not consideration enough to keep this in view, and accommodate himself accordingly, he will lose in a great measure the satisfaction and comfort of having a son. I knew a father who was a violent whig, and used to attack his son for being a tory, upbraiding him with being deficient in "noble sentiments of liberty," while at the same time he made this son live under his roof in such bondage, that he was not only afraid to stir from home without leave like a child, but durst scarcely open his mouth in his father's presence. This was sad living. Yet I would rather see such an excess of awe than a degree of familiarity between father and son by which all reverence is destroyed. I have seen only one instance of this. They were associates in profligacy. It shocked me so much that I abhor the recollection of it.

The natural inclination to take care of our offspring is, I believe, as strong as the principle of duty which is afterwards established by reason and reflection. It is remarkable that in the divine law it is not thought necessary to inculcate parental duty, whereas that of children is one of the ten commandments, "Honour thy father and thy mother, that thy days may be long in the land which the Lord thy GOD giveth thee." This is a proof that children might be safely trusted to the affection of their parents; but that on the other hand the return which children ought to make required to be specially enjoined. The Athenians found it necessary to make a law by which children should be punished for ingratitude to their parents.

The persuasion that children are truly a part of their parents, should, one would think never fail to produce mutual affection. And indeed it must be acknowledged that at least while children are young, and the feelings of parents not deadened by being long habituated to the world, there is almost universally much love between them. *Justus Lipsius,* immediately after what I have taken for my motto, has these words: "*Et non quidem anima (absit hoc dicere) sed tamen indoles et igniculi in eos transeunt et amamus eos et amamur*—And not indeed the soul (far distant be such a thought) but our disposition and spirits are transferred into them; and we love them and are beloved by them." It is curious to observe the extreme orthodox caution with which the worthy author guards against giving the least countenance to an opinion that soul may be transfused. The theory of generation is to be sure quite a mystery as vitality itself is. But however philosophers may differ, they all agree in the females having such a share, or such an influence in the formation of children, as should make a man very studious to choose a good mother to his children, and justify the trite satire that many of our nobility and gentry are more anxious for the pedigree of their horses than for that of their children. We are told by *Cornelius Nepos* that *Iphicrates,* whose father was an Athenian, and his mother a Thracian, being asked whether he valued most his father or his mother? answered his mother; and when every one wondered at this, he said, "My father did what he could to make me a Thracian, but my mother did what she could to make me an Athenian."

It cannot be denied that it is most agreeable and interesting to have children when in their earlier years. *Justus Lipsius,* talking to a friend on marriage, says, "*Jam voluptas alia quanta et quam penetrans? videre natos liberos lusitantes, balbutientes, mox garrientes, fovere sinu, jungere ori, apprimere pectori: et habere in egressu in regressu tristibus etiam rebus lætificantem hunc occursum*—Then how great, how exquisite is another pleasure, to see your children smiling, lisping, and then prattling; to cherish them in your bosom, to kiss them, to press them to your breast, and when you go out and return to have, even amidst misfortunes, such cheering interviews." This is truly pleasing, and perhaps one is never fonder of one's children than when they are about three years old, just in the state that Lipsius describes; nor does one suffer more keenly by their death than when they are so engaging. One would then wish to take in a literal sense our

Saviour's words as to the little children, "of such is the kingdom of Heaven." And how that may be we cannot tell. There is something of a peculiar pleasing fanciful consolation in the letter from a child of two years old in Heaven to its disconsolate surviving mother, in Mrs. Rowe's Letters from the Dead to the Living.

I remember once observing to a friend that children are like nettles, very innocent when young, but sting you when they grow up. I trust, that this observation, though plausible, is not just; for, I believe it is often a father's own fault if his children do not give him increasing satisfaction as they advance in life. If he does the reverse of what he ought to do by indulging them when very young, and restraining them at the time he should relax, it is in the nature of things that they should be hurt by his treatment of them, and should be apt to dislike him. But if he has managed them with rational discipline while totally unfit to manage themselves, and allowed them a suitable freedom and confidence when older; has stored their minds with good instruction, and enabled them to acquire virtuous and pious habits, he will probably find them a joyful credit to him in life, and a support and comfort at death, so that he shall be sensible of the truth of that verse of the Psalmist, "Lo, children are an heritage of the Lord."

MRS. BATTLE'S OPINIONS ON WHIST

Charles Lamb

"A CLEAR FIRE, a clean hearth,[1] and the rigour of the game." This was the celebrated *wish* of old Sarah Battle (now with God), who, next to her devotions, loved a good game of whist. She was none of your lukewarm gamesters, your half-and-half players, who have no objection to take a hand, if you want one to make up a rubber; who affirm that they have no pleasure in winning; that they like to win one game and lose another; that they can while away an hour very agreeably at a card-table, but are indifferent whether they play or no; and will desire an adversary, who has slipped a wrong card, to take it up and play another.[2] These insufferable triflers are the curse of a table. One of these flies will spoil a whole pot. Of such it may be said that they do not play at cards, but only play at playing at them.

Sarah Battle was none of that breed. She detested them, as I do, from her heart and soul, and would not, save upon a striking emergency, willingly seat herself at the same table with them. She loved a thorough-paced partner, a determined enemy. She took, and gave, no concessions. She hated favours. She never made a revoke, nor ever passed it over in her adversary without exacting the utmost forfeiture. She fought a good fight: cut and thrust. She held not her good sword (her cards) "like a dancer." She sate bolt upright; and neither showed you her cards, nor desired to see yours. All people have their blind side—their superstitions; and I have heard her declare, under the rose, that Hearts was her favourite suit.

I never in my life—and I knew Sarah Battle many of the best years of it—saw her take out her snuff-box when it was her turn to play; or snuff

---

[1] This was before the introduction of rugs, Reader. You must remember the intolerable crash of the unswept cinders betwixt your foot and the marble. [Lamb's note.]

[2] As if a sportsman should tell you he liked to kill a fox one day and lose him the next. [Lamb's note.]

a candle in the middle of a game; or ring for a servant, till it was fairly over. She never introduced, or connived at, miscellaneous conversation during its process. As she emphatically observed, cards were cards; and if I ever saw unmingled distaste in her fine last-century countenance, it was at the airs of a young gentleman of a literary turn, who had been with difficulty persuaded to take a hand; and who, in his excess of candour, declared, that he thought there was no harm in unbending the mind now and then, after serious studies, in recreations of that kind! She could not bear to have her noble occupation, to which she wound up her faculties, considered in that light. It was her business, her duty, the thing she came into the world to do,—and she did it. She unbent her mind afterwards— over a book.

Pope was her favourite author: his *Rape of the Lock* her favourite work. She once did me the favour to play over with me (with the cards) his celebrated game of Ombre in that poem; and to explain to me how far it agreed with, and in what points it would be found to differ from, tradrille. Her illustrations were apposite and poignant; and I had the pleasure of sending the substance of them to Mr. Bowles; but I suppose they came too late to be inserted among his ingenious notes upon that author.

Quadrille, she has often told me, was her first love; but whist had engaged her maturer esteem. The former, she said, was showy and specious, and likely to allure young persons. The uncertainty and quick shifting of partners—a thing which the constancy of whist abhors; the dazzling supremacy and regal investiture of Spadille—absurd, as she justly observed, in the pure aristocracy of whist, where his crown and garter give him no proper power above his brother-nobility of the Aces;—the giddy vanity, so taking to the inexperienced, of playing alone; above all, the overpowering attractions of a *Sans Prendre Vole,*—to the triumph of which there is certainly nothing parallel or approaching, in the contingencies of whist;—all these, she would say, make quadrille a game of captivation to the young and enthusiastic. But whist was the *solider* game: that was her word. It was a long meal; not like quadrille, a feast of snatches. One or two rubbers might co-extend in duration with an evening. They gave time to form rooted friendships, to cultivate steady enmities. She despised the chance-started, capricious, and ever-fluctuating alliances of the other. The skirmishes of quadrille, she would say, reminded her of the petty ephemeral embroilments of the little Italian states, depicted by Machiavel: perpetually changing postures and connexions; bitter foes to-day, sugared darlings to-morrow; kissing and scratching in a breath;—but the wars of whist were comparable to the long, steady, deep-rooted, rational antipathies of the great French and English nations.

A grave simplicity was what she chiefly admired in her favourite game.

There was nothing silly in it, like the nob in cribbage—nothing super-fluous. No *flushes*—that most irrational of all pleas that a reasonable being can set up:—that any one should claim four by virtue of holding cards of the same mark and colour, without reference to the playing of the game, or the individual worth or pretensions of the cards themselves! She held this to be a solecism; as pitiful an ambition at cards as alliteration is in authorship. She despised superficiality, and looked deeper than the colours of things.—Suits were soldiers, she would say, and must have a uniformity of array to distinguish them: but what should we say to a foolish squire, who should claim a merit from dressing up his tenantry in red jackets, that never were to be marshalled—never to take the field?—She even wished that whist were more simple than it is; and, in my mind, would have stripped it of some appendages, which, in the state of human frailty, may be venially, and even commendably, allowed of. She saw no reason for the deciding of the trump by the turn of the card. Why not one suit always trumps?—Why two colours, when the mark of the suit would have sufficiently distinguished them without it?

"But the eye, my dear madam, is agreeably refreshed with the variety. Man is not a creature of pure reason—he must have his senses delightfully appealed to. We see it in Roman Catholic countries, where the music and the paintings draw in many to worship, whom your quaker spirit of unsensualising would have kept out.—You yourself have a pretty collec-tion of paintings—but confess to me, whether, walking in your gallery at Sandham, among those clear Vandykes, or among the Paul Potters in the ante-room, you ever felt your bosom glow with an elegant delight, at all comparable to *that* you have it in your power to experience most evenings over a well-arranged assortment of the court-cards?—the pretty antic habits, like heralds in a procession—the gay triumph-assuring scarlets—the contrasting deadly-killing sables—the 'hoary majesty of spades'—Pam in all his glory!—

"All these might be dispensed with; and with their naked names upon the drab pasteboard, the game might go on very well, pictureless; but the *beauty* of cards would be extinguished for ever. Stripped of all that is imaginative in them, they must degenerate into mere gambling. Imagine a dull deal board, or drum head, to spread them on, instead of that nice verdant carpet (next to nature's), fittest arena for those courtly combat-ants to play their gallant jousts and turneys in!—Exchange those deli-cately-turned ivory markers—(work of Chinese artist, unconscious of their symbol,—or as profanely slighting their true application as the arrantest Ephesian journeyman that turned out those little shrines for the goddess)—exchange them for little bits of leather (our ancestors' money), or chalk and a slate!"—

The old lady, with a smile, confessed the soundness of my logic; and to her approbation of my arguments on her favourite topic that evening I have always fancied myself indebted for the legacy of a curious cribbage-board, made of the finest Sienna marble, which her maternal uncle (old Walter Plumer, whom I have elsewhere celebrated) brought with him from Florence:—this, and a trifle of five hundred pounds, came to me at her death.

The former bequest (which I do not least value) I have kept with religious care; though she herself, to confess a truth, was never greatly taken with cribbage. It was an essentially vulgar game, I have heard her say,—disputing with her uncle, who was very partial to it. She could never heartily bring her mouth to pronounce *"Go,"* or *"That's a go."* She called it an ungrammatical game. The pegging teased her. I once knew her to forfeit a rubber (a five-dollar stake) because she would not take advantage of the turn-up knave, which would have given it her, but which she must have claimed by the disgraceful tenure of declaring *"two for his heels."* There is something extremely genteel in this sort of self-denial. Sarah Battle was a gentlewoman born.

Piquet she held the best game at the cards for two persons, though she would ridicule the pedantry of the terms—such as pique—repique—the capot—they savoured (she thought) of affectation. But games for two, or even three, she never greatly cared for. She loved the quadrate, or square. She would argue thus:—Cards are warfare: the ends are gain, with glory. But cards are war, in disguise of a sport: when single adversaries encounter, the ends proposed are too palpable. By themselves, it is too close a fight; with spectators, it is not much bettered. No looker-on can be interested, except for a bet, and then it is a mere affair of money; he cares not for your luck *sympathetically,* or for your play.—Three are still worse; a mere naked war of every man against every man, as in cribbage, without league or alliance; or a rotation of petty and contradictory interests, a succession of heartless leagues, and not much more hearty infractions of them, as in tradrille.—But in square games *(she meant whist),* all that is possible to be attained in card-playing is accomplished. There are the incentives of profit with honour, common to every species—though the *latter* can be but very imperfectly enjoyed in those other games, where the spectator is only feebly a participator. But the parties in whist are spectators and principals too. They are a theatre to themselves, and a looker-on is not wanted. He is rather worse than nothing, and an impertinence. Whist abhors neutrality, or interests beyond its sphere. You glory in some surprising stroke of skill or fortune, not because a cold—or even an interested—bystander witnesses it, but because your *partner* sympathises in the contingency. You win for two. You triumph for two. Two are exalted. Two again are mortified; which divides their disgrace, as the conjunction doubles (by taking off the invidiousness) your glories. Two losing to two are better reconciled, than one to one in that close butchery. The hostile feeling is weakened by multiplying the channels. War becomes a civil game. By such reasonings as these the old lady was accustomed to defend her favourite pastime.

No inducement could ever prevail upon her to play at any game, where chance entered into the composition, *for nothing*. Chance, she would argue—and here again, admire the subtlety of her conclusion;—chance is nothing, but where something else depends upon it. It is obvious that cannot be *glory*. What rational cause of exultation could it give to a man to turn up size ace a hundred times together by himself? or before spectators, where no stake was depending?—Make a lottery of a hundred thousand tickets with but one fortunate number—and what possible principle of our nature, except stupid wonderment, could it gratify to gain that number as many times successively, without a prize? Therefore she disliked the mixture of chance in backgammon, where it was not played for money. She called it foolish, and those people idiots, who were taken with a lucky hit under such circumstances. Games of pure skill were as little to her fancy. Played for a stake, they were a mere system of over-reaching. Played for glory, they were a mere setting of one man's wit,—his memory, or combination-faculty rather—against another's; like a mock-engagement at a review, bloodless and profitless. She could not conceive a *game* wanting the spritely infusion of chance, the handsome excuses of good fortune. Two people playing at chess in a corner of a room, whilst whist was stirring in the centre, would inspire her with insufferable horror and ennui. Those well-cut similitudes of Castles and Knights, the *imagery* of the board, she would argue (and I think in this case justly), were entirely misplaced and senseless. Those hard-head contests can in no instance ally with the fancy. They reject form and colour. A pencil and dry slate (she used to say) were the proper arena for such combatants.

To those puny objectors against cards, as nurturing the bad passions, she would retort, that man is a gaming animal. He must be always trying to get the better in something or other:—that this passion can scarcely be more safely expended than upon a game at cards: that cards are a temporary illusion; in truth, a mere drama; for we do but *play* at being mightily concerned, where a few idle shillings are at stake, yet, during the illusion, we *are* as mightily concerned as those whose stake is crowns and kingdoms. They are a sort of dream-fighting; much ado; great battling, and little bloodshed; mighty means for disproportioned ends: quite as diverting, and a great deal more innoxious, than many of those more serious *games* of life, which men play without esteeming them to be such.

With great deference to the old lady's judgment on these matters, I think I have experienced some moments in my life, when playing at cards *for nothing* has even been agreeable. When I am in sickness, or not in the best spirits, I sometimes call for the cards, and play a game at piquet *for love* with my cousin Bridget—Bridget Elia.

I grant there is something sneaking in it; but with a toothache or a sprained ankle,—when you are subdued and humble,—you are glad to put up with an inferior spring of action.

There is such a thing in nature, I am convinced, as *sick whist.*

I grant it is not the highest style of man—I deprecate the manes of Sarah Battle—she lives not, alas! to whom I should apologise.

At such times, those *terms* which my old friend objected to, come in as something admissible—I love to get a tierce or a quatorze, though they mean nothing. I am subdued to an inferior interest. Those shadows of winning amuse me.

That last game I had with my sweet cousin (I capotted her)—(dare I tell thee, how foolish I am?)—I wished it might have lasted for ever, though we gained nothing, and lost nothing, though it was a mere shade of play: I would be content to go on in that idle folly for ever. The pip-kin should be ever boiling, that was to prepare the gentle lenitive to my foot, which Bridget was doomed to apply after the game was over: and, as I do not much relish appliances, there it should ever bubble. Bridget and I should be ever playing.

A BACHELOR'S COMPLAINT OF THE
BEHAVIOUR OF MARRIED PEOPLE

Charles Lamb

As A single man, I have spent a good deal of my time in noting down the infirmities of Married People, to console myself for those superior pleasures, which they tell me I have lost by remaining as I am.

I cannot say that the quarrels of men and their wives ever made any great impression upon me, or had much tendency to strengthen me in those anti-social resolutions which I took up long ago upon more substantial considerations. What oftenest offends me at the houses of married persons where I visit, is an error of quite a different description;—it is that they are too loving.

Not too loving neither: that does not explain my meaning. Besides, why should that offend me? The very act of separating themselves from the rest of the world, to have the fuller enjoyment of each other's society, implies that they prefer one another to all the world.

But what I complain of is, that they carry this preference so undisguisedly, they perk it up in the faces of us single people so shamelessly, you cannot be in their company a moment without being made to feel, by some indirect hint or open avowal, that *you* are not the object of this preference. Now there are some things which give no offence, while implied or taken for granted merely; but expressed, there is much offence in them. If a man were to accost the first homely-featured or plain-dressed young woman of his acquaintance, and tell her bluntly, that she was not handsome or rich enough for him, and he could not marry her, he would deserve to be kicked for his ill-manners; yet no less is implied in the fact, that having access and opportunity of putting the question to her, he has never yet thought fit to do it. The young woman understands this as clearly as if it were put into words; but no reasonable young woman would think of making this the ground of a quarrel. Just as little right have a married couple to tell me by speeches, and looks that are scarce less plain than speeches, that I am not the happy man,—the lady's choice. It is enough that I know I am not: I do not want this perpetual reminding.

The display of superior knowledge or riches may be made sufficiently mortifying, but these admit of a palliative. The knowledge which is brought out to insult me, may accidentally improve me; and in the rich man's houses and pictures,—his parks and gardens, I have a temporary usufruct at least. But the display of married happiness has none of these palliatives: it is throughout pure, unrecompensed, unqualified insult.

Marriage by its best title is a monopoly, and not of the least invidious sort. It is the cunning of most possessors of any exclusive privilege to keep their advantage as much out of sight as possible, that their less favoured neighbours, seeing little of the benefit, may the less be disposed to question the right. But these married monopolists thrust the most obnoxious part of their patent into our faces.

Nothing is to me more distasteful than that entire complacency and satisfaction which beam in the countenances of a new-married couple, —in that of the lady particularly: it tells you, that her lot is disposed of in this world: that *you* can have no hopes of her. It is true, I have none: nor wishes either, perhaps: but this is one of those truths which ought, as I said before, to be taken for granted, not expressed.

The excessive airs which those people give themselves, founded on the ignorance of us unmarried people, would be more offensive if they were less irrational. We will allow them to understand the mysteries belonging to their own craft better than we, who have not had the happiness to be made free of the company: but their arrogance is not content within these limits. If a single person presume to offer his opinion in their presence, though upon the most indifferent subject, he is immediately silenced as an incompetent person. Nay, a young married lady of my acquaintance, who, the best of the jest was, had not changed her condition above a fortnight before, in a question on which I had the misfortune to differ from her, respecting the properest mode of breeding oysters for the London market, had the assurance to ask with a sneer, how such an old Bachelor as I could pretend to know anything about such matters!

But what I have spoken of hitherto is nothing to the airs which these creatures give themselves when they come, as they generally do, to have children. When I consider how little of a rarity children are,—that every street and blind alley swarms with them,—that the poorest people commonly have them in most abundance,—that there are few marriages that are not blest with at least one of these bargains,—how often they turn out ill, and defeat the fond hopes of their parents, taking to vicious courses, which end in poverty, disgrace, the gallows, etc.—I cannot for my life tell what cause for pride there can possibly be in having them. If they were young phœnixes, indeed, that were born but one in a year, there might be a pretext. But when they are so common—

I do not advert to the insolent merit which they assume with their husbands on these occasions. Let *them* look to that. But why *we,* who are not their natural-born subjects, should be expected to bring our spices, myrrh, and incense,—our tribute and homage of admiration,—I do not see.

"Like as the arrows in the hand of the giant, even so are the young children"; so says the excellent office in our Prayer-book appointed for the churching of women. "Happy is the man that hath his quiver full of them." So say I; but then don't let him discharge his quiver upon us that are weaponless;—let them be arrows, but not to gall and stick us. I have generally observed that these arrows are double-headed: they have two forks, to be sure to hit with one or the other. As for instance, where you come into a house which is full of children, if you happen to take no notice of them (you are thinking of something else, perhaps, and turn a deaf ear to their innocent caresses), you are set down as untractable, morose, a hater of children. On the other hand, if you find them more than usually engaging,—if you are taken with their pretty manners, and set about in earnest to romp and play with them,—some pretext or other is sure to be found for sending them out of the room; they are too noisy or boisterous, or Mr.—— does not like children. With one or other of these forks the arrow is sure to hit you.

I could forgive their jealousy, and dispense with toying with their brats, if it gives them any pain; but I think it unreasonable to be called upon to *love* them, where I see no occasion,—to love a whole family, perhaps eight, nine, or ten indiscriminately,—to love all the pretty dears, because children are so engaging!

I know there is a proverb, "Love me, love my dog": that is not always so very practicable, particularly if the dog be set upon you to tease you or snap at you in sport. But a dog, or a lesser thing—any inanimate substance, as a keepsake, a watch or a ring, a tree, or the place where we last parted when my friend went away upon a long absence, I can make shift to love, because I love him, and anything that reminds me of him; provided it be in its nature indifferent, and apt to receive whatever hue fancy can give it. But children have a real character, and an essential being of themselves: they are amiable or unamiable *per se*; I must love or hate them as I see cause for either in their qualities. A child's nature is too serious a thing to admit of its being regarded as a mere appendage to another being, and to be loved or hated accordingly; they stand with me upon their own stock, as much as men and women do. Oh! but you will say, sure it is an attractive age,—there is something in the tender years of infancy that of itself charms us. That is the very reason why I am more nice about them. I know that a sweet child is the sweetest thing in nature, not even excepting the delicate creatures which bear them; but the prettier the kind of a thing is, the more desirable it is that it should be pretty of its kind. One daisy differs not much from another in glory; but a violet should look and smell the daintiest.—I was always rather squeamish in my women and children.

But this is not the worst: one must be admitted into their familiarity at least, before they can complain of inattention. It implies visits, and some kind of intercourse. But if the husband be a man with whom you have lived on a friendly footing before marriage,—if you did not come in on the wife's side—if you did not sneak into the house in her train, but were an old friend in fast habits of intimacy before their courtship was so much as thought on,—look about you—your tenure is precarious—before a twelve-month shall roll over your head, you shall find your old friend gradually grow cool and altered towards you, and at last seek opportunities of breaking with you. I have scarce a married friend of my acquaintance, upon whose firm faith I can rely, whose friendship did not commence *after the period of his marriage*. With some limitations they can endure that? but that the good man should have dared to enter into a solemn league of friendship in which they were not consulted, though it happened before they knew him,—before they that are now man and wife ever met,—this is intolerable to them. Every long friendship, every old authentic intimacy, must he brought into their office to be new stamped with their currency, as a sovereign prince calls in the good old money that was coined in some reign before he was born or thought of, to be new marked and minted with the stamp of his authority, before he will let it pass current in the world. You may guess what luck generally befalls such a rusty piece of metal as I am in these *new mintings*.

Innumerable are the ways which they take to insult and worm you out of their husband's confidence. Laughing at all you say with a kind of wonder, as if you were a queer kind of fellow that said good things, *but an oddity,* is one of the ways;—they have a particular kind of stare for the purpose;—till at last the husband, who used to defer to your judgment, and would pass over some excrescences of understanding and manner for the sake of a general vein of observation (not quite vulgar) which he perceived in you, begins to suspect whether you are not altogether a humorist,—a fellow well enough to have consorted with in his bachelor days, but not quite so proper to be introduced to ladies. This may be called the staring way; and is that which has oftenest been put in practice against me.

Then there is the exaggerating way, or the way of irony; that is, where they find you an object of especial regard with their husband, who is not so easily to be shaken from the lasting attachment founded on esteem which he has conceived towards you, by never qualified exaggerations to cry up all that you say or do, till the good man, who understands well enough that it is all done in compliment to him, grows weary of the debt of gratitude which is due to so much candour, and by relaxing a little on his part, and taking down a peg or two in his enthusiasm, sinks at length to that kindly level of moderate esteem—that "decent affection and complacent kindness" towards you, where she herself can join in sympathy with him without much stretch and violence to her sincerity.

Another way (for the ways they have to accomplish so desirable a purpose are infinite) is, with a kind of innocent simplicity, continually to mistake what it was which first made their husband fond of you. If an esteem for something excellent in your moral character was that which riveted the chain which she is to break, upon any imaginary discovery of a want of poignancy in your conversation, she will cry, "I thought, my dear, you described your friend Mr.——, as a great wit?" If, on the other hand, it was for some supposed charm in your conversation that he first grew to like you, and was content for this to overlook some trifling irregularities in your moral deportment, upon the first notice of any of these she as readily exclaims, "This, my dear, is your good Mr. ——!" One good lady whom I took the liberty of expostulating with for not showing me quite so much respect as I thought due to her husband's old friend, had the candour to confess to me that she had often heard Mr.—— speak of me before marriage, and that she had conceived a great desire to be acquainted with me, but that the sight of me had very much disappointed her expectations; for, from her husband's representations of me, she had formed a notion that she was to see a fine, tall, officer-like looking man (I use her very words), the very reverse of which proved to be the truth. This was candid; and I had the civility not to ask her in return how she came to pitch upon a standard of personal accomplishments for her husband's friends which differed so much from his own; for my friend's dimensions as near as possible approximate to mine; he standing five feet five in his shoes, in which I have the advantage of him by about half an inch; and he no more than myself exhibiting any indications of a martial character in his air or countenance.

These are some of the mortifications which I have encountered in the absurd attempt to visit at their houses. To enumerate them all would be a vain endeavour; I shall therefore just glance at the very common impropriety of which married ladies are guilty,—of treating us as if we were their husbands, and *vice versâ*. I mean, when they use us with familiarity, and their husbands with ceremony. *Testacea,* for instance, kept me the other night two or three hours beyond my usual time of supping, while she was fretting because Mr.—— did not come home, till the oysters were all spoiled, rather than she would be guilty of the impoliteness of touching one in his absence. This was reversing the point of good manners: for ceremony is an invention to take off the uneasy feeling which we derive from knowing ourselves to be less the object of love and esteem with a fellow-creature than some other person is. It endeavors to make up, by superior attentions in little points, for that invidious preference which it is forced to deny in the greater. Had *Testacea* kept the oysters back for me, and withstood her husband's importunities to go to supper, she would have acted according to the strict rules of propriety. I know no ceremony that ladies are bound to observe to their husbands, beyond the point of a modest behaviour and decorum: therefore I must protest against the vicarious gluttony of *Cerasia,* who at her own table sent away a dish of Morellas, which I was applying to with great good-will, to her husband at the other end of the table, and recommended a plate of less extraordinary gooseberries to my unwedded palate in their stead. Neither can I excuse the wanton affront of——

But I am weary of stringing up all my married acquaintance by Roman denominations. Let them amend and change their manners, or I promise to record the full-length English of their names, to the terror of all such desperate offenders in future.

THE SUPERANNUATED MAN

Charles Lamb

Sera tamen respexit
Libertas.—VIRGIL.

A Clerk I was in London gay.—O'KEEFE.

IF PERADVENTURE, Reader, it has been thy lot to waste the golden years of thy life—thy shining youth—in the irksome confinement of an office; to have thy prison days prolonged through middle age down to decrepitude and silver hairs, without hope of release or respite; to have lived to forget that there are such things as holidays, or to remember them but as the prerogatives of childhood; then, and then only, will you be able to appreciate my deliverance.

It is now six and thirty years since I took my seat at the desk in Mincing-lane. Melancholy was the transition at fourteen from the abundant play-time, and the frequently-intervening vacations of school days, to the eight, nine, and sometimes ten hours' a-day attendance at a counting-house. But time partially reconciles us to anything. I gradually became content—doggedly contented, as wild animals in cages.

It is true I had my Sundays to myself; but Sundays, admirable as the institution of them is for purposes of worship, are for that very reason the very worst adapted for days of unbending and recreation. In particular, there is a gloom for me attendant upon a city Sunday, a weight in the air. I miss the cheerful cries of London, the music, and the ballad-singers— the buzz and stirring murmur of the streets. Those eternal bells depress me. The closed shops repel me. Prints, pictures, all the glittering and endless succession of knacks and gewgaws, and ostentatiously displayed wares of tradesmen, which make a week-day saunter through the less busy parts of the metropolis so delightful—are shut out. No book-stalls deliciously to idle over—No busy faces to recreate the idle man who contemplates them ever passing by—the very face of business a charm by contrast to his temporary relaxation from it. Nothing to be seen but unhappy countenances—or half-happy at best—of emancipated 'prentices and little tradesfolks, with here and there a servant maid that has got leave to go out, who, slaving all the week, with the habit has lost almost the capacity of enjoying a free hour; and livelily expressing the hollowness of a day's pleasuring. The very strollers in the fields on that day look anything but comfortable.

But besides Sundays I had a day at Easter, and a day at Christmas, with a full week in the summer to go and air myself in my native fields of Hertfordshire. This last was a great indulgence; and the prospect of its recurrence, I believe, alone kept me up through the year, and made my durance tolerable. But when the week came round, did the glittering phantom of the distance keep touch with me? or rather was it not a series of seven uneasy days, spent in restless pursuit of pleasure, and a wearisome anxiety to find out how to make the most of them? Where was the quiet, where the promised rest? Before I had a taste of it, it was vanished. I was at the desk again, counting upon the fifty-one tedious weeks that must intervene before such another snatch would come. Still the prospect of its coming threw something of an illumination upon the darker side of my captivity. Without it, as I have said, I could scarcely have sustained my thraldom.

Independently of the rigours of attendance, I have ever been haunted with a sense (perhaps a mere caprice) of incapacity for business. This, during my latter years, had increased to such a degree, that it was visible in the lines of my countenance. My health and my good spirits flagged. I had perpetually a dread of some crisis, to which I should be found unequal. Besides my day-light servitude, I served over again all night in my sleep, and would awake with terrors of imaginary false entries, errors in my accounts, and the like. I was fifty years of age, and no prospect of emancipation presented itself. I had grown to my desk, as it were; and the wood had entered into my soul.

My fellows in the office would sometimes rally me upon the trouble legible in my countenance; but I did not know that it had raised the suspicions of any of my employers, when, on the 5th of last month, a day ever to be remembered by me, L——, the junior partner in the firm, calling me on one side, directly taxed me with my bad looks, and frankly inquired the cause of them. So taxed, I honestly made confession of my infirmity, and added that I was afraid I should eventually be obliged to resign his service. He spoke some words of course to hearten me, and there the matter rested. A whole week I remained labouring under the impression that I had acted imprudently in my disclosure that I had foolishly given a handle against myself, and had been anticipating my own dismissal. A week passed in this manner, the most anxious one, I verily believe, in my whole life, when on the evening of the 12th of April, just

as I was about quitting my desk to go home (it might be about eight
o'clock) I received an awful summons to attend the presence of the
whole assembled firm in the formidable back parlour. I thought, now my
time is surely come, I have done for myself, I am going to be told that
they have no longer occasion for me. L—— I could see, smiled at the
terror I was in, which was a little relief to me,—when to my utter astonishment B——, the eldest partner, began a formal harangue to me on the
length of my services, my very meritorious conduct during the whole of
the time (the deuce, thought I, how did he find out that? I protest I never
had the confidence to think as much). He went on to descant on the
expediency of retiring at a certain time of life (how my heart panted!)
and asking me a few questions as to the amount of my own property, of
which I have a little, ended with a proposal, to which his three partners
nodded a grave assent, that I should accept from the house, which I had
served so well, a pension for life to the amount of two-thirds of my
accustomed salary—a magnificent offer! I do not know what I answered
between surprise and gratitude, but it was understood that I accepted
their proposal, and I was told that I was free from that hour to leave their
service. I stammered out a bow, and at just ten minutes after eight I went
home—for ever. This noble—benefit gratitude forbids me to conceal
their names—I owe to the kindness of the most munificent firm in the
world—the house of Boldero, Merryweather, Bosanquet, and Lacy.

Esto perpetua!

For the first day or two I felt stunned, overwhelmed. I could only
apprehend my felicity; I was too confused to taste it sincerely. I wandered
about, thinking I was happy, and knowing that I was not. I was in the
condition of a prisoner in the old Bastile, suddenly let loose after a forty
years' confinement. I could scarce trust myself with myself. It was like
passing out of Time into Eternity—for it is a sort of Eternity for a man
to have his Time all to himself. It seemed to me that I had more time on
my hands than I could ever manage. From a poor man, poor in Time, I
was suddenly lifted up into a vast revenue; I could see no end of my possessions; I wanted some steward, or judicious bailiff, to manage my estates
in Time for me. And here let me caution persons grown old in active
business, not lightly, nor without weighing their own resources, to forego
their customary employment all at once, for there may be danger in it. I
feel it by myself, but I know that my resources are sufficient; and now
that those first giddy raptures have subsided, I have a quiet home-feeling
of the blessedness of my condition. I am in no hurry. Having all holidays,
I am as though I had none. If Time hung heavy upon me, I could walk
it away; but I do not walk all day long, as I used to do in those old tran-

sient holidays, thirty miles a day, to make the most of them. If Time were troublesome, I could read it away, but I do not read in that violent measure, with which, having no Time my own but candle-light Time, I used to weary out my head and eyesight in by-gone winters. I walk, read or scribble (as now) just when the fit seizes me. I no longer hunt after pleasure; I let it come to me. I am like the man

> —That's born, and has his years come to him,
> In some green desart.

"Years," you will say! "what is this superannuated simpleton calculating upon? He has already told us, he is past fifty."

I have indeed lived nominally fifty years, but deduct out of them the hours which I have lived to other people, and not to myself, and you will find me still a young fellow. For that is the only true time, which a man can properly call his own, that which he has all to himself; the rest, though in some sense he may be said to live it, is other people's time, not his. The remnant of my poor days, long or short, is at least multiplied for me three-fold. My ten next years, if I stretch so far, will be as long as any preceding thirty. 'Tis a fair rule-of-three sum.

Among the strange fantasies which beset me at the commencement of my freedom, and of which all traces are not yet gone, one was, that a vast tract of time had intervened since I quitted the Counting House. I could not conceive of it as an affair of yesterday. The partners, and the clerks, with whom I had for so many years, and for so many hours in each day of the year, been closely associated—being suddenly removed from them—they seemed as dead to me. There is a fine passage, which may serve to illustrate this fancy, in a Tragedy by Sir Robert Howard, speaking of a friend's death:

> —'Twas but just now he went away;
> I have not since had time to shed a tear;
> And yet the distance does the same appear
> As if he had been a thousand years from me.
> Time takes no measure in Eternity.

To dissipate this awkward feeling, I have been fain to go among them once or twice since; to visit my old desk-fellows—my co-brethren of the quill—that I had left below in the state militant. Not all the kindness with which they received me could quite restore to me that pleasant familiarity, which I had heretofore enjoyed among them. We cracked some of our old jokes, but methought they went off but faintly. My old desk; the peg there I hung my hat, were appropriated to another. I knew it must be, but I could not take it kindly. D——l take me, if I could not feel some remorse—beast, if I had not,—at quitting my old compeers, the faithful partners of my toils for six and thirty years, that smoothed for me with their jokes and conundrums the ruggedness of my professional road. Had it been so rugged then after all? or was I a coward simply? Well, it is too late to repent; and I also know, that these suggestions are a common fallacy of the mind on such occasions. But my heart smote me. I had violently broken the bands betwixt us. It was at least not courteous. I shall be some time before I get quite reconciled to the separation. Farewell, old cronies, yet not for long, for again and again I will come among ye, if I shall have your leave. Farewell Ch——, dry, sarcastic, and friendly! Do——, mild, slow to move, and gentlemanly! Pl——, officious to do, and to volunteer, good services!—and thou, thou dreary pile, fit mansion for a Gresham or a Whittington of old, stately House of merchants; with thy labyrinthine passages, and light-excluding, pent-up offices, where candles for one half the year supplied the place of the sun's light; unhealthy contributor to my weal, stern fosterer of my living, farewell! In thee remain, and not in the obscure collection of some wandering bookseller, my "works!" There let them rest, as I do from my labours, piled on thy massy shelves, more MSS. in folio than ever Aquinas left, and full as useful! My mantle I bequeath among ye. A fortnight has passed since the date of my first communication. At that period I was approaching to tranquillity, but had not reached it. I boasted of a calm indeed, but it was comparative only. Something of the first flutter was left; an unsettling sense of novelty; the dazzle to weak eyes of unaccustomed light. I missed my old chains, forsooth, as if they had been some necessary part of my apparel. I was a poor Carthusian, from strict cellular discipline suddenly by some revolution returned upon the world. I am now as if I had never been other than my own master. It is natural to me to go where I please, to do what I please. I find myself at eleven o'clock in the day in Bond-street, and it seems to me that I have been sauntering there at that very hour for years past. I digress into Soho, to explore a book-stall. Methinks I have been thirty years a collector. There is nothing strange nor new in it. I find myself before a fine picture in a morning. Was it ever otherwise? What is become of Fish-street Hill? Where is Fenchurch-street? Stones of old Mincing-lane, which I have worn with my daily pilgrimage for six and thirty years, to the footsteps of what toilworn clerk are your everlasting flints now vocal? I indent the gayer flags of Pall Mall. It is Change time, and I am strangely among the Elgin marbles. It was no hyperbole when I ventured to compare the change in my condition to a passing into another world. Time stands still in a manner to me. I have lost all distinction of season. I do not know the day of the week, or of the month. Each day used to be individually felt by me in its reference to the foreign post days; in its distance from, or propinquity to, the next Sunday. I had my Wednesday feelings, my Saturday nights' sensations. The genius of each day was upon me distinctly during the whole of it, affecting my appetite, spirits, &c. The phantom of the next day, with the dreary five to follow, sate as a load upon my poor Sabbath recreations. What charm has washed that Ethiop white? What is gone of Black Monday? All days are the same. Sunday itself—that unfortunate failure of a holyday as it too often proved, what with my sense of its fugitiveness, and over-care to get the greatest quantity of pleasure out of it—is melted down into a week day. I can spare to go to church now, without grudging the huge cantle which it used to seem to cut out of the holyday. I have Time for everything. I can visit a sick friend. I can interrupt the man of much occupation when he is busiest. I can insult over him with an invitation to take a day's pleasure with me to Windsor this fine May-morning. It is Lucretian pleasure to behold the poor drudges, whom I have left behind in the world, carking and caring; like horses in a mill, drudging on in the same eternal round—and what is it all for? A man can never have too much Time to himself, nor too little to do. Had I a little son, I would christen him NOTHING-TO-DO; he should do nothing. Man, I verily believe, is out of his element as long as he is operative. I am altogether for the life contemplative. Will no kindly earthquake come and swallow up those accursed cotton mills? Take me that lumber of a desk there, and bowl it down

> As low as to the fiends.

I am no longer ******, clerk to the Firm of &c. I am Retired Leisure. I am to be met with in trim gardens. I am already come to be known by my vacant face and careless gesture, perambulating at no fixed pace, nor with any settled purpose. I walk about; not to and from. They tell me, a certain *cum dignitate* air, that has been buried so long with my other good parts, has begun to shoot forth in my person. I grow into gentility perceptibly. When I take up a newspaper, it is to read the state of the opera. *Opus operatum est.* I have done all that I came into this world to do. I have worked task work, and have the rest of the day to myself.

OLD CHINA
Charles Lamb

I HAVE AN almost feminine partiality for old china. When I go to see any great house, I enquire for the china-closet, and next for the picture gallery. I cannot defend the order of preference, but by saying, that we have all some taste or other, of too ancient a date to admit of our remembering distinctly that it was an acquired one. I can call to mind the first play, and the first exhibition, that I was taken to; but I am not conscious of a time when china jars and saucers were introduced into my imagination.

I had no repugnance then—why should I now have?—to those little, lawless, azure-tinctured grotesques, that under the notion of men and women, float about, uncircumscribed by any element, in that world before perspective—a china tea-cup.

I like to see my old friends—whom distance cannot diminish—figuring up in the air (so they appear to our optics) yet on *terra firma* still—so we must in courtesy interpret that speck of deeper blue,—which the decorous artist, to prevent absurdity, has made to spring up beneath their sandals.

I love the men with women's faces, and the women, if possible, with still more womanish expressions.

Here is a young and courtly Mandarin, handing tea to a lady from a salver—two miles off. See how distance seems to set off respect! And here the same lady, or another—for likeness is identity on tea-cups—is stepping into a little fairy boat, moored on the hither side of this calm garden river, with a dainty mincing foot, which in a right angle of incidence (as angles go in our world) must infallibly land her in the midst of a flowery mead—a furlong off on the other side of the same strange stream!

Farther on—if far or near can be predicated of their world—see horses, trees, pagodas, dancing the hays.

Here—a cow and rabbit couchant, and co-extensive—so objects show, seen through the lucid atmosphere of fine Cathay.

I was pointing out to my cousin last evening, over our Hyson, (which we are old fashioned enough to drink unmixed still of an afternoon) some of these *speciosa miracula* upon a set of extraordinary old blue china (a recent purchase) which we were now for the first time using; and could not help remarking, how favourable circumstances had been to us of late years, that we could afford to please the eye sometimes with trifles of this sort—when a passing sentiment seemed to overshade the brows of my companion. I am quick at detecting these summer clouds in Bridget.

"I wish the good old times would come again," she said, "when we were not quite so rich. I do not mean, that I want to be poor; but there was a middle state"—so she was pleased to ramble on,—"in which I am sure we were a great deal happier. A purchase is but a purchase, now that you have money enough and to spare. Formerly it used to be a triumph. When we coveted a cheap luxury (and, O! how much ado I had to get you to consent in those times!)—we were used to have a debate two or three days before, and to weigh the *for* and *against,* and think what we might spare it out of, and what saving we could hit upon, that should be an equivalent. A thing was worth buying then, when we felt the money that we paid for it.

"Do you remember the brown suit, which you made to hang upon you, till all your friends cried shame upon you, it grew so thread-bare— and all because of that folio Beaumont and Fletcher, which you dragged home late at night from Barker's in Covent Garden? Do you remember how we eyed it for weeks before we could make up our minds to the purchase, and had not come to a determination till it was near ten o'clock of the Saturday night, when you set off from Islington, fearing you should be too late—and when the old bookseller with some grumbling opened his shop, and by the twinkling taper (for he was setting bedwards) lighted out the relic from his dusty treasures—and when you lugged it home, wishing it were twice as cumbersome—and when you presented it to me—and when we were exploring the perfectness of it (*collating* you called it)—and while I was repairing some of the loose leaves with paste, which your impatience would not suffer to be left till day-break—was there no pleasure in being a poor man? or can those neat black clothes which you wear now, and are so careful to keep brushed, since we have become rich and finical, give you half the honest vanity, with which you flaunted it about in that overworn suit—your old corbeau—for four or five weeks longer than you should have done, to pacify your conscience for the mighty sum of fifteen—or sixteen shillings was it?—a great affair we thought it then—which you had lavished on the old folio. Now you can afford to buy any book that pleases you, but I do not see that you ever bring me home any nice old purchases now."

"When you came home with twenty apologies for laying out a less number of shillings upon that print after Lionardo, which we christened the 'Lady Blanch'; when you looked at the purchase, and thought of the money—and thought of the money, and looked again at the picture—was there no pleasure in being a poor man. Now, you have nothing to do but to walk into Colnaghi's, and buy a wilderness of Lionardos. Yet do you?

"Then, do you remember our pleasant walks to Enfield, and Potter's Bar, and Waltham, when we had a holyday—holydays, and all other fun, are gone, now we are rich—and the little hand-basket in which I used to deposit our day's fare of savoury cold lamb and salad—and how you would pry about at noon-tide for some decent house, where we might go in, and produce our store—only paying for the ale that you must call for—and speculate upon the looks of the landlady, and whether she was likely to allow us a table-cloth—and wish for such another honest hostess, as Izaak Walton has described many a one on the pleasant banks of the Lea, when he went a fishing—and sometimes they would prove obliging enough, and sometimes they would look grudgingly upon us—but we had cheerful looks still for one another, and would eat our plain food savorily, scarcely grudging Piscator his Trout Hall? Now,—when we go out a day's pleasuring, which is seldom moreover, we *ride* part of the way—and go into a fine inn, and order the best of dinners, never debating the expense—which, after all, never has half the relish of those chance country snaps, when we were at the mercy of uncertain usage, and a precarious welcome.

"You are too proud to see a play anywhere now but in the pit. Do you remember where it was we used to sit, when we saw the Battle of Hexham, and the Surrender of Calais, and Bannister and Mrs. Bland in the Children in the Wood—when we squeezed out our shillings a-piece to sit three or four times in a season in the one-shilling gallery—where you felt all the time that you ought not to have brought me—and more strongly I felt obligation to you for having brought me—and the pleasure was the better for a little shame—and when the curtain drew up, what cared we for our place in the house, or what mattered it where we were sitting, when our thoughts were with Rosalind in Arden, or with Viola at the Court of Illyria? You used to say, that the Gallery was the best place of all for enjoying a play socially—that the relish of such exhibitions must be in proportion to the infrequency of going—that the company we met there, not being in general readers of plays, were obliged to attend the more, and did attend, to what was going on, on the stage—because a word lost would have been a chasm, which it was impossible for them to fill up. With such reflections we consoled our pride then—and I appeal to you, whether, as a woman, I met generally with less attention and accommodation, than I have done since in more expensive situations in the house? The getting in indeed, and the crowd-ing up those inconvenient staircases, was bad enough,—but there was still a law of civility to woman recognised to quite as great an extent as we ever found in the other passages—and how a little difficulty overcome heightened the snug seat, and the play, afterwards. Now we can only pay our money and walk in. You cannot see, you say, in the galleries now. I am sure we saw, and heard too, well enough then—but sight, and all, I think, is gone with our poverty."

"There was pleasure in eating strawberries, before they became quite common—in the first dish of peas, while they were yet dear—to have them for a nice supper, a treat. What treat can we have now? If we were to treat ourselves now—that is, to have dainties a little above our means, it would be selfish and wicked. It is the very little more that we allow ourselves beyond what the actual poor can get at, that makes what I call a treat—when two people living together, as we have done, now and then indulge themselves in a cheap luxury, which both like; while each apologises, and is willing to take both halves of the blame to his single share. I see no harm in people making much of themselves in that sense of the word. It may give them a hint how to make much of others. But now—what I mean by the word—we never do make much of ourselves. None but the poor can do it. I do not mean the veriest poor of all, but persons as we were, just above poverty."

"I know what you were going to say, that it is mighty pleasant at the end of the year to make all meet,—and much ado we used to have every Thirty-first Night of December to account for our exceedings—many a long face did you make over your puzzled accounts, and in contriving to make it out how we had spent so much—or that we had not spent so much—or that it was impossible we should spend so much next year— and still we found our slender capital decreasing—but then, betwixt ways, and projects, and compromises of one sort or another, and talk of curtailing this charge, and doing without that for the future—and the hope that youth brings, and laughing spirits (in which you were never poor till now) we pocketed up our loss, and in conclusion, with 'lusty brimmers' (as you used to quote it out of *hearty cheerful Mr. Cotton,* as you called him), we used to welcome in the 'coming guest.' Now we have no reckoning at all at the end of the old year—no flattering promises about the new year doing better for us."

Bridget is so sparing of her speech on most occasions, that when she gets into a rhetorical vein, I am careful how I interrupt it. I could not help, however, smiling at the phantom of wealth which her dear imagi-nation had conjured up out of a clear income of a poor—hundred pounds a year. "It is true we were happier when we were poorer, but we were also younger, my cousin. I am afraid we must put up with the excess, for if we were to shake the superflux into the sea, we should not much mend ourselves. That we had much to struggle with, as we grew up together, we have reason to be most thankful. It strengthened, and knit our compact closer. We could never have been what we have been to each other, if we had always had the sufficiency which you now complain of. The resisting power—those natural dilations of the youthful spirit, which circumstances cannot straighten—with us are long since passed away. Competence to age is supplementary youth, a sorry supplement indeed, but I fear the best that is to be had. We must ride, where we formerly walked: live better, and lie softer—and shall be wise to do so—than we had means to do in those good old days you speak of. Yet could those days return—could you and I once more walk our thirty miles a-day—could Bannister and Mrs. Bland again be young, and you and I be young to see them—could the good old one-shilling gallery days return—they are dreams, my cousin, now—but could you and I at this moment, instead of this quiet argument, by our well-carpeted fireside, sitting on this luxurious sofa—be once more struggling up those inconvenient stair cases, pushed about, and squeezed, and elbowed by the poorest rabble of poor gallery scramblers—could I once more hear those anxious shrieks of yours—and the delicious *Thank God, we are safe,* which always followed when the topmost stair, conquered, let in the first light of the whole cheerful theatre down beneath us—I know not the fathom line that ever touched a descent so deep as I would be willing to bury more wealth in than Crœsus had, or the great Jew R—— is supposed to have, to purchase it. And now do just look at that merry little Chinese waiter holding an umbrella, big enough for a bed-tester, over the head of that pretty insipid half-Madonaish chit of a lady in that very blue summer house."

ON FAMILIAR STYLE

William Hazlitt

IT IS not easy to write a familiar style. Many people mistake a familiar for a vulgar style, and suppose that to write without affectation is to write at random. On the contrary, there is nothing that requires more precision, and, if I may so say, purity of expression, than the style I am speaking of. It utterly rejects not only all unmeaning pomp, but all low, cant phrases, and loose, unconnected, *slipshod* allusions. It is not to take the first word that offers, but the best word in common use; it is not to throw words together in any combinations we please, but to follow and avail ourselves of the true idiom of the language. To write a genuine familiar or truly English style, is to write as any one would speak in common conversation, who had a thorough command and choice of words, or who could discourse with ease, force, and perspicuity, setting aside all pedantic and oratorical flourishes. Or, to give another illustration, to write naturally is the same thing in regard to common conversation, as to read naturally is in regard to common speech. It does not follow that it is an easy thing to give the true accent and inflection to the words you utter, because you do not attempt to rise above the level of ordinary life and colloquial speaking. You do not assume indeed the solemnity of the pulpit, or the tone of stage-declamation: neither are you at liberty to gabble on at a venture, without emphasis or discretion, or to resort to vulgar dialect or clownish pronunciation. You must steer a middle course. You are tied down to a given and appropriate articulation, which is determined by the habitual associations between sense and sound, and which you can only hit by entering into the author's meaning, as you must find the proper words and style to express yourself by fixing your thoughts on the subject you have to write about. Any one may mouth out a passage with a theatrical cadence, or get upon stilts to tell his thoughts: but to write or speak with propriety and simplicity is a more difficult task. Thus it is easy to affect a pompous style, to use a word twice as big as the thing you want to express: it is not so easy to pitch upon the very word that exactly fits it. Out of eight or ten words equally common, equally intelligible, with nearly equal pretensions, it is a matter of some nicety and discrimination to pick out the very one, the preferableness of which is scarcely perceptible, but decisive. The reason why I object to Dr. Johnson's style is, that there is no discrimination, no selection, no variety in it. He uses none but "tall, opaque words," taken from the "first row of the rubric:"—words with the greatest number of syllables, or Latin phrases with merely English terminations. If a fine style depended on this sort of arbitrary pretension, it would be fair to judge of an author's elegance by the measurement of his words, and the substitution of foreign circumlocutions (with no precise associations) for the mother-tongue. How simple is it to be dignified without ease, to be pompous without meaning! Surely, it is but a mechanical rule for avoiding what is low to be always pedantic and affected. It is clear you cannot use a vulgar English word, if you never use a common English word at all. A fine tact is shown in adhering to those which are perfectly common, and yet never falling into any expressions which are debased by disgusting circumstances, or which owe their signification and point to technical or professional allusions. A truly natural or familiar style can never be quaint or vulgar, for this reason, that it is of universal force and applicability, and that quaintness and vulgarity arise out of the immediate connection of certain words with coarse and disagreeable, or with confined ideas. The last form what we understand by *cant* or *slang* phrases.—To give an example of what is not very clear in the general statement. I should say that the phrase *To cut with a knife,* or *To cut a piece of wood,* is perfectly free from vulgarity, because it is perfectly common: but to *cut an acquaintance* is not quite unexceptionable, because it is not perfectly common or intelligible, and has hardly yet escaped out of the limits of slang phraseology. I should hardly therefore use the word in this sense without putting it in italics as a license of expression, to be received *cum grano salis.* All provincial or bye-phrases come under the same mark of reprobation—all such as the writer transfers to the page from his fireside or a particular *coterie,* or that he invents for his own sole use and convenience. I conceive that words are like money, not the worse for being common, but that it is the stamp of custom alone that gives them circulation or value. I am fastidious in this respect, and would almost as soon coin the currency of the realm as counterfeit the King's English. I never invented or gave a new and unauthorised meaning to any word but one single one (the term *impersonal* applied to feelings) and that was in an abstruse metaphysical discussion to express a very difficult distinction. I have been (I know) loudly accused of revelling in vulgarisms and broken English. I cannot speak to that point: but so far I plead guilty to the determined use of acknowledged idioms and common elliptical expressions. I am not sure that the critics in question know the one from the other, that is, can distinguish any medium between formal pedantry and the most barbarous solecism. As an author, I endeavour to employ plain words and popular modes of construction, as were I a chapman and dealer, I should common weights and measures.

The proper force of words lies not in the words themselves, but in their application. A word may be a fine-sounding word, of an unusual length, and very imposing from its learning and novelty, and yet in the connection in which it is introduced, may be quite pointless and irrelevant. It is not pomp or pretension, but the adaptation of the expression to the idea that clenches a writer's meaning:—as it is not the size or glossiness of the materials, but their being fitted each to its place, that gives strength to the arch; or as the pegs and nails are as necessary to the support of the building as the larger timbers, and more so than the mere showy, unsubstantial ornaments. I hate anything that occupies more space than it is worth. I hate to see a load of bandboxes go along the street, and I hate to see a parcel of big words without anything in them. A person who does not deliberately dispose of all his thoughts alike in cumbrous draperies and flimsy disguises, may strike out twenty varieties of familiar every-day language, each coming somewhat nearer to the feeling he wants to convey, and at last not hit upon that particular and only one, which may be said to be identical with the exact impression in his mind. This would seem to show that Mr. Cobbett is hardly right in saying that the first word that occurs is always the best. It may be a very good one; and yet a better may present itself on reflection or from time to time. It should be suggested naturally, however, and spontaneously, from a fresh and lively conception of the subject. We seldom succeed by trying at improvement, or by merely substituting one word for another that we are not satisfied with, as we cannot recollect the name of a place or person by merely plaguing ourselves about it. We wander farther from the point by persisting in a wrong scent; but it starts up accidentally in the memory when we least expected it, by touching some link in the chain of previous association.

There are those who hoard up and make a cautious display of nothing but rich and rare phraseology;—ancient medals, obscure coins, and Spanish pieces of eight. They are very curious to inspect; but I myself would neither offer nor take them in the course of exchange. A sprinkling of archaisms is not amiss; but a tissue of obsolete expressions is more fit *for keep than wear.* I do not say I would not use any phrase that had been brought into fashion before the middle or the end of the last century: but I should be shy of using any that had not been employed by any approved author during the whole of that time. Words, like clothes, get old-fashioned, or mean and ridiculous, when they have been for some time laid aside. Mr. Lamb is the only imitator of old English style I can read with pleasure; and he is so thoroughly imbued with the spirit of his authors, that the idea of imitation is almost done away. There is an inward unction, a marrowy vein both in the thought and feeling, an intuition, deep and lively, of his subject, that carries off any quaintness or awkwardness arising from an antiquated style and dress. The matter is completely his own, though the manner is assumed. Perhaps his ideas are altogether so marked and individual, as to require their point and pungency to be neutralised by the affectation of a singular but traditional form of conveyance. Tricked out in the prevailing costume, they would probably seem more startling and⁻ out of the way. The old English authors, Burton, Fuller, Coryat, Sir Thomas Browne, are a kind of mediators between us and the more eccentric and whimsical modern, reconciling us to his peculiarities. I do not however know how far this is the case or not, till he condescends to write like one of us. I must confess that what I like best of his papers under the signature of Elia (still I do not presume, amidst such excellence, to decide what is most excellent) is the account of "Mrs. Battle's Opinions on Whist," which is also the most free from obsolete allusions and turns of expression—

A well of native English undefiled.

To those acquainted with his admired prototypes, these Essays of the ingenious and highly-gifted author have the same sort of charm and relish, that Erasmus's Colloquies or a fine piece of modern Latin have to the classical scholar. Certainly, I do not know any borrowed pencil that has more power or felicity of execution than the one of which I have here been speaking.

It is as easy to write a gaudy style without ideas, as it is to spread a pallet of showy colours, or to smear in a flaunting transparency. "What do you read?"—"Words, words, words."—"What is the matter?"—"*Nothing,*" it might be answered. The florid style is the reverse of the familiar. The last is employed as an unvarnished medium to convey ideas; the first is resorted to as a spangled veil to conceal the want of them. When there is nothing to be set down but words, it costs little to have them fine. Look through the dictionary, and cull out a *florilegium,* rival the *tulippomania. Rouge* high enough, and never mind the natural complexion. The vulgar, who are not in the secret, will admire the look of preternatural health and vigour; and the fashionable, who regard only appearances, will be delighted with the imposition. Keep to your sounding generalities, your tinkling phrases, and all will be well. Swell out an unmeaning truism to a perfect tympany of style. A thought, a distinction is the rock on which all this brittle cargo of verbiage splits at once. Such writers have merely *verbal* imaginations, that retain nothing but words. Or their puny thoughts have dragon-wings, all green and gold. They soar far above the vulgar failing of the *Sermo humi obrepens*—their most ordinary speech is never short of an hyperbole, splendid, imposing, vague, incomprehensible, magniloquent, a cento of sounding common-places. If some of us, whose "ambition is more lowly," pry a little too narrowly into nooks and corners to pick up a number of "unconsidered trifles," they never once direct their eyes or lift their hands to seize on any but the most gorgeous, tarnished, thread bare patch-work set of phrases, the left-off finery of poetic extravagance, transmitted down through successive generations of barren pretenders. If they criticise actors and actresses, a huddled phantasmagoria of feathers, spangles, floods of light, and oceans of sound float before their morbid sense, which they paint in the style of Ancient Pistol. Not a glimpse can you get of the merits or defects of the performers: they are hidden in a profusion of barbarous epithets and wilful rhodomontade. Our hypercritics are not thinking of these little fantoccini beings—

That strut and fret their hour upon the stage—

but of tall phantoms of words, abstractions, *genera* and *species,* sweeping clauses, periods that unite the Poles, forced alliterations, astounding antitheses—

And on their pens *Fustian* sits plumed.

If they describe kings and queens, it is an Eastern pageant. The Coronation at either House is nothing to it. We get at four repeated images—a curtain, a throne, a sceptre, and a footstool. These are with them the wardrobe of a lofty imagination; and they turn their servile strains to servile uses. Do we read a description of pictures? It is not a reflection of tones and hues which "nature's own sweet and cunning hand laid on," but piles of precious stones, rubies, pearls, emeralds, Golconda's mines, and all the blazonry of art. Such persons are in fact besotted with words, and their brains are turned with the glittering, but empty and sterile phantoms of things. Personifications, capital letters, seas of sunbeams, visions of glory, shining inscriptions, the figures of a transparency, Britannia with her shield, or Hope leaning on an anchor, make up their stock in trade. They may be considered *hieroglyphical* writers. Images stands out in their minds isolated and important merely in themselves, without any ground-work of feeling—there is no context in their imaginations. Words affect them in the same way, by the mere sound, that is, by their possible, not by their actual application to the subject in hand.

They are fascinated by first appearances, and have no sense of consequences. Nothing more is meant by them than meets the ear: they understand or feel nothing more than meets their eye. The web and texture of the universe, and of the heart of man, is a mystery to them: they have no faculty that strikes a chord in unison with it. They cannot get beyond the daubings of fancy, the varnish of sentiment. Objects are not linked to feelings, words to things, but images revolve in splendid mockery, words represent themselves in their strange rhapsodies. The categories of such a mind are pride and ignorance—pride in outside show, to which they sacrifice everything, and ignorance of the true worth and hidden structure both of words and things. With a sovereign contempt for what is familiar and natural, they are the slaves of vulgar affectation—of a routine of high-flown phrases. Scorning to imitate realities, they are unable to invent anything, to strike out one original idea. They are not copyists of nature, it is true: but they are the poorest of all plagiarists, the plagiarists of words. All is far fetched, dear-bought, artificial, oriental, in subject and allusion: all is mechanical, conventional, vapid, formal, pedantic in style and execution. They startle and confound the understanding of the reader, by the remoteness and obscurity to their illustrations: they soothe the ear by the monotony of the same everlasting round of circuitous metaphors. They are the *mock-school* in poetry and prose. They flounder about between fustian in expression, and bathos in sentiment. They tantalise the fancy, but never reach the head nor touch the heart. Their Temple of Fame is like a shadowy structure raised by Dulness to Vanity, or like Cowper's description of the Empress of Russia's palace of ice, "as worthless as in show 'twas glittering"—

It smiled, and it was cold!

ON GOING A JOURNEY
William Hazlitt

ONE OF the pleasantest things in the world is going a journey; but I like to go by myself. I can enjoy society in a room; but out of doors, nature is company enough for me. I am then never less alone than when alone.

> The fields his study, nature was his book.

I cannot see the wit of walking and talking at the same time. When I am in the country, I wish to vegetate like the country. I am not for criticising hedge-rows and black cattle. I go out of town in order to forget the town and all that is in it. There are those who for this purpose go to watering-places, and carry the metropolis with them. I like more elbow-room, and fewer incumbrances. I like solitude, when I give myself up to it, for the sake of solitude; nor do I ask for

> —a friend in my retreat,
> Whom I may whisper solitude is sweet.

The soul of a journey is liberty, perfect liberty, to think, feel, do, just as one pleases. We go a journey chiefly to be free of all impediments and of all inconveniences; to leave ourselves behind much more to get rid of others. It is because I want a little breathing-space to muse on indifferent matters, where Contemplation

> May plume her feathers and let grow her wings,
> That in the various bustle of resort
> Were all too ruffled, and sometimes impair'd,

that I absent myself from the town for a while, without feeling at a loss the moment I am left by myself. Instead of a friend in a postchaise or in a Tilbury, to exchange good things with, and vary the same stale topics over again, for once let me have a truce with impertinence. Give me the clear blue sky over my head, and the green turf beneath my feet, a winding road before me, and a three hours' march to dinner—and then to thinking! It is hard if I cannot start some game on these lone heaths. I laugh, I run, I leap, I sing for joy. From the point of yonder rolling cloud, I plunge into my past being, and revel there, as the sun-burnt Indian plunges headlong into the wave that wafts him to his native shore. Then long-forgotten things, like "sunken wrack and sumless treasuries," burst upon my eager sight, and I begin to feel, think, and be myself again. Instead of an awkward silence, broken by attempts at wit or dull common-places, mine is that undisturbed silence of the heart which alone is perfect eloquence. No one likes puns, alliterations, antitheses, argument, and analysis better than I do; but I sometimes had rather be without them. "Leave, oh, leave me to my repose!" I have just now other business in hand, which would seem idle to you, but is with me "very stuff o' the conscience." Is not this wild rose sweet without a comment? Does not this daisy leap to my heart set in its coat of emerald? Yet if I were to explain to you the circumstance that has so endeared it to me, you would only smile. Had I not better then keep it to myself, and let it serve me to brood over, from here to yonder craggy point, and from thence onward to the far-distant horizon? I should be but bad company all that way, and therefore prefer being alone. I have heard it said that you may, when the moody fit comes on, walk or ride on by yourself, and indulge your reveries. But this looks like a breach of manners, a neglect of others, and you are thinking all the time that you ought to rejoin your party. "Out upon such half-faced fellowship," say I. I like to be either entirely to myself, or entirely at the disposal of others; to talk or be silent, to walk or sit still, to be sociable or solitary. I was pleased with an observation of Mr. Cobbett's, that "he thought it a bad French custom to drink our wine with our meals, and that an Englishman ought to do only one thing at a time." So I cannot talk and think, or indulge in melancholy musing and lively conversation by fits and starts. "Let me have a companion of my way," says Sterne, "were it but to remark how the shadows lengthen as the sun declines." It is beautifully said: but in my opinion, this continual comparing of notes interferes with the involuntary impression of things upon the mind, and hurts the sentiment. If you only hint what you feel in a kind of dumb show, it is insipid: if you have to explain it, it is making a toil of a pleasure. You cannot read the book of nature without being perpetually put to the trouble of translating it for the benefit of others. I am for this synthetical method on a journey in preference to the analytical. I am content to lay in a stock of ideas then, and to examine and anatomise them afterwards. I want to see my vague notions float like the down of the thistle before the breeze, and not to have them entangled in the briars and thorns of controversy. For once, I like to have it all my own way; and this is impossible unless you are alone, or in such company as I do not covet. I have no objection to argue a point with any one for twenty miles of measured road, but not for pleasure. If you remark the scent of a bean-field crossing the road, perhaps your fellow-traveller has no smell. If you point to a distant object, perhaps he is short-sighted, and has to take out his glass to look at it. There is a feeling in the air, a tone in the colour of a cloud which hits your fancy, but the effect of which you are unable to account for. There is then no sympathy, but an uneasy craving after it, and a dissatisfaction which pursues you on the way, and in the end probably produces ill-humour. Now I never quarrel with myself, and take all my own conclusions for granted till I find it necessary to defend them against objections. It is not merely that you may not be of accord on the objects and circumstances that present themselves before you—these may recall a number of objects, and lead to associations too delicate and refined to be possibly communicated to others. Yet these I love to cherish, and sometimes still fondly clutch them, when I can escape from the throng to do so. To give way to our feelings before company seems extravagance or affectation; and on the other hand, to have to unravel this mystery of our being at every turn, and to make others take an equal interest in it (otherwise the end is not answered), is a task to which few are competent. We must "give it an understanding, but no tongue." My old friend Coleridge, however, could do both. He could go on in the most delightful explanatory way over hill and dale a summer's day, and convert a landscape into a didactic poem or a Pindaric ode. "He talked far above singing." If I could so clothe my ideas in sounding and flowing words, I might perhaps wish to have some one with me to admire the swelling theme; or I could be more content, were it possible for me still to hear his echoing voice in the woods of All-Foxden. They had "that fine madness in them which our first poets had"; and if they could have been caught by some rare instrument, would have breathed such strains as the following:—

> —Here be woods as green
> As any, air likewise as fresh and sweet
> As when smooth Zephyrus plays on the fleet
> Face of the curled streams, with flow'rs as many
> As the young spring gives, and as choice as any;
> Here be all new delights, cool streams and wells,
> Arbours o'ergrown with woodbines, caves and dells;
> Choose where thou wilt, whilst I sit by and sing,
> Or gather rushes to make many a ring
> For thy long fingers; tell thee tales of love,
> How the pale Phoebe, hunting in a grove,

First saw the boy Endymion, from whose eyes
She took eternal fire that never dies;
How she convey'd him softly in a sleep,
His temples bound with poppy, to the steep
Head of old Latmos, where she stoops each night,
Gilding the mountain with her brother's light,
To kiss her sweetest.—

Had I words and images at command like these, I would attempt to wake the thoughts that lie slumbering on golden ridges in the evening clouds: but at the sight of nature my fancy, poor as it is, droops and closes up its leaves, like flowers at sunset. I can make nothing out on the spot:—I must have time to collect myself.

In general, a good thing spoils out-of-door prospects: it should be reserved for Table-talk. Lamb is for this reason, I take it, the worst company in the world out of doors; because he is the best within. I grant, there is one subject on which it is pleasant to talk on a journey; and that is, what one shall have for supper when we get to our inn at night. The open air improves this sort of conversation or friendly altercation, by setting a keener edge on appetite. Every mile of the road heightens the flavour of the viands we expect at the end of it. How fine it is to enter some old town, walled and turreted, just at approach of nightfall, or to come to some straggling village, with the lights streaming through the surrounding gloom; and then after inquiring for the best entertainment that the place affords, to "take one's ease at one's inn!" These eventful moments in our lives' history are too precious, too full of solid, heartfelt happiness to be frittered and dribbled away in imperfect sympathy. I would have them all to myself, and drain them to the last drop: they will do to talk of or to write about afterwards. What a delicate speculation it is, after drinking whole goblets of tea,

The cups that cheer, but not inebriate,

and letting the fumes ascend into the brain, to sit considering what we shall have for supper—eggs and a rasher, a rabbit smothered in onions, or an excellent veal-cutlet! Sancho in such a situation once fixed on cow-heel; and his choice, though he could not help it, is not to be disparaged. Then, in the intervals of pictured scenery and Shandean contemplation, to catch the preparation and the stir in the kitchen [getting ready for the gentleman in the parlour.] *Procul, O procul este profani!* These hours are sacred to silence and to musing, to be treasured up in the memory, and to feed the source of smiling thoughts hereafter. I would not waste them in idle talk; or if I must have the integrity of fancy broken in upon, I would rather it were by a stranger than a friend. A stranger takes his hue and character from the time and place; he is a part of the furniture and costume of an inn. If he is a Quaker, or from the West Riding of Yorkshire, so much the better. I do not even try to sympathise with him, and he breaks no squares. How I love to see the camps of the gypsies, and to sigh my soul into that sort of life. If I express this feeling to another, he may qualify and spoil it with some objection. I associate nothing with my travelling companion but present objects and passing events. In his ignorance of me and my affairs, I in a manner forget myself. But a friend reminds one of other things, rips up old grievances, and destroys the abstraction of the scene. He comes in ungraciously between us and our imaginary character. Something is dropped in the course of conversation that gives a hint of your profession and pursuits; or from having some one with you that knows the less sublime portions of your history, it seems that other people do. You are no longer a citizen of the world; but your "unhoused free condition is put into circumspection and confine." The *incognito* of an inn is one of its striking privileges—"lord of one's self, uncumber'd with a name." Oh! it is great to shake off the trammels of the world and of public opinion—to lose our importunate, tormenting, everlasting personal identity in the elements of nature, and become the creature of the moment, clear of all ties—to hold to the universe only by a dish of sweetbreads, and to owe nothing but the score of the evening— and no longer seeking for the applause and meeting with contempt, to be known by no other title than *the Gentleman in the parlour!* One may take one's choice of all characters in this romantic state of uncertainty as to one's real pretensions, and become indefinitely respectable and nega- tively right-worshipful. We baffle prejudice and disappoint conjecture; and from being so to others, begin to be objects of curiosity and won- der even to ourselves. We are no more those hackneyed commonplaces that we appear in the world; an inn restores us to the level of nature, and quits scores with society! I have certainly spent some enviable hours at inns—sometimes when I have been left entirely to myself, and have tried to solve some metaphysical problem, as once at Witham Common, where I found out the proof that likeness is not a case of the association of ideas—at other times, when there have been pictures in the room, as at St. Neot's, (I think it was) where I first met with Gribelin's engravings of the Cartoons, into which I entered at once, and at a little inn on the borders of Wales, where there happened to be hanging some of Westall's drawings which I compared triumphantly (for a theory that I had, not for the admired artist) with the figure of a girl who had ferried me over the Severn, standing up in a boat between me and the twilight—at other times I might mention luxuriating in books, with a peculiar interest in this way, as I remember sitting up half the night to read Paul and Virginia, which I picked up at an inn at Bridgewater, after being drenched in the rain all day; and at the same place I got through two volumes of Madame D'Arblay's Camilla. It was on the 10th of April, 1798, that I sat down to a volume of the New Eloise, at the inn at Llangollen, over a bottle of sherry and a cold chicken. The letter I chose was that in which St. Preux describes his feelings as he first caught a glimpse from the heights of the Jura of the Pays de Vaud, which I had brought with me as a *bon bouche* to crown the evening with. It was my birthday, and I had for the first time come from a place in the neighbourhood to visit this delightful spot. The road to Llangollen turns off between Chirk and Wrexham; and on passing a certain point, you come all at once upon the valley, which opens like an amphitheatre, broad, barren hills rising in majestic state on either side, with "green upland swells that echo to the bleat of flocks" below, and the river Dee babbling over its stony bed in the midst of them. The valley at this time "glittered green with sunny showers," and a budding ash-tree dipped its tender branches in the chiding stream. How proud, how glad I was to walk along the high road that overlooks the delicious prospect, repeating the lines which I have just quoted from Mr. Coleridge's poems! But besides the prospect which opened beneath my feet, another also opened to my inward sight, a heavenly vision, on which were written, in letters large as Hope could make them, these four words, LIBERTY, GENIUS, LOVE, VIRTUE; which have since faded in the light of common day, or mock my idle gaze.

> The Beautiful is vanished, and returns not.

Still I would return some time or other to this enchanted spot; but I would return to it alone. What other self could I find to share that influx of thoughts, of regret, and delight, the fragments of which I could hardly conjure up myself, so much have they been broken and defaced. I could stand on some tall rock, and overlook the precipice of years that separates me from what I then was. I was at that time going shortly to visit the poet whom I have above named. Where is he now? Not only I myself have changed; the world, which was then new to me, has become old and incorrigible. Yet will I turn to thee in thought, O sylvan Dee, in joy, in youth and gladness as thou then wert; and thou shalt always be to me the river of Paradise, where I will drink the waters of life freely!

There is hardly anything that shows the short-sightedness or capriciousness of the imagination more than travelling does. With change of place we change our ideas; nay, our opinions and feelings. We can by an effort indeed transport ourselves to old and long-forgotten scenes, and then the picture of the mind revives again; but we forget those that we have just left. It seems that we can think but of one place at a time. The canvas of the fancy is but of a certain extent, and if we paint one set of objects upon it, they immediately efface every other. We cannot enlarge our conceptions, we can only shift our point of view. The landscape bares its bosom to the enraptured eye, we take our fill of it, and seem as if we could form no other image of beauty or grandeur. We pass on, and think no more of it: the horizon that shuts it from our sight also blots it from our memory like a dream. In travelling through a wild barren country, I can form no idea of a woody and cultivated one. It appears to me that all the world must be barren, like what I see of it. In the country we forget the town, and in the town we despise the country. "Beyond Hyde Park," says Sir Topling Flutter, "all is a desert." All that part of the map which we do not see before us is blank. The world in our conceit of it is not much bigger than a nutshell. It is not one prospect expanded into another, country joined to country, kingdom to kingdom, land to seas, making an image voluminous and vast;—the mind can form no larger idea of space than the eye can take in at a single glance. The rest is a name written in a map, a calculation of arithmetic. For instance, what is the true signification of that immense mass of territory and population, known by the name of China to us? An inch of pasteboard on a wooden globe, of no more account than a China orange! Things near us are seen of the size of life: things at a distance are diminished to the size of the understanding. We measure the universe by ourselves, and even comprehend the texture of our own being only piecemeal. In this way, however, we remember an infinity of things and places. The mind is like a mechanical instrument that plays a great variety of tunes, but it must play them in succession. One idea recalls another, but it at the same time excludes all others. In trying to renew old recollections, we cannot as it were unfold the whole web of our existence; we must pick out the single threads. So in coming to a place where we have formerly lived, and with which we have intimate associations, every one must have found that the feeling grows more vivid the nearer we approach the spot, from the mere anticipation of the actual impression: we remember circumstances, feelings, persons, faces, names that we had not thought of for years; but for the time all the rest of the world is forgotten!—To return to the question I have quitted above:—

I have no objection to go to see ruins, aqueducts, pictures, in company with a friend or a party, but rather the contrary, for the former reason reversed. They are intelligible matters, and will bear talking about. The sentiment here is not tacit, but communicable and overt. Salisbury Plain is barren of criticism, but Stonehenge will bear a discussion antiquarian, picturesque, and philosophical. In setting out on a party of pleasure, the first consideration is always where we shall go to: in taking a solitary ramble, the question is what we shall meet with by the way. "The mind is its own place"; nor are we anxious to arrive at the end of our journey. I can myself do the honours indifferently well to works of art and curiosity. I once took a party to Oxford with no mean *éclat*—showed them that seat of the Muses at a distance,

> With glistering spires and pinnacles adorn'd—

descanted on the learned air that breathes from the grassy quadrangles and stone walls of halls and colleges—was at home in the Bodleian; and at Blenheim quite superseded the powdered Cicerone that attended us, and that pointed in vain with his wand to common-place beauties in matchless pictures. As another exception to the above reasoning, I should not feel confident in venturing on a journey in a foreign country without a companion. I should want at intervals to hear the sound of my own language. There is an involuntary antipathy in the mind of an Englishman to foreign manners and notions that requires the assistance of social sympathy to carry it off. As the distance from home increases, this relief, which was at first a luxury, becomes a passion and an appetite. A person would almost feel stifled to find himself in the deserts of Arabia without friends and countrymen: there must be allowed to be something in the view of Athens or old Rome that claims the utterance of speech; and I own that the Pyramids are too mighty for any single contemplation. In such situations, so opposite to all one's ordinary train of ideas, one seems a species by one's-self, a limb torn off from society, unless one can meet with instant fellowship and support. Yet I did not feel this want or craving very pressing once, when I first set foot on the laughing shores of France. Calais was peopled with novelty and delight. The confused, busy murmur of the place was like oil and wine poured into my ears; nor did the mariners' hymn, which was sung from the top of an old crazy vessel in the harbour, as the sun went down, send an alien sound into my soul. I only breathed the air of general humanity. I walked over "the vine-covered hills and gay regions of France," erect and satisfied; for the image of man was not cast down and chained to the foot of arbitrary thrones: I was at no loss for language, for that of all the great schools of painting was open to me. The whole is vanished like a shade. Pictures, heroes, glory, freedom, all are fled: nothing remains but the Bourbons and the French people!—There is undoubtedly a sensation in travelling into foreign parts that is to be had nowhere else: but it is more pleasing at the time than lasting. It is too remote from our habitual associations to be a common topic of discourse or reference, and, like a dream or another state of existence, does not piece into our daily modes of life. It is an animated but a momentary hallucination. It demands an effort to exchange our actual for our ideal identity; and to feel the pulse of our old transports revive very keenly, we must "jump" all our present comforts and connexions. Our romantic and itinerant character is not to be domesticated. Dr. Johnson remarked how little foreign travel added to the facilities of conversation in those who had been abroad. In fact, the time we have spent there is both delightful, and in one sense instructive; but it appears to be cut out of our substantial, downright existence, and never to join kindly on to it. We are not the same, but another, and perhaps more enviable individual, all the time we are out of our own country. We are lost to ourselves, as well as our friends. So the poet somewhat quaintly sings,

> Out of my country and myself I go.

Those who wish to forget painful thoughts, do well to absent themselves for a while from the ties and objects that recall them: but we can be said only to fulfil our destiny in the place that gave us birth. I should on this account like well enough to spend the whole of my life in travelling abroad, if I could anywhere borrow another life to spend afterwards at home!

A FEW THOUGHTS ON SLEEP

Leigh Hunt

THIS IS an article for the reader to think of, when he or she is warm in bed, a little before he goes to sleep, the clothes at his ear, and the wind moaning in some distant crevice.

"Blessings," exclaimed Sancho, "on him that first invented sleep! It wraps a man all round like a cloak." It is a delicious moment certainly—that of being well nestled in bed, and feeling that you shall drop gently to sleep. The good is to come, not past; the limbs have been just tired enough to render the remaining in one posture delightful: the labor of the day is done. A gentle failure of the perceptions comes creeping over one:—the spirit of consciousness disengages itself more and more, with slow and hushing degrees, like a mother detaching her hand from that of her sleeping child;—the mind seems to have a balmy lid closing over it, like the eye:—'tis closing;—'tis more closing;—'tis closed. The mysterious spirit has gone to make its airy rounds.

It is said that sleep is best before midnight; and Nature herself, with her darkness and chilling dews informs us so. There is another reason for going to bed betimes: for it is universally acknowledged that lying late in the morning is a great shortener of life. At least, it is never found in company with longevity. It also tends to make people corpulent. But these matters belong rather to the subject of early rising, than of sleep.

Sleep at a late hour in the morning is not half so pleasant as the more timely one. It is sometimes however excusable, especially to a watchful or overworked head; neither can we deny the seducing merits of "t'other doze,"—the pleasing wilfulness of nestling in a new posture, when you know you ought to be up, like the rest of the house. But then you cut up the day, and your sleep the next night.

In the course of the day, few people think of sleeping, except after dinner; and then it is often rather a hovering and nodding on the borders of sleep than sleep itself. This is a privilege allowable, we think, to none but the old, or the sickly, or the very tired and care-worn; and it should be well understood, before it is exercised in company. To escape into slumber by an argument; or to take it as an affair of course, only between you and your biliary duct; or to assent with involuntary nods to all that you have just been disputing, is not so well: much less, to sit nodding and tottering beside a lady; or to be in danger of dropping your head into the fruit-plate or your host's face; or of waking up, and saying, "Just so," to the bark of a dog; or "Yes, Madam," to the black at your elbow.

Care-worn people, however, might refresh themselves oftener with day-sleep than they do; if their bodily state is such as to dispose them to it. It is a mistake to suppose that all care is wakeful. People sometimes sleep, as well as wake, by reason of their sorrow. The difference seems to depend upon the nature of their temperament; though in the *most* excessive cases, sleep is perhaps Nature's never-failing relief, as swooning is upon the rack. A person with jaundice in his blood shall lie down and go to sleep at noon-day, when another of different complexion shall find his eyes as uncloseable as a statue's, though he has had no sleep for nights together. Without meaning to lessen the dignity of suffering, which has quite enough to do with its waking hours, it is this that may often account for the profound sleeps enjoyed the night before hazardous battles, executions, and other demands upon an over-excited spirit.

The most complete and healthy sleep that can be taken in the day, is in summer-time, out in a field. There is perhaps no solitary sensation so exquisite as that of slumbering on the grass or hay, shaded from the hot sun by a tree, with the consciousness of a fresh but light air running through the wide atmosphere, and the sky stretching far overhead upon all sides. Earth, and heaven, and a placid humanity, seem to have the creation to themselves. There is nothing between the slumberer and the naked and glad innocence of nature.

Next to this, but at a long interval, the most relishing snatch of slumber out of bed, is the one which a tired person takes, before he retires for the night, while lingering in his sitting-room. The consciousness of being very sleepy and of having the power to go to bed immediately, gives great zest to the unwillingness to move. Sometimes he sits nodding in his chair; but the suddenness and leaden jerks of the head to which a state of great sleepiness renders him liable, are generally too painful for so luxurious a moment; and he gets into a more legitimate posture, sitting sideways with his head on the chair-back, or throwing his legs up at once on another chair, and half reclining. It is curious, however, to find how long an inconvenient posture will be borne for the sake of this foretaste of repose. The worst of it is, that on going to bed, the charm sometimes vanishes; perhaps from the colder temperature of the chamber; for a fireside is a great opiate.

Speaking of the painful positions into which a sleepy lounger will get himself, it is amusing to think of the more fantastic attitudes that so often take place in bed. If we could add anything to the numberless things that have been said about sleep by the poets, it would be upon this point. Sleep never shows himself a greater leveller. A man in his waking moments may look as proud and self-possessed as he pleases. He may walk proudly, he may sit proudly, he may eat his dinner proudly; he may shave himself with an air of infinite superiority; in a word, he may show himself grand and absurd upon the most trifling occasions. But Sleep plays the petrifying magician. He arrests the proudest lord as well as the humblest clown in the most ridiculous postures: so that if you could draw a grandee from his bed without waking him, no limb-twisting fool in a pantomime should create wilder laughter. The toy with the string between its legs, is hardly a posture-master more extravagant. Imagine a despot lifted up to the gaze of his valets, with his eyes shut, his mouth open, his left hand under his right ear, his other twisted and hanging helplessly before him like an idiot's, one knee lifted up, and the other leg stretched out, or both knees huddled up together;—what a scarecrow to lodge majestic power in!

But Sleep is kindly, even in his tricks; and the poets have treated him with reverence. According to the ancient mythologists, he had even one of the Graces to wife. He had a thousand sons, of whom the chief were Morpheus, or the Shaper; Icelos, or the Likely; Phantasus, the Fancy; and Phobetor, the Terror. His dwelling some writers place in a dull and darkling part of the earth; others, with greater compliment, in heaven; and others, with another kind of propriety, by the seashore. There is a good description of it in Ovid; but in these abstracted tasks of poetry, the moderns outvie the ancients; and there is nobody who has built his bower for him so finely as Spenser. Archimago in the first book of the *Faerie Queene* (Canto I. st. 39), sends a little spirit down to Morpheus to fetch him a Dream:

> He, making speedy way through spersed ayre,
> And through the world of waters, wide and deepe,
> To Morpheus' house doth hastily repaire
> Amid the bowels of the earth full steepe
> And low, where dawning day doth never peepe,
> His dwelling is. There, Tethys his wet bed
> Doth ever wash; and Cynthia still doth steepe
> In silver dew his ever-drouping head,
> Whiles sad Night over him her mantle black doth spred

> And more to lull him in his slumber soft
> A trickling streame from high rocke tumbling downe,
> And ever-drizzling rain upon the loft,

> Mixed with a murmuring winde, much like the soune
> Of swarming bees, did cast him in a swoune.
> No other noise, nor people's troublous cryes,
> As still are wont to annoy the walled towne,
> Might there be heard; but carelesse Quiet lyes,
> Wrapt in eternall silence, far from enimyes.

Chaucer has drawn the cave of the same god with greater simplicity; but nothing can have a more deep and sullen effect than his cliffs and cold running waters. It seems as real as an actual solitude, or some quaint old picture in a book of travels in Tartary. He is telling the story of Ceyx and Alcyone in the poem called his Dream. Juno tells a messenger to go to Morpheus and "bid him creep into the body" of the drowned king, to let his wife know the fatal event by his apparition.

> This messenger tooke leave, and went
> Upon his way; and never he stent
> Till he came to the dark valley,
> That stant betweene rockes twey.
> There never yet grew corne, ne gras,
> Ne tree, ne naught that aught was,
> Beast, ne man, ne naught else;
> Save that there were a few wells
> Came running fro the cliffs adowne,
> That made a deadly sleeping soune,
> And runnen downe right by a cave,
> That was under a rocky grave,
> Amid the valley, wonder-deepe.
> There these goddis lay asleepe,
> Morpheus and Eclympasteire,
> That was the god of Sleepis heire,
> That slept and did none other worke.

Where the credentials of this new son and heir Eclympasteire are to be found, we know not; but he acts very much, it must be allowed, like an heir presumptive, in sleeping, and doing "none other work."

We dare not trust ourselves with many quotations upon sleep from the poets: they are so numerous as well as beautiful. We must content ourselves with mentioning that our two most favorite passages are one in the *Philoctetes* of Sophocles, admirable for its contrast to a scene of terrible agony, which it closes; and the other the following address in Beaumont and Fletcher's tragedy of *Valentinian,* the hero of which is also a sufferer under bodily torment. He is in a chair, slumbering; and these most exquisite lines are gently sung with music.

> Care-charming Sleep, thou easer of all woes.
> Brother to Death, sweetly thyself dispose
> On this afflicted prince. Fall like a cloud
> In gentle showers: give nothing that is loud
> Or painful to his slumbers: easy, sweet,
> And as a purling stream, thou son of Night,
> Pass by his troubled senses; sing his pain
> Like hollow murmuring wind, or silver rain:
> Into this prince, gently, oh gently slide,
> And kiss him into slumbers, like a bride.

How earnest and prayer-like are these pauses! How lightly sprinkled, and yet how deeply settling, like rain, the fancy! How quiet, affectionate, and perfect the conclusion!

Sleep is most graceful in an infant; soundest, in one who has been tired in the open air; completest, to the seaman after a hard voyage; most welcome, to the mind haunted with one idea; most touching to look at, in the parent that has wept; lightest, in the playful child; proudest, in the bride adored.

GETTING UP ON COLD MORNINGS
Leigh Hunt

AN ITALIAN author—Giulio Cordara, a Jesuit—has written a poem upon insects, which he begins by insisting, that those troublesome and abominable little animals were created for our annoyance, and that they were certainly not inhabitants of Paradise. We of the north may dispute this piece of theology; but on the other hand, it is as clear as the snow on the housetops, that Adam was not under the necessity of shaving; and that when Eve walked out of her delicious bower, she did not step upon ice three inches thick.

Some people say it is a very easy thing to get up of a cold morning. You have only, they tell you, to take the resolution; and the thing is done. This may be very true; just as a boy at school has only to take a flogging, and the thing is over. But we have not at all made up our minds upon it; and we find it a very pleasant exercise to discuss the matter, candidly, before we get up. This at least is not idling, though it may be lying. It affords an excellent answer to those, who ask how lying in bed can be indulged in by a reasoning being—a rational creature. How! Why with the argument calmly at work in one's head, and the clothes over one's shoulder. Oh! it is a fine way of spending a sensible, impartial half-hour.

If these people would be more charitable, they would get on with their argument better. But they are apt to reason so ill, and to assert so dogmatically, that one could wish to have them stand round one's bed of a bitter morning, and *lie* before their faces. They ought to hear both sides of the bed, the inside and out. If they cannot entertain themselves with their own thoughts for half an hour or so, it is not the fault of those who can.

Candid inquiries into one's decumbency, besides the greater or less privileges to be allowed a man in proportion to his ability of keeping early hours, was the work given his faculties, &c., will at least concede their due merits to such representations as the following. In the first place, says the injured but calm appealer, I have been warm all night, and find my system in a state perfectly suitable to a warm-blooded animal. To get out of this state into the cold, besides the inharmonious and uncritical abruptness of the transition, is so unnatural to such a creature, that the poets, refining upon the tortures of the damned, make one of their greatest agonies consist in being suddenly transported from heat to cold—from fire to ice. They are "haled" out of their "beds," says Milton, by "harpy-footed furies,"—fellows who come to call them. On my first movement towards the anticipation of getting up, I find that such parts of the sheets and bolster as are exposed to the air of the room, are stone-cold. On opening my eyes, the first thing that meets them is my own breath rolling forth, as if in the open air, like smoke out of a chimney. Think of this symptom. Then I turn my eyes sideways, and see the window all frozen over. Think of that. Then the servant comes in. 'It is very cold this morning, is it not?"—"Very cold, sir."—"Very cold indeed, isn't it?"—"Very cold indeed, sir."—"More than usually so, isn't it, even for this weather?" (Here the servant's wit and good nature are put to a considerable test, and the inquirer lies on thorns for the answer.) "Why, sir, . . . I think it *is.*" (Good creature! There is not a better, or more truth-telling servant going.) "I must rise, however—get me some warm water."—Here comes a fine interval between the departure of the servant and the arrival of the hot water; during which, of course, it is of "no use?" to get up. The hot water comes. "Is it quite hot?"—"Yes, sir."—"Perhaps too hot for shaving; I must wait a little?"—"No, sir, it will just do." (There is an over-nice propriety sometimes, an officious zeal of virtue, a little troublesome.) "Oh—the shirt—you must air my clean shirt;—linen gets very damp this weather."—"Yes, sir." Here another delicious five minutes. A knock at the door. "Oh, the shirt—very well. My stockings—I think the stockings had better be aired too."—"Very well, sir."—Here another interval. At length everything is ready, except myself. I now, continues our incumbent (a happy word, by the bye, for a country vicar)—I now cannot help thinking a good deal—who can?—upon the unnecessary and villainous custom of shaving: it is a thing so unmanly (here I nestle closer)—so effeminate (here I recoil from an unlucky step into the colder part of the bed).—No wonder that the Queen of France took part with the rebels against that degenerate King, her husband, who first affronted her smooth visage with a face like her own. The Emperor Julian never showed the luxuriancy of his genius to better advantage than in reviving the flowing beard. Look at Cardinal Bembo's picture—at Michael Angelo's—at Titian's—at Shakespeare's—at Fletcher's—at Spenser's—at Chaucer's—at Alfred's—at Plato's—I could name a great man for every tick of my watch.—Look at the Turks, a grave and otiose people.—Think of Haroun al Raschid and Bed-ridden Hassan.—Think of Wortley Montague, the worthy son of his mother, above the prejudice of his time.—Look at the Persian gentle-men, whom one is ashamed of meeting about the suburbs, their dress and appearance are so much finer than our own.—Lastly, think of the razor itself—how totally opposed to every sensation of bed—how cold, how edgy, how hard! how utterly different from anything like the warm and circling amplitude, which

> Sweetly recommends itself
> Unto our gentle senses.

Add to this, benumbed fingers, which may help you to cut yourself, a quivering body, a frozen towel, and a ewer full of ice; and he that says there is nothing to oppose in all this, only shows that he has no merit in opposing it.

Thomson, the poet, who exclaims in his Seasons—

> Falsely luxurious! Will not man awake?

used to lie in bed till noon, because he said he had no motive in getting up. He could imagine the good of rising; but then he could also imagine the good of lying still; and his exclamation it must be allowed, was made upon summer-time, not winter. We must proportion the argument to the individual character. A money-getter may be drawn out of his bed by three or four pence; but this will not suffice for a student. A proud man may say, "What shall I think of myself, if I don't get up?" but the more humble one will be content to waive this prodigious notion of himself, out of respect to his kindly bed. The mechanical man shall get up without any ado at all; and so shall the barometer. An ingenious lier in bed will find hard matter of discussion even on the score of health and longevity. He will ask us for our proofs and precedents of the ill effects of lying later in cold weather; and sophisticate much on the advantages of an even temperature of body; of the natural propensity (pretty univer-sal) to have one's way; and of the animals that roll themselves up, and sleep all the winter. As to longevity, he will ask whether the longest is of necessity the best; and whether Holborn is the handsomest street in London.

TUNBRIDGE TOYS

William Makepeace Thackeray

I WONDER WHETHER those little silver pencil-cases with a moveable almanack at the butt-end are still favourite implements with boys, and whether pedlers still hawk them about the country? Are there pedlars and hawkers still, or are rustics and children grown too sharp to deal with them? Those pencil-cases, as far as my memory serves me, were not of much use. The screw, upon which the moveable almanack turned, was constantly getting loose. The 1 of the table would work from its moorings, under Tuesday or Wednesday, as the case might be, and you would find, on examination, that Th. or W. was the 23½ of the month (which was absurd on the face of the thing), and in a word your cherished pencil-case an utterly unreliable timekeeper. Nor was this a matter of wonder. Consider the position of a pencil-case in a boy's pocket. You had hard-bake in it; marbles, kept in your purse when the money was all gone; your mother's purse knitted so fondly and supplied with a little bit of gold, long since—prodigal little son!—scattered amongst the swine—I mean amongst brandy-balls, open tarts, three-cornered puffs, and similar abominations. You had a top and string; a knife; a piece of cobbler's wax; two or three bullets; a *Little Warbler*; and I, for my part, remember, for a considerable period, a brass-barrelled pocket-pistol (which would fire beautifully, for with it I shot off a button from Butt Major's jacket);—with all these things, and ever so many more, clinking and rattling in your pockets, and your hands, of course, keeping them in perpetual movement, how could you expect your moveable almanack not to be twisted out of its place now and again—your pencil-case to be bent—your liquorice water not to leak out of your bottle over the cobbler's wax, your bull's-eyes not to ram up the lock and barrel of your pistol, and so forth?

In the month of June, thirty-seven years ago, I bought one of those pencil-cases from a boy whom I shall call Hawker, and who was in my form. Is he dead? Is he a millionaire? Is he a bankrupt now? He was an immense screw at school, and I believe to this day that the value of the thing for which I owed and eventually paid three-and-sixpence, was in reality not one-and-nine.

I certainly enjoyed the case at first a good deal, and amused myself with twiddling round the moveable calendar. But this pleasure wore off. The jewel, as I said, was not paid for, and Hawker, a large and violent boy, was exceedingly unpleasant as a creditor. His constant remark was, "When are you going to pay me that three-and-sixpence? What sneaks your relations must be? They come to see you. You go out to them on Saturdays and Sundays, and they never give you anything! Don't tell *me,* you little humbug!" and so forth. The truth is that my relations were respectable; but my parents were making a tour in Scotland; and my friends in London, whom I used to go and see, were most kind to me, certainly, but somehow never tipped me. That term, of May to August, 1823, passed in agonies then, in consequence of my debt to Hawker. What was the pleasure of a calendar pencil-case in comparison with the doubt and torture of mind occasioned by the sense of the debt, and the constant reproach of that fellow's scowling eyes and gloomy, coarse reminders? How was I to pay off such a debt out of sixpence a week? ludicrous! Why did not some one come to see me, and tip me? Ah! my dear sir, if you have any little friends at school, go and see them, and do the natural thing by them. You won't miss the sovereign. You don't know what a blessing it will be to them. Don't fancy they are too old— try 'em. And they will remember you, and bless you in future days; and their gratitude shall accompany your dreary after life; and they shall meet you kindly when thanks for kindness are scant. O mercy! shall I ever forget that sovereign you gave me, Captain Bob? or the agonies of being in debt to Hawker? In that very term, a relation of mine was going to India. I actually was fetched from school in order to take leave of him. I am afraid I told Hawker of this circumstance. I own I speculated upon my friend's giving me a pound. A pound? Pooh! A relation going to India, and deeply affected at parting from his darling kinsman, might give five pounds to the dear fellow! ∗ ∗ ∗ There was Hawker when I came back— of course there he was. As he looked in my scared face, his turned livid with rage. He muttered curses, terrible from the lips of so young a boy. My relation, about to cross the ocean to fill a lucrative appointment, asked me with much interest about my progress at school, heard me construe a passage of Eutropius, the pleasing Latin work on which I was then engaged; gave me a God bless you, and sent me back to school; upon my word of honour, without so much as a half-crown! It is all very well, my dear sir, to say that boys contract habits of expecting tips from their parents' friends, that they become avaricious, and so forth. Avaricious! fudge! Boys contract habits of tart and toffee eating, which they do not carry into after life. On the contrary, I wish I *did* like 'em. What raptures of pleasure one could have now for five shillings, if one could but pick it off the pastrycook's tray! No. If you have any little friends at school, out with your half-crowns, my friend, and impart to those little ones the little fleeting joys of their age.

Well, then. At the beginning of August, 1823, Bartlemy-tide holidays came, and I was to go to my parents, who were at Tunbridge Wells. My place in the coach was taken by my tutor's servants—Bolt-in-Tun, Fleet Street, seven o'clock in the morning, was the word. My Tutor, the Rev. Edward P——, to whom I hereby present my best compliments, had a parting interview with me: gave me my little account for my governor: the remaining part of the coach-hire; five shillings for my own expenses; and some five-and-twenty shillings on an old account which had been overpaid, and was to be restored to my family.

Away I ran and paid Hawker his three-and-six. Ouf! what a weight it was off my mind! (He was a Norfolk boy, and used to go home from Mrs. Nelson's Bell Inn, Aldgate—but that is not to the point.) The next morning, of course, we were an hour before the time. I and another boy shared a hackney-coach; two-and-six: porter for putting luggage on coach, threepence. I had no more money of my own left. Rasherwell, my companion, went into the Bolt-in-Tun coffee-room, and had a good breakfast. I couldn't; because, though I had five-and-twenty shillings of my parents' money, I had none of my own, you see.

I certainly intended to go without breakfast, and still remember how strongly I had that resolution in my mind. But there was that hour to wait. A beautiful August morning—I am very hungry. There is Rasherwell "tucking" away in the coffee-room. I pace the street, as sadly almost as if I had been coming to school, not going thence. I turned into a court by mere chance—I vow it was by mere chance—and there I see a coffee-shop with a placard in the window, *Coffee Twopence. Round of buttered toast, Twopence*. And here am I hungry, penniless, with five-and-twenty shillings of my parents' money in my pocket.

What would you have done? You see I had had my money, and spent it in that pencil-case affair. The five-and-twenty shillings were a trust—by me to be handed over.

But then would my parents wish their only child to be actually without breakfast? Having this money, and being so hungry, so *very* hungry, mightn't I take ever so little? Mightn't I at home eat as much as I chose?

Well, I went into the coffee-shop, and spent fourpence. I remember the taste of the coffee and toast to this day—a peculiar, muddy, not-sweet-enough, most fragrant coffee—a rich, rancid, yet not-buttered-enough, delicious toast. The waiter had nothing. At any rate, fourpence I know was the sum I spent. And the hunger appeased, I got on the coach a guilty being.

At the last stage,—what is its name? I have forgotten in seven-and-thirty years,—there is an inn with a little green and trees before it; and by the trees there is an open carriage. It is our carriage. Yes, there are Prince and Blucher, the horses; and my parents in the carriage. Oh! how I had been counting the days until this one came! Oh! how happy had I been to see them yesterday! But there was that fourpence. All the journey down the toast had choked me, and the coffee poisoned me.

I was in such a state of remorse about the fourpence, that I forgot the maternal joy and caresses, the tender paternal voice. I pull out the twenty-four shillings and eightpence with a trembling hand.

"Here's your money," I gasp out, "which Mr. P. owes you, all but fourpence. I owed three-and-sixpence to Hawker out of my money for a pencil-case, and I had none left, and I took fourpence of yours, and had some coffee at a shop."

I suppose I must have been choking whilst uttering this confession.

"My dear boy," says the governor, "why didn't you go and breakfast at the hotel?"

"He must be starved," says my mother.

I had confessed; I had been a prodigal; I had been taken back to my parents' arms again. It was not a very great crime as yet, or a very long career of prodigality; but don't we know that a boy who takes a pin which is not his own, will take a thousand pounds when occasion serves, bring his parents' grey heads with sorrow to the grave, and carry his own to the gallows? Witness the career of Dick Idle, upon whom our friend Mr. Sala has been discoursing. Dick only began by playing pitch-and-toss on a tombstone: playing fair, for what we know: and even for that sin he was promptly caned by the beadle. The bamboo was ineffectual to cane that reprobate's bad courses out of him. From pitch-and-toss he proceeded to manslaughter if necessary: to highway robbery; to Tyburn and the rope there. Ah! heaven be thanked, my parents' heads are still above the grass, and mine still out of the noose.

As I look up from my desk, I see Tunbridge Wells Common and the rocks, the strange familiar place which I remember forty years ago. Boys saunter over the green with stumps and cricket-bats. Other boys gallop by on the riding-master's hacks. I protest it is *Cramp, Riding Master*, as it used to be in the reign of George IV., and that Centaur Cramp must be at least a hundred years old. Yonder comes a footman with a bundle of novels from the library. Are they as good as *our* novels? Oh! how delightful they were! Shades of Valancour, awful ghost of Manfroni, how I shudder at your appearance! Sweet image of Thaddeus of Warsaw, how often has this almost infantile hand tried to depict you in a Polish cap and richly embroidered tights! And as for Corinthian Tom in light blue pantaloons and Hessians, and Jerry Hawthorn from the country, can all the fashion, can all the splendour of real life which these eyes have subsequently beheld, can all the wit I have heard or read in later times, compare with your fashion, with your brilliancy, with your delightful grace, and sparkling vivacious rattle?

Who knows? They *may* have kept those very books at the library still—at the well-remembered library on the Pantiles, where they sell that delightful, useful Tunbridge ware. I will go and see. I went my way to the Pantiles, the queer little old-world Pantiles, where, a hundred years since, so much good company came to take its pleasure. Is it possible, that in the past century, gentlefolks of the first rank (as I read lately in a lecture on George II. in the *Cornhill Magazine*) assembled here and entertained each other with gaming, dancing, fiddling, and tea? There are fiddlers, harpers, and trumpeters performing at this moment in a weak little old balcony, but where is the fine company? Where are the earls, duchesses, bishops, and magnificent embroidered gamesters? A half dozen of children and their nurses are listening to the musicians; an old lady or two in a poke bonnet passes, and for the rest, I see but an uninteresting population of native tradesmen. As for the library, its window is full of pictures of burly theologians, and their works, sermons, apologues, and so forth. Can I go in and ask the young ladies at the counter for "Manfroni, or the One-Handed Monk," and "Life in London, or the Adventures of Corinthian Tom, Jeremiah Hawthorn, Esq., and their friend Bob Logic?"—absurd. I turn away abashed from the casement—from the Pantiles—no longer Pantiles, but Parade. I stroll over the Common and survey the beautiful purple hills around, twinkling with a thousand bright villas, which have sprung up over this charming ground since first I saw it. What an admirable scene of peace and plenty! What a delicious air breathes over the heath, blows the cloud shadows across it, and murmurs through the full-clad trees! Can the world show a land fairer, richer, more cheerful? I see a portion of it when I look up from the window at which I write. But fair scene, green woods, bright terraces gleaming in sunshine, and purple clouds swollen with summer rain—nay, the very pages over which my head bends—disappear from before my eyes. They are looking backwards, back into forty years off, into a dark room, into a little house hard by on the Common here, in the Bartlemy-tide holidays. The parents have gone to town for two days: the house is all his own, his own and a grim old maid-servant's, and a little boy is seated at night in the lonely drawing-room, poring over "Manfroni, or the One-Handed Monk," so frightened that he scarcely dares to turn round.

LYING AWAKE

Charles Dickens

"MY UNCLE lay with his eyes half closed, and his nightcap drawn almost down to his nose. His fancy was already wandering, and began to mingle up the present scene with the crater of Vesuvius, the French Opera, the Coliseum at Rome, Dolly's Chop-house in London, and all the farrago of noted places with which the brain of a traveller is crammed; in a word, he was just falling asleep."

Thus, that delightful writer, Washington Irving, in his *Tales of a Traveller*. But, it happened to me the other night to be lying: not with my eyes half closed, but with my eyes wide open; not with my nightcap drawn almost down to my nose, for on sanitary principles I never wear a nightcap: but with my hair pitchforked and touzled all over the pillow; not just falling asleep by any means, but glaringly, persistently, and obstinately, broad awake. Perhaps, with no scientific intention or invention, I was illustrating the theory of the Duality of the Brain; perhaps one part of my brain, being wakeful, sat up to watch the other part which was sleepy. Be that as it may, something in me was as desirous to go to sleep as it possibly could be, but something else in me *would not* go to sleep, and was as obstinate as George the Third.

Thinking of George the Third—for I devote this paper to my train of thoughts as I lay awake: most people lying awake sometimes, and having some interest in the subject—put me in mind of Benjamin Franklin, and so Benjamin Franklin's paper on the art of procuring pleasant dreams, which would seem necessarily to include the art of going to sleep, came into my head. Now, as I often used to read that paper when I was a very small boy, and as I recollect everything I read then as perfectly as I forget everything I read now, I quoted "Get out of bed, beat up and turn your pillow, shake the bed-clothes well with at least twenty shakes, then throw the bed open and leave it to cool; in the meanwhile, continuing undrest, walk about your chamber. When you begin to feel the cold air unpleasant, then return to your bed, and you will soon fall asleep, and your sleep will be sweet and pleasant." Not a bit of it! I performed the whole ceremony, and if it were possible for me to be more saucer-eyed than I was before, that was the only result that came of it.

Except Niagara. The two quotations from Washington Irving and Benjamin Franklin may have put it in my head by an American association of ideas; but there I was, and the Horse-shoe Fall was thundering and tumbling in my eyes and ears, and the very rainbows that I left upon the spray when I really did last look upon it, were beautiful to see. The night-light being quite as plain, however, and sleep seeming to be many thousand miles further off than Niagara, I made up my mind to think a little about Sleep; which I no sooner did than I whirled off in spite of myself to Drury Lane Theatre, and there saw a great actor and dear friend of mine (whom I had been thinking of in the day) playing Macbeth, and heard him apostrophising "the death of each day's life," as I have heard him many a time, in the days that are gone.

But, Sleep. I *will* think about Sleep. I am determined to think (this is the way I went on) about Sleep. I must hold the word Sleep, tight and fast, or I shall be off at a tangent in half a second. I feel myself unaccountably straying, already, into Clare Market. Sleep. It would be curious, as illustrating the equality of sleep, to inquire how many of its phenomena are common to all classes, to all degrees of wealth and poverty, to every grade of education and ignorance. Here, for example, is her Majesty Queen Victoria in her palace, this present blessed night, and here is Winking Charley, a sturdy vagrant, in one of her Majesty's jails. Her Majesty has fallen, many thousands of times, from that same Tower, which *I* claim a right to tumble off now and then. So has Winking Charley. Her Majesty in her sleep has opened or prorogued Parliament, or has held a Drawing Room, attired in some very scanty dress, the deficiencies and improprieties of which have caused her great uneasiness. I, in my degree, have suffered unspeakable agitation of mind from taking the chair at a public dinner at the London Tavern in my night-clothes, which not all the courtesy of my kind friend and host Mr. Bathe could persuade me were quite adapted to the occasion. Winking Charley has been repeatedly tried in a worse condition. Her Majesty is no stranger to a vault or firmament, of a sort of floorcloth, with an indistinct pattern distantly resembling eyes, which occasionally obtrudes itself on her repose. Neither am I. Neither is Winking Charley. It is quite common to all three of us to skim along with airy strides a little above the ground; also to hold, with the deepest interest, dialogues with various people, all represented by ourselves; and to be at our wit's end to know what they are going to tell us; and to be indescribably astonished by the secrets they disclose. It is probable that we have all three committed murders and hidden bodies. It is pretty certain that we have all desperately wanted to cry out, and have had no voice; that we have all gone to the play and not been able to get in; that we have all dreamed much more of our youth than of our later lives; that—I have lost it! The thread's broken.

And up I go. I, lying here with the night-light before me, up I go, for no reason on earth that I can find out, and drawn by no links that are visible to me, up the Great Saint Bernard! I have lived in Switzerland, and rambled among the mountains; but, why I should go there now, and why up the Great Saint Bernard in preference to any other mountain, I have no idea. As I lie here broad awake, and with every sense so sharpened that I can distinctly hear distant noises inaudible to me at another time, I make that journey, as I really did, on the same summer day, with the same happy party—ah! two since dead, I grieve to think—and there is the same track, with the same black wooden arms to point the way, and there are the same storm-refuges here and there; and there is the same snow falling at the top, and there are the same frosty mists, and there is the same intensely cold convent with its ménagerie smell, and the same breed of dogs fast dying out, and the same breed of jolly young monks whom I mourn to know as humbugs, and the same convent parlour with its piano and the sitting round the fire, and the same supper, and the same lone night in a cell, and the same bright fresh morning when going out into the highly rarefied air was like a plunge into an icy bath. Now, see here what comes along; and why does this thing stalk into my mind on the top of a Swiss mountain!

It is a figure that I once saw, just after dark, chalked upon a door in a little back lane near a country church—my first church. How young a child I may have been at the time I don't know, but it horrified me so intensely—in connexion with the churchyard, I suppose, for it smokes a pipe, and has a big hat with each of its ears sticking out in a horizontal line under the brim, and is not in itself more oppressive than a mouth from ear to ear, a pair of goggle eyes, and hands like two bunches of carrots, five in each, can make it—that it is still vaguely alarming to me to recall (as I have often done before, lying awake) the running home, the looking behind, the horror, of its following me; though whether disconnected from the door, or door and all, I can't say, and perhaps never could. It lays a disagreeable train. I must resolve to think of something on the voluntary principle.

The balloon ascents of this last season. They will do to think about, while I lie awake, as well as anything else. I must hold them tight though, for I feel them sliding away, and in their stead are the Mannings, husband and wife, hanging on the top of Horsemonger Lane Jail. In connexion with which dismal spectacle, I recall this curious fantasy of the mind. That, having beheld that execution, and having left those two forms dangling on the top of the entrance gateway—the man's, a limp, loose suit of clothes as if the man had gone out of them; the woman's a fine shape, so elaborately corseted and artfully dressed, that it was quite unchanged in its trim appearance as it slowly swung from side to side—I never could, by my uttermost efforts, for some weeks, present the outside of that prison to myself (which the terrible impression I had received continually obliged me to do) without presenting it with the two figures still hanging in the morning air. Until, strolling past the gloomy place one night, when the street was deserted and quiet, and actually seeing that the bodies were not there, my fancy was persuaded, as it were, to take them down and bury them within the precincts of the jail, where they have lain ever since.

The balloon ascents of last season. Let me reckon them up. There were the horse, the bull, the parachute, and the tumbler hanging on—chiefly by his toes, I believe—below the car. Very wrong, indeed, and decidedly to be stopped. But, in connexion with these and similar dangerous exhibitions, it strikes me that that portion of the public whom they entertain, is unjustly reproached. Their pleasure is in the difficulty overcome. They are a public of great faith, and are quite confident that the gentleman will not fall off the horse, or the lady off the bull or out of the parachute, and that the tumbler has a firm hold with his toes. They do not go to see the adventurer vanquished, but triumphant. There is no parallel in public combats between men and beasts, because nobody can answer for the particular beast—unless it were always the same beast, in which case it would be a mere stage-show, which the same public would go in the same state of mind to see, entirely believing in the brute being beforehand safely subdued by the man. That they are not accustomed to calculate hazards and dangers with any nicety, we may know from their rash exposure of themselves in overcrowded steamboats, and unsafe conveyances and places of all kinds. And I cannot help thinking that instead of railing, and attributing savage motives to a people naturally well disposed and humane, it is better to teach them, and lead them argumentatively and reasonably—for they are very reasonable, if you will discuss a matter with them—to more considerate and wise conclusions.

This is a disagreeable intrusion! Here is a man with his throat cut, dashing towards me as I lie awake! A recollection of an old story of a kinsman of mine, who, going home one foggy winter night to Hampstead, when London was much smaller and the road lonesome, suddenly encountered such a figure rushing past him, and presently two keepers from a madhouse in pursuit. A very unpleasant creature indeed, to come into my mind unbidden, as I lie awake.

—The balloon ascents of last season. I must return to the balloons. Why did the bleeding man start out of them? Never mind; if I inquire, he will be back again. The balloons. This particular public have inher-

ently a great pleasure in the contemplation of physical difficulties overcome; mainly, as I take it, because the lives of a large majority of them are
exceedingly monotonous and real, and further, are a struggle against continual difficulties, and further still, because anything in the form of accidental injury, or any kind of illness or disability is so very serious in their
own sphere. I will explain this seeming paradox of mine. Take the case
of a Christmas Pantomime. Surely nobody supposes that the young
mother in the pit who falls into fits of laughter when the baby is boiled
or sat upon, would be at all diverted by such an occurrence off the stage.
Nor is the decent workman in the gallery, who is transported beyond the
ignorant present by the delight with which he sees a stout gentleman
pushed out of a two pair of stairs window, to be slandered by the suspi-
cion that he would be in the least entertained by such a spectacle in any
street in London, Paris, or New York. It always appears to me that the
secret of this enjoyment lies in the temporary superiority to the common
hazards and mischances of life; in seeing casualties, attended when they
really occur with bodily and mental suffering, tears, and poverty, happen
through a very rough sort of poetry without the least harm being done
to any one—the pretence of distress in a pantomime being so broadly
humourous as to be no pretence at all. Much as in the comic fiction I
can understand the mother with a very vulnerable baby at home, greatly
relishing the invulnerable baby on the stage, so in the Cremorne reality
I can understand the mason who is always liable to fall off a scaffold in
his working jacket and to be carried to the hospital, having an infinite
admiration of the radiant personage in spangles who goes into the clouds
upon a bull, or upside down, and who, he takes it for granted—not
reflecting upon the thing—has, by uncommon skill and dexterity, conquered such mischances as those to which he and his acquaintance are
continually exposed.

I wish the Morgue in Paris would not come here as I lie awake, with
its ghastly beds, and the swollen saturated clothes hanging up, and the
water dripping, dripping all day long, upon that other swollen saturated
something in the corner, like a heap of crushed over-ripe figs that I have
seen in Italy! And this detestable Morgue comes back again at the head
of a procession of forgotten ghost stories. This will never do. I must think
of something else as I lie awake; or, like that sagacious animal in the
United States who recognised the colonel who was such a dead shot, I
am a gone 'Coon. What shall I think of? The late brutal assaults. Very
good subject. The late brutal assaults.

(Though whether, supposing I should see, here before me as I lie
awake, the awful phantom described in one of those ghost stories, who,
with a head-dress of shroud, was always seen looking in through a certain glass door at a certain dead hour—whether, in such a case it would

be the least consolation to me to know on philosophical grounds that it was merely my imagination, is a question I can't help asking myself by the way.)

The late brutal assaults. I strongly question the expediency of advocating the revival of whipping for those crimes. It is a natural and generous impulse to be indignant at the perpetration of inconceivable brutality, but I doubt the whipping panacea gravely. Not in the least regard or pity for the criminal, whom I hold in far lower estimation than a mad wolf, but in consideration for the general tone and feeling, which is very much improved since the whipping times. It is bad for a people to be familiarised with such punishments. When the whip went out of Bridewell, and ceased to be flourished at the cart's tail and at the whipping-post, it began to fade out of madhouses, and workhouses, and schools and families, and to give place to a better system everywhere, than cruel driving. It would be hasty, because a few brutes may be inadequately punished, to revive, in any aspect, what, in so many aspects, society is hardly yet happily rid of. The whip is a very contagious kind of thing, and difficult to confine within one set of bounds. Utterly abolish punishment by fine—a barbarous device, quite as much out of date as wager by battle, but particularly connected in the vulgar mind with this class of offence—at least quadruple the term of imprisonment for aggravated assaults—and above all let us, in such cases, have no Pet Prisoning, vain glorifying, strong soup, and roasted meats, but hard work, and one unchanging and uncompromising dietary of bread and water, well or ill; and we shall do much better than by going down into the dark to grope for the whip among the rusty fragments of the rack, and the branding iron, and the chains and gibbet from the public roads, and the weights that pressed men to death in the cells of Newgate.

I had proceeded thus far, when I found I had been lying awake so long that the very dead began to wake too, and to crowd into my thoughts most sorrowfully. Therefore, I resolved to lie awake no more, but to get up and go out for a night walk—which resolution was an acceptable relief to me, as I dare say it may prove now to a great many more.

A WALK IN A WOOD

Anthony Trollope

THE MOST difficult thing that a man has to do is to think. There are many who can never bring themselves really to think at all, but do whatever thinking is done by them in a chance fashion, with no effort, using the faculty which the Lord has given them because they cannot, as it were, help themselves. To think is essential, all will agree. That it is difficult most will acknowledge who have tried it. If it can be compassed so as to become pleasant, brisk, and exciting as well as salutary, much will have been accomplished. My purpose here is to describe how this operation, always so difficult, often so repugnant to us, becomes easier out among the woods, with the birds and the air and the leaves and the branches around us, than in the seclusion of any closet.

But I have nothing to show for it beyond my own experience, and no performances of thought to boast of beyond the construction of combinations in fiction, countless and unimportant as the sand on the sea-shore. For in these operations of thinking it is not often the entire plot of a novel,—the plot of a novel as a whole,—that exercises the mind. That is a huge difficulty;—one so arduous as to have been generally found by me altogether beyond my power of accomplishment. Efforts are made, no doubt,—always out in the open air, and within the precincts of a wood if a wood be within reach; but to construct a plot so as to know, before the story is begun, how it is to end, has always been to me a labour of Hercules beyond my reach. I have to confess that my incidents are fabricated to fit my story as it goes on, and not my story to fit my incidents. I wrote a novel once in which a lady forged a will; but I had not myself decided that she had forged it till the chapter before that in which she confesses her guilt. In another a lady is made to steal her own diamonds,—a grand tour-de-force, as I thought,—but the brilliant idea only struck me when I was writing the page in which the theft is described. I once heard an unknown critic abuse my workmanship because a certain lady had been made to appear too frequently in my pages. I went home and killed her immediately. I say this to show that the process of thinking to which I am alluding has not generally been applied to any great effort of construction. It has expended itself on the minute ramifications of tale-telling;—how this young lady should be made to behave herself with that young gentleman;—how this mother or that father would be affected by the ill conduct or the good of a son or a daughter;—how these words or those other would be most appropriate and true to nature if used on some special occasion. Such plottings as these, with a fabricator of fiction, are infinite in number as they are infinitesimal in importance,—and are therefore, as I have said, like the sand of the sea-shore. But not one of them can be done fitly without thinking. My little effort will miss its wished-for result, unless I be true to nature; and to be true to nature I must think what nature would produce. Where shall I go to find my thoughts with the greatest ease and most perfect freedom?

Bad noises, bad air, bad smells, bad light, an inconvenient attitude, ugly surroundings, little misfortunes that have lately been endured, little misfortunes that are soon to come, hunger and thirst, overeating and overdrinking, want of sleep or too much of it, a tight boot, a starched collar, are all inimical to thinking. I do not name bodily ailments. The feeling of heroism which is created by the magnanimity of overcoming great evils will sometimes make thinking easy. It is not the sorrows but the annoyances of life which impede. Were I told that the bank had broken in which my little all was kept for me I could sit down and write my love story with almost a sublimated vision of love; but to discover that I had given half a sovereign instead of sixpence to a cabman would render a great effort necessary before I could find the fitting words for a lover. These little lacerations of the spirit, not the deep wounds, make the difficulty. Of all the nuisances named noises are the worst. I know a hero who can write his leading article for a newspaper in a club smoking-room while all the chaff of all the Joneses and all the Smiths is sounding in his ears;—but he is a hero because he can do it. To think with a barrel organ within hearing is heroic. For myself I own that a brass band altogether incapacitates me. No sooner does the first note of the opening burst reach my ear than I start up, fling down my pen, and cast my thoughts disregarded into the abyss of some chaos which is always there ready to receive them. Ah, how terrible, often how vain, is the work of fishing, to get them out again! Here, in our quiet square, the beneficent police have done wonders for our tranquillity,—not, however, without creating for me personally a separate trouble in having to encounter the stern reproaches of the middle-aged leader of the band when he asks me in mingled German and English accents whether I do not think that he too as well as I,—he with all his comrades, and then he points to the nine

stalwart, well-cropped, silent and sorrowing Teutons around him,—
whether he and they should not be allowed to earn their bread as well as
I. I cannot argue the matter with him. I cannot make him understand
that in earning my own bread I am a nuisance to no one. I can only
assure him that I am resolute, being anxious to avoid the gloom which
was cast over the declining years of one old philosopher. I do feel, however, that this comparative peace within the heart of a huge city is purchased at the cost of many tears. When, as I walk-abroad, I see in some
small crowded street the ill-shod feet of little children spinning round in
the perfect rhythm of a dance, two little tots each holding the other by
their ragged duds while an Italian boy grinds at his big box, each footfall
true to its time, I say to myself that a novelist's schemes, or even a philosopher's figures, may be purchased too dearly by the silencing of the music
of the poor.

Whither shall a man take himself to avoid these evils, so that he may
do his thinking in peace,—in silence if it may be possible? And yet it is
not silence that is altogether necessary. The wood-cutter's axe never
stopped a man's thought, nor the wind through the branches, nor the
flowing of water, nor the singing of birds, nor the distant tingling of a
chapel bell. Even the roaring of the sea and the loud splashing of the
waves among the rocks do not impede the mind. No sounds coming
from water have the effect of harassing. But yet the sea-shore has its dis-
advantages. The sun overhead is hot or the wind is strong,—or the very
heaviness of the sand creates labour and distraction. A high road is ugly,
dusty, and too near akin to the business of the world. You may calculate
your five per cents and your six per cents with precision as you tramp
along a high road. They have a weight of material interest which rises
above dust. But if your mind flies beyond this;—if it attempts to deal
with humour, pathos, irony, or scorn, you should take it away from the
well-constructed walks of life. I have always found it impossible to utilise
railroads for delicate thinking. A great philosopher once cautioned me
against reading in railway carriages. "Sit still," said he, "and label your
thoughts." But he was a man who had stayed much at home himself.
Other men's thoughts I can digest when I am carried along at the rate of
thirty miles an hour; but not my own.

Any carriage is an indifferent vehicle for thinking, even though the
cushions be plump, and the road gracious,—not rough nor dusty,—and
the horses going at their ease. There is a feeling attached to the carriage
that it is there for a special purpose,—as though to carry one to a fixed
destination; and that purpose, hidden perhaps but still inherent, clogs the
mind. The end is coming, and the sooner it is reached, the better. So at
any rate thinks the driver. If you have been born to a carriage, and carried about listlessly from your childhood upwards, then, perhaps, you

may use it for free mental exercise; but you must have been coaching it from your babyhood to make it thus effective.

On horseback something may be done. You may construct your villain or your buffoon as you are going across country. All the noise of an assize court or the low rattle of a gambling table may thus be arranged. Standing by the covert side I myself have made a dozen little plots, and were I to go back to the tales I could describe each point at the covert side at which the incident or the character was moulded and brought into shape. But this, too, is only good for rough work. Solitude is necessary for the task we have in hand; and the bobbing up and down of the horse's head is antagonistic to solitude.

I have found that I can best command my thoughts on foot, and can do so with the most perfect mastery when wandering through a wood. To be alone is of course essential. Companionship requires conversation,—for which indeed the spot is most fit; but conversation is not now the object in view. I have found it best even to reject the society of a dog, who, if he be a dog of manners, will make some attempt at talking. And though he should be silent the sight of him provokes words and caresses and sport. It is best to be away from cottages, away from children, away as far as may be from other chance wanderers. So much easier is it to speak than to think that any slightest temptation suffices to carry away the idler from the harder to the lighter work. An old woman with a bundle of sticks becomes an agreeable companion, or a little girl picking wild fruit. Even when quite alone, when all the surroundings seem to be fitted for thought, the thinker will still find a difficulty in thinking. It is not that the mind is inactive, but that it will run exactly whither it is not bidden to go. With subtle ingenuity it will find for itself little easy tasks instead of settling itself down on that which it is its duty to do at once. With me, I own, it is so weak as to fly back to things already done,— which require no more thinking, which are perhaps unworthy of a place even in the memory,—and to revel in the ease of contemplating that which has been accomplished rather than to struggle for further performance. My eyes which should become moist with the troubles of the embryo heroine, shed tears as they call to mind the early sorrow of Mr. ——, who was married and made happy many years ago. Then,—when it comes to this,—a great effort becomes necessary, or that day will for him have no results. It is so easy to lose an hour in maundering over the past, and to waste the good things which have been provided in remembering instead of creating!

But a word about the nature of the wood! It is not always easy to find a wood, and sometimes when you have got it, it is but a muddy, plashy, rough-hewn congregation of ill-grown trees,—a thicket rather than a wood,—in which even contemplation is difficult and thinking is out of the question. He who has devoted himself to wandering in woods will know at the first glance whether the place will suit his purpose. A crowded undergrowth of hazel, thorn, birch, and alder, with merely a track through it, will by no means serve the occasion. The trees around you should be big and noble. There should be grass at your feet. There should be space for the felled or fallen princes of the forest. A roadway, with the sign of wheels that have passed long since, will be an advantage, so long as the branches above head shall meet or seem to meet each other. I will not say that the ground should not be level, lest by creating difficulties I shall seem to show that the fitting post may be too difficult to be found; but, no doubt, it will be an assistance in the work to be done if occasionally you can look down on the tops of the trees as you descend, and again look up to them as with increasing height they rise high above your head. And it should be a wood,—perhaps a forest,—rather than a skirting of timber. You should feel that, if not lost, you are lose-able. To have trees around you is not enough unless you have many. You must have a feeling as of Adam in the garden. There must be a confirmed assurance in your mind that you have got out of the conventional into the natural,—which will not establish itself unless there be a consciousness of distance between you and the next ploughed field. If possible you should not know the East from the West, or, if so, only by the setting of the sun. You should recognise the direction in which you must return simply by the fall of water.

But where shall the wood be found? Such woodlands there are still in England, though, alas, they are becoming rarer every year. Profit from the timber-merchant or dealer in firewood is looked to, or else, as is more probable, drives are cut broad and straight, like spokes of a wheel radiating to a nave or centre, good only for the purposes of the slayer of multitudinous pheasants. I will not say that a wood prepared, not as the home but the slaughter-ground of game, is altogether inefficient for our purpose. I have used such even when the sound of the guns has been near enough to warn me to turn my steps to the right or to the left. The scents are pleasant even in winter, the trees are there, and sometimes even yet the delightful feeling may be encountered that the track on which you are walking leads to some far off vague destination, in reaching which there may be much of delight because it will be new,—something also of peril because it will be distant. But the wood if possible should seem to be purposeless. It should have no evident consciousness of being their either for game or fagots. The felled trunk on which you sit should seem to have been selected for some accidental purpose of house-building, as though a neighbour had searched for what was wanting and had found it. No idea should be engendered that it was let out at so much an acre to a contractor who would cut the trees in order and sell them in the next market. The mind should conceive that this wood never had been planted by hands, but had come there from the direct beneficence of the Creator,—as the first woods did come,—before man had been taught to recreate them systematically, and as some still remain to us, so much more lovely in their wildness than when reduced to rows and quincunces, and made to accommodate themselves to laws of economy and order.

England, dear England,—and certainly with England Scotland also,—has advanced almost too far for this. There are still woods, but they are so divided, and marked, and known, so apportioned out among game-keepers, park rangers, and other custodians, that there is but little left of wildness in them. It is too probable that the stray wanderer may be asked his purpose; and if so, how will it be with him if he shall answer to the custodian that he has come thither only for the purpose of thinking? "But it's here my lord turns out his young pheasants!" "Not a feather from the wing of one of them shall be the worse for me," answers the thinker. "I dun-na know," says the civil custodian; "but it's here my lord turns out his young pheasants." It is then explained that the stile into the field is but a few yards off,—for our woodland distances are seldom very great,—and the thinker knows that he must go and think elsewhere. Then his work for that day will be over with him. There are woods, however, which may with more or less of difficulty be utilised. In Cumberland and Westmoreland strangers are so rife that you will hardly be admitted beyond the paths recognised for tourists. You may succeed on the sly, and if so the sense of danger adds something to the intensity of your thought. In Northamptonshire, where John the planter lived, there are miles of woodland,—but they consist of avenues rather than of trees. Here you are admitted and may trespass, but still with a feeling that game is the lord of all. In Norfolk, Suffolk, and Essex the gamekeepers will meet you at every turn,—or rather at every angle, for turns there are none. The woods have been all re-fashioned with measuring rod and tape. Two lines crossing each other, making what they call in Essex a four-want way, has no special offence, though if they be quite rectangular they tell something too plainly of human regularity; but four lines thus converging and radiating, displaying the brazen-faced ingenuity of an artificer, are altogether destructive of fancy. In Devonshire there are still some sweet woodland nooks, shaws, and holts, and pleasant spinneys, through which clear water brooks run, and the birds sing sweetly, and the primroses bloom early, and the red earth pressing up here and there gives a glow of colour,—and the gamekeeper does not seem quite as yet to dominate everything. Here, perhaps, in all fair England the solitary thinker may have his fairest welcome.

But though England be dear, there are other countries not so small, not so crowded, in which every inch of space has not been made so available either for profit or for pleasure, in which the woodland rambler may have a better chance of solitude amidst the unarranged things of nature. They who have written and they who have read about Australia say little and hear little as to its charm of landscape, but here the primeval forests running for uninterrupted miles, with undulating land and broken timber, with ways open everywhere through the leafy wilderness, where loneliness is certain till it be interrupted by the kangaroo, and where the silence is only broken by the noises of quaint birds high above your head, offer all that is wanted by him whose business it is to build his castles carefully in the air. Here he may roam at will and be interrupted by no fence, feel no limits, be wounded by no art, and have no sense of aught around him but the forest, the air, and the ground. Here too he may lose himself in truth till he shall think it well if he come upon a track leading to a shepherd's hut.

But the woods of Australia, New Zealand, California, or South Africa are too far afield for the thinker for whom I am writing. If he is to take himself out of England it must be somewhere among the forests of Europe. France has still her woodlands;—though for these let him go somewhat far afield, nor trust himself to the bosky dells through which Parisian taste will show him the way by innumerable finger posts. In the Pyrenees he may satisfy himself, or on the sides of Jura. The chesnut groves of Lucca, and the oak woods of Tuscany are delightful where the autumnal leaves of Vallombrosa lie thick,—only let him not trust himself to the mid-day sun. In Belgium, as far as I know it, the woods are of recent growth, and smack of profitable production. But in Switzerland there are pure forests still, standing or appearing to stand as nature caused them to grow, and here the poet or the novelist may wander and find all as he would have it. Or, better still, let him seek the dark shadows of the Black Forest, and there wander, fancy free,—if that indeed can be freedom which demands a bondage of its own.

Were I to choose the world all round I should take certain districts in the Duchy of Baden as the hunting ground for my thoughts. The reader will probably know of the Black Forest that it is not continual wood. Nor, indeed, are the masses of timber, generally growing on the mountain sides, or high among the broad valleys, or on the upland plateaux, very large. They are interspersed by pleasant meadows and occasional cornfields, so that the wanderer does not wander on among them, as he does, perhaps hopelessly, in Australia. But as the pastures are interspersed through the forest, so is the forest through the pastures; and when you shall have come to the limit of this wood, it is only to be lured on into the confines of the next. You go upwards among the ashes and beeches, and oaks, till you reach the towering pines. Oaks have the pride of magnificence; the smooth beech with its nuts thick upon it is a tree laden with tenderness; the sober ash has a savour of solitude, and of truth; the birch with its may-day finery springing thick about it boasts the brightest green which nature has produced; the elm,—the useless elm,—savours of decorum and propriety; but for sentiment, for feeling, for grandeur, and for awe, give me the forest of pines. It is when they are round me that, if ever, I can use my mind aright and bring it to the work which is required of it. There is a scent from them which reaches my brain and soothes it. There is a murmur among their branches, best heard when the moving breath of heaven just stirs the air, which reminds me of my duty without disturbing me. The crinkling fibres of their blossom are pleasant to my feet as I walk over them. And the colours which they produce are at the same time sombre and lovely, never paining the eye and never exciting it. If I can find myself here of an afternoon when there shall be another two hours for me, safe before the sun set, with my stick in my hand, and my story half-conceived in my mind, with some blotch of a character or two, just daubed out roughly on the canvas, then if ever I can go to work, and decide how he and she, and they shall do their work.

They will not come at once, those thoughts which are so anxiously expected,—and in the process of coming they are apt to be troublesome, full of tricks, and almost traitorous. They must be imprisoned, or bound with thongs, when they come, as was Proteus when Ulysses caught him amidst his sea-calves,—as was done with some of the fairies of old, who would, indeed, do their beneficent work, but only under compulsion. It may be that your spirit should on an occasion be as obedient as Ariel, but that will not be often. He will run backwards,—as it were downhill,—because it is so easy, instead of upward and onward. He will turn to the right and to the left, making a show of doing fine work, only not the work that is demanded of him that day. He will skip hither and thither, with pleasant bright gambols, but will not put his shoulder to the wheel, his neck to the collar, his hand to the plough. Has my reader ever driven a pig to market? The pig will travel on freely, but will always take the wrong turning, and then when stopped for the tenth time, will head backwards, and try to run between your legs. So it is with the tricksy Ariel,—that Ariel which every man owns, though so many of us fail to use him for much purpose, which but few of us have subjected to such discipline as Prospero had used before he had brought his servant to do his bidding at the slightest word.

It is right that a servant should do his master's bidding; and, with judicious discipline, he will do it. The great thinkers, no doubt, are they who have made their servant perfect in obedience, and quick at a moment's notice for all work. To them no adjuncts of circumstances are necessary. Solitude, silence, and beauty of surroundings are unnecessary. Such a one can bid his mind go work, and the task shall be done, whether in town or country, whether amid green fields, or congregated books or crowded assemblies. Such a master no doubt was Prospero. Such were Homer, and Cicero, and Dante. Such were Bacon and Shakespeare. They had so tamed, and trained, and taught their Ariels that each, at a moment's notice, would put a girdle round the earth. With us, though the attendant Spirit will come at last and do something at our bidding, it is but driving an unwilling pig to market.

But at last I feel that I have him,—perhaps by the tail, as the Irishman drives his pig. When I have got him I have to be careful that he shall not escape me till that job of work be done. Gradually as I walk, or stop, as I seat myself on a bank, or lean against a tree, perhaps as I hurry on waving my stick above my head till with my quick motion the sweat-drops come out upon my brow, the scene forms itself for me. I see, or fancy that I see, what will be fitting, what will be true, how far virtue may be made to go without walking upon stilts, what wickedness may do without breaking the link which binds it to humanity, how low ignorance may grovel, how high knowledge may soar, what the writer may teach without repelling by severity, how he may amuse without descending to buffoonery; and then the limits of pathos are searched, and words are weighed which shall suit, but do no more than suit, the greatness or the smallness of the occasion. We, who are slight, may not attempt lofty things, or make ridiculous with our little fables the doings of the gods. But for that which we do there are appropriate terms and boundaries which may be reached but not surpassed. All this has to be thought of and decided upon in reference to those little plotlings of which I have spoken, each of which has to be made the receptacle of pathos or of humour, of honour or of truth, as far as the thinker may be able to furnish them. He has to see, above all things, that in his attempts he shall not sin against nature, that in striving to touch the feelings he shall not excite ridicule, that in seeking for humour he does not miss his point, that in quest of honour and truth he does not become bombastic and straight-laced. A clergyman in his pulpit may advocate an altitude of virtue fitted to a millennium here or to a heaven hereafter;—nay, from the nature of his profession, he must do so. The poet too may soar as high as he will, and if words suffice to him, need never fear to fail because his ideas are too lofty. But he who tells tales in prose can hardly hope to be effective as a teacher unless he binds himself by the circumstances of the world which he finds around him. Honour and truth there should be, and pathos and humour, but he should so constrain them that they shall not seem to mount into nature beyond the ordinary habitations of men and women.

Such rules as to construction have probably been long known to him.

It is not for them he is seeking as he is roaming listlessly or walking rapidly through the trees. They have come to him from much observation, from the writings of others, from that which we call study,—in which imagination has but little immediate concern. It is the fitting of the rules to the characters which he has created, the filling in with living touches and true colours those daubs and blotches on his canvas which have been easily scribbled with a rough hand, that the true work consists. It is here that he requires that his fancy should be undisturbed; that the trees should overshadow him, that the birds should comfort him, that the green and yellow mosses should be in unison with him,—that the very air should be good to him. The rules are there fixed,—fixed as far as his judgment can fix them, and are no longer a difficulty to him. The first coarse outlines of his story he has found to be a matter almost indifferent to him. It is with these little plotlings that he has to contend. It is for them that he must catch his Ariel, and bind him fast;—but yet so bind him that not a thread shall touch the easy action of his wings. Every little scene must be arranged so that,—if it may be possible,—the proper words may be spoken and the fitting effect produced.

Alas, with all these struggles, when the wood has been found, when all external things are propitious, when the very heavens have lent their aid, it is so often that it is impossible! It is not only that your Ariel is untrained, but that the special Ariel which you may chance to own is no better than a rustic Hobgoblin, or a Peaseblossom, or Mustard Seed at the best. You cannot get the pace of the race-horse from a farm-yard colt, train him as you will. How often is one prompted to fling one's self down in despair, and, weeping between the branches, to declare that it is not that the thoughts will wander, it is not that the mind is treacherous. That which it can do it will do;—but the pace required from it should be fitted only for the farm-yard.

Nevertheless, before all be given up, let a walk in a wood be tried.

THE CLOUDS *ARE THERE*
John Ruskin

HAVING BEEN myself long a cloud-worshipper, and passed many hours of life in the pursuit of them from crag to crag, I must consider what can possibly be submitted in their defence, and in Turner's.

The first and principal thing to be submitted is, that the clouds *are there.* Whether we like them or not, it is a fact that by far the largest spaces of the habitable world are full of them. That is Nature's will in the matter; and whatever we may theoretically determine to be expedient or beautiful, she has long ago determined what shall *be.* We may declare that clear horizons and blue skies form the most exalted scenery; but for all that, the bed of the river in the morning will still be traced by its line of white mist, and the mountain peaks will be seen at evening only in the rents between their blue fragments of towering cloud. Thus it is, and that so constantly, that it is impossible to become a faithful landscape painter without continually getting involved in effects of this kind. We may, indeed, avoid them systematically, but shall become narrow mannerists if we do.

But not only is there a *partial* and variable mystery thus caused by clouds and vapors throughout great spaces of landscape; there is a continual mystery caused throughout *all* spaces, caused by the absolute infinity of things. WE NEVER SEE ANYTHING CLEARLY. . . . The fact is, that everything we look at, be it large or small, near or distant, has an equal quantity of mystery in it; and the only question is, not how much mystery there is, but at what part of the object mystification begins. We suppose we see the ground under our feet clearly, but if we try to number its grains of dust, we shall find that it is as full of confusion and doubtful form as anything else; so that there is literally *no* point of clear sight, and there never can be. What we call seeing a thing clearly, is only seeing enough of it to *make out what it is*; this point of intelligibility varying in distance for different magnitudes and kinds of things, while the appointed quantity of mystery remains nearly the same for all. Thus: throwing an open book and an embroidered handkerchief on a lawn, at a distance of half a mile we cannot tell which is which; that is the point of mystery for the whole of those things. They are then merely white spots of indistinct shape. We approach them, and perceive that one is a book, the other a handkerchief, but cannot read the one, nor trace the embroidery of the other. The mystery has ceased to be in the whole things, and has gone into their details. We go nearer, and can now read the text and trace the embroidery, but cannot see the fibres of the paper, nor the threads of the stuff. The mystery has gone into a third place. We take both up and look closely at them; we see the watermark and the threads, but not the hills and dales in the paper's surface, nor the fine fibres which shoot off from every thread. The mystery has gone into a fourth place, where it must stay, till we take a microscope, which will send it into a fifth, sixth, handredth, or thousandth place, according to the power we use. When, therefore, we say, we see the book *clearly*, we mean only that we know it is a book. When we say that we see the letters clearly, we mean that we know what letters they are; and artists feel that they are drawing objects at a convenient distance when they are so near them as to know, and to be able in painting to show that they know, what the objects are, in a tolerably complete manner; but this power does not depend on any definite distance of the object, but on its size, kind, and distance, together; so that a small thing in the foreground may be precisely in the same *phase* or place of a mystery as a large thing far away.

The other day, as I was lying down to rest on the side of the hill round which the Rhone sweeps in its main angle, opposite Martigny, and looking carefully across the valley to the ridge of the hill which rises above Martigny itself, then distant about four miles, a plantain seed-vessel about an inch long, and a withered head of a scabious half an inch broad, happened to be seen rising up, out of the grass near me, across the outline of the distant hill, so as seemingly to set themselves closely beside the large pines and chestnuts which fringed that distant ridge. The plantain was eight yards from me, and the scabious seven; and to my sight, at these distances, the plantain and the far away pines were equally clear (it being a clear day, and the sun stooping to the west). The pines, four miles off, showed their branches, but I could not count them; and two or three young and old Spanish chestnuts beside them showed their broken masses distinctly; but I could not count those masses, only I knew the trees to be chestnuts by their general look. The plantain and scabious in like manner I knew to be a plantain and scabious by their general look. I saw the plantain seed-vessel to be, somehow, rough, and that there were two little projections at the bottom of the scabious head, which I knew to mean the leaves of the calyx; but I could no more count distinctly the seeds of the plantain, or the group of leaves forming the calyx of the scabious, than I could count the branches of the far-away pines.

Under these circumstances, it is quite evident that neither the pine nor plantain could have been rightly represented by a single dot or stroke of color. Still less could they be represented by a definite drawing, on a small scale, of a pine with all its branches clear, or of a plantain with all its seeds clear. The round dot or long stroke would represent nothing, and the clear delineation too much. They were not mere dots of color which I saw on the hill, but something full of essence of pine; out of which I could gather which were young and which were old, and discern the distorted and crabbed pines from the symmetrical and healthy pines; and feel how the evening sun was sending its searching threads among their dark leaves;—assuredly they were more than dots of color. And yet not one of their boughs or outlines could be distinctly made out, or distinctly drawn. Therefore, if I had drawn either a definite pine, or a dot, I should have been equally wrong, the right lying in an inexplicable, almost inimitable, confusion between the two.

"But is this only the case with pines four miles away, and with plantains eight yards?"

Not so. Everything in the field of sight is equally puzzling, and can only be drawn rightly on the same difficult conditions. Try it fairly. Take the commonest, closest, most familiar thing, and strive to draw it verily as you see it. Be sure of this last face, for otherwise you will find yourself continually drawing, not what you *see,* but what you *know.* The best practice to begin with is, sitting about three yards from a bookcase (not your own, so that you may *know* none of the titles of the books), to try to draw the books accurately, with the titles on the backs, and patterns on the bindings, as you see them. You are not to stir from your place to look what they are, but to draw them simply as they appear, giving the perfect look of neat lettering; which, nevertheless, must be (as you find it on most of the books) absolutely illegible. Next try to draw a piece of patterned muslin or lace (of which you do not know the pattern) a little way off, and rather in the shade; and be sure you get all the grace and *look* of the pattern without going a step nearer to see what it is. Then try to draw a bank of grass, with all its blades; or a bush, with all its leaves; and you will soon begin to understand under what a universal law of obscurity we live, and perceive that all *distinct* drawing must be *bad* drawing, and that nothing can be right, till it is unintelligible.

PERSONAL STYLE
John Addington Symonds

A SURVEY of language, however superficial, makes it evident that when we speak of style, we have to take into account those qualities of national character which are embodied in national speech. If two men could be born of precisely the same physical, mental, and moral nature, at precisely the same moment of history, and under precisely the same social conditions; and if these men learned different languages in the cradle, and used those languages in after life, they would be unable to deliver exactly the same message to the world through literature. The dominant qualities of each mother-tongue would impose definite limitations on their power of expressing thoughts, however similar or identical those thoughts might be.

We cannot conceive two men born with the same physical, mental, and moral nature, at the same moment, under precisely the same conditions, and using the same language. They would be identical; and everything they uttered would be clothed with exactly the same words. The absurdity of this conception brings home to us the second aspect of style. Style is not merely a sign of those national qualities which are generic to established languages, and which constitute the so-called genius of a race. It is also the sign of personal qualities, specific to individuals, which constitute the genius of a man. Whatever a man utters from his heart and head is the index of his character. The more remarkable a person is, the more strongly he is differentiated from the average of human beings, the more salient will be the characteristic notes of his expression. But even the commonest people have, each of them, a specific style. The marks of difference become microscopical as we descend from Dante or Shakespeare to the drudges of the clerk's desk in one of our great cities. Yet these marks exist, and are no less significant of individuality than the variations between leaf and leaf upon the lime-trees of an avenue.

It may be asked whether the manner of expression peculiar to any person is a complete index to his character—whether, in other words, there is "an art to find the mind's construction" in the style. Not altogether and exhaustively. Not all the actions and the utterances of an individual betray the secret of his personality. You may live with men and women through years, by day, by night, yet you will never know the whole about them. No human being knows the whole about himself.

The deliberate attitude adopted by a literary writer implies circumspection; invites suppression, reservation, selection; is compatible with affectation, dissimulation, hypocrisy. So much cannot be claimed for critical analysis as that we should pretend to reproduce a man's soul after close examination of his work. What we may assert with confidence is that the qualities of style are intimately connected with the qualities and limitations of the writer, and teach us much about him. He wrote thus and thus, because he was this or this. In the exercise of style it is impossible for any one to transcend his inborn and acquired faculties of ideation, imagination, sense-perception, verbal expression—just as it is impossible in the exercise of strength for an athlete to transcend the limits of his physical structure, powers of innervation, dexterity and courage. The work of art produced by a writer is therefore, of necessity, complexioned and determined by the inborn and acquired faculties of the individual. This is what we mean by the hackneyed epigram: "Le style c'est l'homme."

II

Certain broad distinctions of moral and emotional temperament may undoubtedly be detected in literary style. A tendency toward exaggeration, toward self-revelation, toward emphasis upon the one side; a tendency to reserve, to diminished tone in colouring, to parsimony of rhetorical resource upon the other; these indicate expansiveness or reticence in the writer. Victor Hugo differs by the breadth of the whole heavens from Leopardi. One man is ironical by nature, another sentimental. Sterne and Heine have a common gift of humour; but the quality of humour in each case is conditioned by sympathetic or by caustic undercurrents of emotion. Sincerity and affectation, gaiety and melancholy, piety and scepticism, austerity and sensuality penetrate style so subtly and unmistakably that a candid person cannot pose as the mere slave of convention, a boon companion cannot pass muster for an anchorite, the founder of a religious sect cannot play the part of an agnostic. In dramatic work the artist creates characters alien from his own personality, and exhibits people widely different from himself acting and talking as they ought to do. This he achieves by sympathy and intuition. Yet all except the very greatest fail to render adequately what they have not felt and been. In playwrights of the second order, like our Fletcher, or of the third order, like our Byron, the individual who writes the tragedy and shapes the characters is always apparent under every mask he chooses to assume. And even the style of the greatest, their manner of presenting the varieties of human nature, betrays individual peculiarities. Æschylus sees men and women differently from Sophocles, Corneille from Racine, Shakespeare from Goethe.

In like manner the broad distinctions of mental temperament may be traced in style. The abstract thinker differs from the concrete thinker in his choice of terms; the analytical from the synthetic; the ratiocinative from the intuitive; the logical from the imaginative; the scientific from the poetical. One man thinks in images, another in formal propositions. One is diffuse, and gets his thought out by reiterated statement. Another makes epigrams, and finds some difficulty in expanding their sense or throwing light upon them by illustrations. One arrives at conclusions by the way of argument. Another clothes assertion with the tropes and metaphors of rhetoric.

The same is true of physical and æsthetical qualities. They are felt inevitably in style. The sedentary student does not use the same figures of speech as come naturally to the muscular and active lover of field sports. According as the sense for colour, or for sound, or for light, or for form shall preponderate in a writer's constitution, his language will abound in references to the world, viewed under conditions of colour, sound, light, or form. He will insensibly dwell upon those aspects of things which stimulate his sensibility and haunt his memory. Thus, too, predilections for sea or mountains, for city-life or rural occupations, for flowers, precious stones, scents, birds, animals, insects, different kinds of food, torrid or temperate climates, leave their mark on literary style.

Acquired faculties and habits find their expression in style no less than inborn qualities. Education, based upon humanism or scientific studies; contact with powerful personalities at an impressible period of youth; enthusiasm aroused for this or that great masterpiece of literature; social environment; high or low birth; professional training for the bar, the church, medicine, or commerce; life in the army, at sea, upon a farm, and so forth, tinge the mind and give a more or less perceptible colour to language.

The use of words itself yields, upon analysis, valuable results illustrative of the various temperaments of authors. A man's vocabulary marks him out as of this sort or that sort—his preference for certain syntactical forms, for short sentences or for periods, for direct or inverted propositions, for plain or figurative statement, for brief or amplified illustrations. Some compose sentences, but do not build paragraphs— like Emerson; some write chapters, but cannot construct a book. Nor is punctuation to be disregarded, inasmuch as stops enable us to measure a writer's sense of time-values, and the importance he attaches to several degrees of rest and pause.

III

It is impossible to do more than indicate some of the leading points which illustrate the meaning of the saying that style is the man; any one can test them and apply them for himself. We not only feel that Walter Scott *did not* write like Thackeray, but we also know that he *could not* write like Thackeray, and *vice versâ*. This impossibility of one man producing work in exactly the same manner as another makes all deliberate attempts at imitation assume the form of parody or caricature. The sacrifice of individuality involved in scrupulous addiction to one great master of Latin prose, Cicero, condemned the best stylists of the Renaissance—men like Muretus—to lifeless and eventually worthless production. Meanwhile the exact psychology is wanting which would render our intuitions regarding the indissoluble link between style and personal character irrefutable.

Literary style is more a matter of sentiment, emotion, involuntary habits of feeling and observing, constitutional sympathy with the world and men, tendencies of curiosity and liking, than of the pure intellect. The style of scientific works, affording little scope for the exercise of these psychological elements, throws less light upon their authors' temperament than does the style of poems, novels, essays, books of travel, descriptive criticism. In the former case all that need be aimed at is lucid exposition of fact and vigorous reasoning. In the latter, the fact to be stated, the truth to be arrived at, being of a more complex nature, involves a process akin to that of the figurative arts. The stylist has here to produce the desired effect by suggestions of infinite subtlety, and to present impressions made upon his sensibility.

Autobiographies, epistolary correspondence, notes of table-talk, are of the highest value in determining the correlation between a writer's self and his style. We not only derive a mass of information about Goethe's life from Eckermann, but we also discover from those conversations in how true a sense the style of Goethe's works grew out of his temperament and experience. Gibbon and Rousseau, Alfieri and Goldoni, Samuel Johnson in his "Life" by Boswell, John Stuart Mill in his autobiographical essay, Petrarch in his "Secretum" and fragment of personal confessions, have placed similar keys within our reach for unlocking the secret of their several manners.

The rare cases in which men of genius have excelled in more than one branch of art are no less instructive. Michel Angelo the sonnet-writer helps us to understand Michel Angelo the sculptor. Rossetti the painter throws light on Rossetti the poet; William Blake the lyrist upon William Blake the draughtsman. We find, on comparing the double series of work offered by such eminent and exceptionally gifted individuals, that their styles in literature and plastic art possess common qualities, which mark the men and issue from their personalities. Michel Angelo in the sonnets is as abstract, as ideal, as form-loving, as indifferent to the charm of brilliant colour, as neglectful of external nature as Michel Angelo in his statues and the frescoes of the Sistine Chapel. Rosseti's pictures, with their wealth of colour, their elaborate execution, their sharp incisive vision, their deep imaginative mysticism and powerful perfume of intellectual sensuousness, present a close analogue to his ballads, sonnets, and descriptive poems. With these and similar instances in our mind, we are prepared to hear that Victor Hugo designed pictures in the style of Gustave Doré; nor would it surprise us to discover that Gustave Doré had left odes or fiction in the manner of Victor Hugo.

The problems suggested by style as a sign and index of personality may be approached from many points of view. I have not aimed at exhaustiveness even of suggestion in my treatment of the topic; and while saying much which will appear perhaps trivial and obvious, have omitted some of the subtler and more interesting aspects of the matter. A systematic criticism of personal style would require a volume, and would demand physiological and psychological knowledge which is rarely found in combination with an extensive study of literatures and arts.

HER OWN VILLAGE

W. H. Hudson

ONE AFTERNOON when cycling among the limestone hills of Derbyshire I came to an unlovely dreary-looking little village named Chilmorton. It was an exceptionally hot June day and I was consumed with thirst: never had I wanted tea so badly. Small gritstone-built houses and cottages of a somewhat sordid aspect stood on either side of the street, but there was no shop of any kind and not a living creature could I see. It was like a village of the dead or sleeping. At the top of the street I came to the church standing in the middle of its churchyard with the public-house for nearest neighbour. Here there was life. Going in I found it the most squalid and evil-smelling village pub I had ever entered. Half a dozen grimy-looking labourers were drinking at the bar, and the landlord was like them in appearance, with his dirty shirt-front open to give his patrons a view of his hairy sweating chest. I asked him to get me tea. "Tea!" he shouted, staring at me as if I had insulted him; "There's no tea here!" A little frightened at his aggressive manner I then meekly asked for soda-water, which he gave me, and it was warm and tasted like a decoction of mouldy straw. After taking a sip and paying for it I went to look at the church, which I was astonished to find open.

It was a relief to be in that cool, twilight, not unbeautiful interior after my day in the burning sun.

After resting and taking a look round I became interested in watching and listening to the talk of two other visitors who had come in before me. One was a slim, rather lean brown-skinned woman, still young but with the incipient crow's-feet, the lines on the forehead, the dusty-looking dark hair, and other signs of time and toil which almost invariably appear in the country labourer's wife before she attains to middle age. She was dressed in a black gown, presumably her best although it was getting a little rusty. Her companion was a fat, red-cheeked young girl in a towny costume, a straw hat decorated with bright flowers and ribbons, and a string of big coloured beads about her neck.

In a few minutes they went out, and when going by me I had a good look at the woman's face, for it was turned towards me with an eager questioning look in her dark eyes and a very friendly smile on her lips. What was the attraction I suddenly found in that sunburnt face?—what did it say to me or remind me of?—what did it suggest?

I followed them out to where they were standing talking among the gravestones, and sitting down on a tomb near them spoke to the woman. She responded readily enough, apparently pleased to have some one to talk to, and pretty soon began to tell me the history of their lives. She told me that Chilmorton was her native place, but that she had been absent from it many many years. She knew just how many years because her child was only six months old when she left and was now fourteen though she looked more. She was such a big girl! Then her man took them to his native place in Staffordshire, where they had lived ever since. But their girl didn't live with them now. An aunt, a sister of her husband, had taken her to the town where she lived, and was having her taught at a private school. As soon as she left school her aunt hoped to get her a place in a draper's shop. For a long time past she had wanted to show her daughter her native place, but had never been able to manage it because it was so far to come and they didn't have much money to spend; but now at last she had brought her and was showing her everything.

Glancing at the girl who stood listening but with no sign of interest in her face, I remarked that her daughter would perhaps hardly think the journey had been worth taking.

"Why do you say that?" she quickly demanded.

"Oh well," I replied, "because Chilmorton can't have much to interest a girl living in a town." Then I foolishly went on to say what I thought of Chilmorton. The musty taste of that warm soda-water was still in my mouth and made me use some pretty strong words.

At that she flared up and desired me to know that in spite of what I thought it Chilmorton was the sweetest, dearest village in England; that she was born there and hoped to be buried in its churchyard where her parents were lying, and her grandparents and many others of her family. She was thirty-six years old now, she said, and would perhaps live to be an old woman, but it would make her miserable for all the rest of her life if she thought she would have to lie in the earth at a distance from Chilmorton.

During this speech I began to think of the soft reply it would now be necessary for me to make, when, having finished speaking, she called sharply to her daughter, "Come, we've others to see yet," and, followed by the girl, walked briskly away without so much as a good-bye, or even a glance!

Oh you poor foolish woman, thought I; why take it to heart like that! and I was sorry and laughed a little as I went back down the street.

It was beginning to wake up now! A man in his shirt sleeves and without a hat, a big angry man, was furiously hunting a rebellious pig all round a small field adjoining a cottage, trying to corner it; he swore and shouted, and out of the cottage came a frowsy-looking girl in a ragged gown with her hair hanging all over her face, to help him with the pig. A little further on I caught sight of yet another human being, a tall gaunt old woman in cap and shawl, who came out of a cottage and moved feebly towards a pile of faggots a few yards from the door. Just as she got to the pile I passed, and she slowly turned and gazed at me out of her dim old eyes. Her wrinkled face was the colour of ashes and was like the face of a corpse, still bearing on it the marks of suffering endured for many miserable years. And these three were the only inhabitants I saw on my way down the street.

At the end of the village the street broadened to a clean white road with high ancient hedgerow elms on either side, their upper branches meeting and forming a green canopy over it. As soon as I got to the trees I stopped and dismounted to enjoy the delightful sensation the shade produced: there out of its power I could best appreciate the sun shining in splendour on the wide green hilly earth and in the green translucent foliage above my head. In the upper branches a blackbird was trolling out his music in his usual careless leisurely manner; when I stopped under it the singing was suspended for half a minute or so, then resumed, but in a lower key, which made it seem softer, sweeter, inexpressibly beautiful.

There are beautiful moments in our converse with nature when all the avenues by which nature comes to our souls seem one, when hearing and seeing and smelling and feeling are one sense, when the sweet sound that falls from a bird, is but the blue of heaven, the green of earth, and the golden sunshine made audible.

Such a moment was mine, as I stood under the elms listening to the blackbird. And looking back up the village street I thought of the woman in the churchyard, her sun-parched eager face, her questioning eyes and friendly smile: what was the secret of its attraction?—what did that face say to me or remind me of?—what did it suggest?

Now it was plain enough. She was still a child at heart, in spite of those marks of time and toil on her countenance, still full of wonder and delight at this wonderful world of Chilmorton set amidst its limestone hills, under the wide blue sky—this poor squalid little village where I couldn't get a cup of tea!

It was the child surviving in her which had attracted and puzzled me; it does not often shine through the dulling veil of years so brightly. And as she now appeared to me as a child in heart I could picture her as a child in years, in her little cotton frock and thin bare legs, a sunburnt little girl of eight, with the wide-eyed, eager, half-shy, half-trustful look, asking you, as the child ever asks, what you think?—what you feel? It was a wonderful world, and the world was the village, its streets of gritstone houses, the people living in them, the comedies and tragedies of their lives and deaths, and burials in the churchyard with grass and flowers to grow over them by-and-by. And the church;—I think its interior must have seemed vaster, more beautiful and sublime to her wondering little soul than the greatest cathedral can be to us. I think that our admiration for the loveliest blooms—the orchids and roses and chrysanthemums at our great annual shows—is a poor languid feeling compared to what she experienced at the sight of any common flower of the field. Best of all perhaps were the elms at the village end, those mighty rough-barked trees that had their tops "so close against the sky." And I think that when a blackbird chanced to sing in the upper branches it was as if some angelic being had dropped down out of the sky into that green translucent cloud of leaves, and seeing the child's eager face looking up had sung a little song of his own celestial country to please her.

DANDY: A STORY OF A DOG
W. H. Hudson

HE WAS of mixed breed, and was supposed to have a strain of Dandy Dinmont blood which gave him his name. A big ungainly animal with a rough shaggy coat of blue-grey hair and white on his neck and clumsy paws. He looked like a Sussex sheep-dog with legs reduced to half their proper length. He was, when I first knew him, getting old and increasingly deaf and dim of sight, otherwise in the best of health and spirits, or at all events very good-tempered.

Until I knew Dandy I had always supposed that the story of Ludlam's dog was pure invention, and I daresay that is the general opinion about it; but Dandy made me reconsider the subject, and eventually I came to believe that Ludlam's dog did exist once upon a time, centuries ago perhaps, and that if he had been the laziest dog in the world Dandy was not far behind him in that respect. It is true he did not lean his head against a wall to bark; he exhibited his laziness in other ways. He barked often, though never at strangers; he welcomed every visitor, even the tax-collector, with tail-waggings and a smile. He spent a good deal of his time in the large kitchen, where he had a sofa to sleep on, and when the two cats of the house wanted an hour's rest they would coil themselves up on Dandy's broad shaggy side, preferring that bed to cushion or rug. They were like a warm blanket over him, and it was a sort of mutual benefit society. After an hour's sleep Dandy would go out for a short constitutional as far as the neighbouring thoroughfare, where he would blunder against people, wag his tail to everybody, and then come back. He had six or eight or more outings each day, and, owing to doors and gates being closed and to his lazy disposition, he had much trouble in getting out and in. First he would sit down in the hall and bark, bark, bark, until some one would come to open the door for him, whereupon he would slowly waddle down the garden path, and if he found the gate closed he would again sit down and start barking. And the bark, bark would go on until some one came to let him out. But if after he had barked about twenty

159

or thirty times no one came, he would deliberately open the gate himself, which he could do perfectly well, and let himself out. In twenty minutes or so he would be back at the gate and barking for admission once more, and finally, if no one paid any attention, letting himself in.

Dandy always had something to eat at mealtimes, but he too liked a snack between meals once or twice a day. The dog-biscuits were kept in an open box on the lower dresser shelf, so that he could get one "whenever he felt so disposed," but he didn't like the trouble this arrangement gave him, so he would sit down and start barking, and as he had a bark which was both deep and loud, after it had been repeated a dozen times at intervals of five seconds, any person who happened to be in or near the kitchen was glad to give him his biscuit for the sake of peace and quietness. If no one gave it him, he would then take it out himself and eat it.

Now it came to pass that during the last year of the war dog-biscuits, like many other articles of food for man and beast, grew scarce, and were finally not to be had at all. At all events, that was what happened in Dandy's town of Penzance. He missed his biscuits greatly and often reminded us of it by barking; then, lest we should think he was barking about something else, he would go and sniff and paw at the empty box. He perhaps thought it was pure forgetfulness on the part of those of the house who went every morning to do the marketing and had fallen into the habit of returning without any dog-biscuits in the basket. One day during that last winter of scarcity and anxiety I went to the kitchen and found the floor strewn all over with the fragments of Dandy's biscuit-box. Dandy himself had done it; he had dragged the box from its place out into the middle of the floor, and then deliberately set himself to bite and tear it into small pieces and scatter them about. He was caught at it just as he was finishing the job, and the kindly person who surprised him in the act suggested that the reason of his breaking up the box in that way was that he got something of the biscuit flavour by biting the pieces. My own theory was that as the box was there to hold biscuits and now held none, he had come to regard it as useless—as having lost its function, so to speak—also that its presence there was an insult to his intelligence, a constant temptation to make a fool of himself by visiting it half a dozen times a day only to find it empty as usual. Better, then, to get rid of it altogether, and no doubt when he did it he put a little temper into the business!

Dandy, from the time I first knew him, was strictly teetotal, but in former and distant days he had been rather fond of his glass. If a person held up a glass of beer before him, I was told, he wagged his tail in joyful anticipation, and a little beer was always given him at meal-time. Then he had an experience, which, after a little hesitation, I have thought it best to relate, as it is perhaps the most curious incident in Dandy's some-what uneventful life.

One day Dandy, who after the manner of his kind, had attached him-self to the person who was always willing to take him out for a stroll, followed his friend to a neighbouring public-house, where the said friend had to discuss some business matter with the landlord. They went into the taproom, and Dandy, finding that the business was going to be a rather long affair, settled himself down to have a nap. Now it chanced that a barrel of beer which had just been broached had a leaky tap, and the landlord had set a basin on the floor to catch the waste. Dandy, wak-ing from his nap and hearing the trickling sound, got up, and going to the basin quenched his thirst, after which he resumed his nap. By-and-by he woke again and had a second drink, and altogether he woke and had a drink five or six times; then, the business being concluded, they went out together, but no sooner were they in the fresh air than Dandy began to exhibit signs of inebriation. He swerved from side to side, colliding with the passers-by, and finally fell off the pavement into the swift stream of water which at that point runs in the gutter at one side of the street. Getting out of the water, he started again, trying to keep close to the wall to save himself from another ducking. People looked curiously at him, and by-and-by they began to ask what the matter was. "Is your dog going to have a fit—or what is it?" they asked. Dandy's friend said he didn't know; something was the matter no doubt, and he would take him home as quickly as possible and see to it.

When they finally got to the house Dandy staggered to his sofa, and succeeded in climbing on to it and, throwing himself on his cushion, went fast asleep, and slept on without a break until the following morn-ing. Then he rose quite refreshed and appeared to have forgotten all about it; but that day when at dinner-time some one said "Dandy" and held up a glass of beer, instead of wagging his tail as usual he dropped it between his legs and turned away in evident disgust. And from that time onward he would never touch it with his tongue, and it was plain that when they tried to tempt him, setting beer before him and smilingly inviting him to drink, he knew they were mocking him, and before turn-ing away he would emit a low growl and show his teeth. It was the one thing that put him out and would make him angry with his friends and life companions.

I should not have related this incident if Dandy had been alive. But he is no longer with us. He was old—half-way between fifteen and sixteen: it seemed as though he had waited to see the end of the war, since no sooner was the armistice proclaimed than he began to decline rapidly. Gone deaf and blind, he still insisted on taking several constitutionals every day, and would bark as usual at the gate, and if no one came to let him out or admit him, he would open it for himself as before. This went on till January, 1919, when some of the boys he knew were coming back to Penzance and to the house. Then he established himself on his sofa, and we knew that his end was near, for there he would sleep all day and all night, declining food. It is customary in this country to chloroform a dog and give him a dose of strychnine to "put him out of his misery." But it was not necessary in this case, as he was not in misery; not a groan did he ever emit, waking or sleeping; and if you put a hand on him he would look up and wag his tail just to let you know that it was well with him. And in his sleep he passed away—a perfect case of euthanasia—and was buried in the large garden near the second apple-tree.

FELLOW TRAVELLERS WITH A BIRD
Alice Meynell

TO ATTEND to a living child is to be baffled in your humour, disappointed of your pathos, and set freshly free from all the pre-occupations. You cannot anticipate him. Blackbirds, overheard year by year, do not compose the same phrases; never two leitmotifs alike. Not the tone, but the note alters. So with the uncovenanted ways of a child you keep no tryst. They meet you at another place, after failing you where you tarried; your former experiences, your documents are at fault. You are the fellow traveller of a bird. The bird alights and escapes out of time to your footing.

No man's fancy could be beforehand, for instance, with a girl of four years old who dictated a letter to a distant cousin, with the sweet and unimaginable message: "I hope you enjoy yourself with your loving dolls." A boy, still younger, persuading his mother to come down from the heights and play with him on the floor, but sensible, perhaps, that there was a dignity to be observed none the less, entreated her, "Mother, do be a lady frog." None ever said their good things before these indeliberate authors. Even their own kind—children—have not preceded them. No child in the past ever found the same replies as the girl of five whose father made that appeal to feeling which is doomed to a different, perverse, and unforeseen success. He was rather tired with writing, and had a mind to snare some of the yet uncaptured flock of her sympathies. "Do you know, I have been working hard, darling? I work to buy things for you." "Do you work," she asked, "to buy the lovely puddin's?" Yes, even for these. The subject must have seemed to her to be worth pursuing. "And do you work to buy the fat? I don't like fat."

The sympathies, nevertheless, are there. The same child was to be soothed at night after a weeping dream that a skater had been drowned in the Kensington Round Pond. It was suggested to her that she should forget it by thinking about the one unfailing and gay subject—her wishes. "Do you know," she said, without loss of time, "what I should like best in

163

all the world? A thundred dolls and a whistle!" Her mother was so over-come by this tremendous numeral, that she could make no offer as to the dolls. But the whistle seemed practicable. "It is for me to whistle for cabs," said the child, with a sudden moderation, "when I go to parties." Another morning she came down radiant. "Did you hear a great noise in the miggle of the night? That was me crying. I cried because I dreamt that Cuckoo [a brother] had swallowed a bead into his nose."

The mere errors of children are unforeseen as nothing is—no, noth-ing feminine—in this adult world. "I've got a lotter than you," is the word of a very young egotist. An older child says, "I'd better go, bettern't I, mother?" He calls a little space at the back of a London house, "the backy-garden." A little creature proffers almost daily the reminder at luncheon—at tart-time: "Father, I hope you will remember that I am the favourite of the crust." Moreover, if an author set himself to invent the naïf things that children might do in their Christmas plays at home, he would hardly light upon the device of the little *troupe* who, having no footlights, arranged upon the floor a long row of candle-shades.

"It's *jolly* dull without you, mother," says a little girl who—gentlest of the gentle—has a dramatic sense of slang, of which she makes no secret. But she drops her voice somewhat to disguise her feats of metathesis, about which she has doubts and which are involuntary: the "stand-wash," the "sweeping-crosser," the "sewing chamine." Genoese peasants have the same prank when they try to speak Italian.

Children forget last year so well that if they are Londoners they should by any means have an impression of the country or the sea annually. A London little girl watches a fly upon the wing, follows it with her point-ing finger, and names it "bird." Her brother, who wants to play with a bronze Japanese lobster, asks "Will you please let me have that tiger?"

At times children give to a word that slight variety which is the most touching kind of newness. Thus, a child of three asks you to save him. How moving a word, and how freshly said! He had heard of the "sav-ing" of other things of interest—especially chocolate creams taken for safe-keeping—and he asks, "Who is going to save me to-day? Nurse is going out, will you save me, mother?" The same little variant upon com-mon use is in another child's courteous reply to a summons to help in the arrangement of some flowers, "I am quite at your ease."

A child, unconscious little author of things told in this record, was taken lately to see a fellow author of somewhat different standing from her own, inasmuch as he is, among other things, a Saturday Reviewer. As he dwelt in a part of the South-west of the town unknown to her, she noted with interest the shops of the neighbourhood as she went, for they might be those of the *fournisseurs* of her friend. "That is his bread shop, and that is his book shop. And that, mother," she said finally, with even heightened sympathy, pausing before a blooming *parterre* of confectionery hard by the abode of her man of letters, "that, I suppose, is where he buys his sugar pigs."

In all her excursions into streets new to her, this same child is intent upon a certain quest—the quest of a genuine collector. We have all heard of collecting butterflies, of collecting china-dogs, of collecting cocked hats, and so forth; but her pursuit gives her a joy that costs her nothing except a sharp look-out upon the proper names over all shop-windows. No hoard was ever lighter than hers. "I began three weeks ago next Monday, mother," she says with precision, "and I have got thirty-nine." "Thirty-nine what?" "Smiths."

The mere gathering of children's language would be much like collecting together a handful of flowers that should be all unique, single of their kind. In one thing, however, do children agree, and that is the rejection of most of the conventions of the authors who have reported them. They do not, for example, say "me is"; their natural reply to "are you?" is "I are." One child, pronouncing sweetly and neatly, will have nothing but the nominative pronoun. "Lift I up and let I see it raining," she bids; and told that it does not rain, resumes, "Lift I up and let I see it not raining."

An elder child had a rooted dislike to a brown corduroy suit ordered for her by maternal authority. She wore the garments under protest, and with some resentment. At the same time it was evident that she took no pleasure in hearing her praises sweetly sung by a poet, her friend. He had imagined the making of this child in the counsels of Heaven, and the decreeing of her soft skin, of her brilliant eyes, and of her hair—"a brown tress." She had gravely heard the words as "a brown dress," and she silently bore the poet a grudge for having been the accessory of Providence in the mandate that she should wear the loathed corduroy. The unpractised ear played another little girl a like turn. She had a phrase for snubbing any anecdote that sounded improbable. "That," she said, more or less after Sterne, "is a cotton-wool story."

The learning of words is, needless to say, continued long after the years of mere learning to speak. The young child now takes a current word into use, a little at random, and now makes a new one, so as to save the interruption of a pause for search. I have certainly detected, in children old enough to show their motives, a conviction that a word of their own making is as good a communication as another, and as intelligible. There is even a general implicit conviction among them that the grown-up people, too, make words by the wayside as occasion befalls. How otherwise should words be so numerous that every day brings forward some hitherto unheard? The child would be surprised to know how irritably poets are refused the faculty and authority which he thinks to belong to the common world.

There is something very cheerful and courageous in the setting-out of a child on a journey of speech with so small baggage and with so much confidence in the chances of the hedge. He goes free, a simple adventurer. Nor does he make any officious effort to invent anything strange or particularly expressive or descriptive. The child trusts genially to his hearer. A very young boy, excited by his first sight of sunflowers, was eager to describe them, and called them, without allowing himself to be checked for the trifle of a name, "summersets." This was simple and unexpected; so was the comment of a sister a very little older. "Why does he call those flowers summersets?" their mother said; and the girl, with a darkly brilliant look of humour and penetration, answered, "because they are so big." There seemed to be no further question possible after an explanation that was presented thus charged with meaning.

To a later phase of life, when a little girl's vocabulary was, somewhat at random, growing larger, belong a few brave phrases hazarded to express a meaning well realized—a personal matter. Questioned as to the eating of an uncertain number of buns just before lunch, the child averred, "I took them just to appetize my hunger." As she betrayed a familiar knowledge of the tariff of an attractive confectioner, she was asked whether she and her sisters had been frequenting those little tables on their way from school. "I sometimes go in there, mother," she confessed; "but I generally speculate outside."

Children sometimes attempt to cap something perfectly funny with something so flat that you are obliged to turn the conversation. Dryden does the same thing, not with jokes, but with his sublimer passages. But sometimes a child's deliberate banter is quite intelligible to elders. Take the letter written by a little girl to a mother who had, it seems, allowed her family to see that she was inclined to be satisfied with something of her own writing. The child has a full and gay sense of the sweetest kinds of irony. There was no need for her to write, she and her mother being both at home, but the words must have seemed to her worthy of a pen:—"My dear mother, I really wonder how you can be proud of that article, if it is worthy to be called a article, which I doubt. Such a unletterary article. I cannot call it letterature. I hope you will not write any more such unconventionan trash."

This is the saying of a little boy who admired his much younger sister, and thought her forward for her age: "I wish people knew just how old she is, mother, then they would know she is onward. They can see she is pretty, but they can't know she is such a onward baby."

Thus speak the naturally unreluctant; but there are other children who in time betray a little consciousness and a slight *méfiance* as to where the adult sense of humour may be lurking in wait for them, obscure. These children may not be shy enough to suffer any self-checking in their talk, but they are now and then to be heard slurring a word of which they do not feel too sure. A little girl whose sensitiveness was barely enough to cause her to stop to choose between two words, was wont to bring a cup of tea to the writing-table of her mother, who had often feigned indignation at the weakness of what her Irish maid always called "the infusion." "I'm afraid it's bosh again, mother," said the child; and then, in a half-whisper, "Is bosh right, or wash, mother?" She was not told, and decided for herself, with doubts, for bosh. The afternoon cup left the kitchen an infusion, and reached the library "bosh" thenceforward.

THE UNREADY

Alice Meynell

IT IS rashly said that the senses of children are quick. They are, on the contrary, unwieldy in turning, unready in reporting, until advancing age teaches them agility. This is not lack of sensitiveness, but mere length of process. For instance, a child nearly newly born is cruelly startled by a sudden crash in the room—a child who has never learnt to fear, and is merely overcome by the shock of sound; nevertheless, that shock of sound does not reach the conscious hearing or the nerves but after some moments, nor before some moments more is the sense of the shock expressed. The sound travels to the remoteness and seclusion of the child's consciousness, as the roar of a gun travels to listeners half a mile away.

So it is, too, with pain, which has learnt to be so instant and eager with us of later age that no point of time is lost in its touches—direct as the unintercepted message of great and candid eyes, unhampered by trivialities; even so immediate is the communication of pain. But you could count five between the prick of a surgeon's instrument upon a baby's arm and the little whimper that answers it. The child is then too young, also, to refer the feeling of pain to the arm that suffers it. Even when pain has groped its way to his mind it hardly seems to bring local tidings thither. The baby does not turn his eyes in any degree towards his arm or towards the side that is so vexed with vaccination. He looks in any other direction at haphazard, and cries at random.

See, too, how slowly the unpractised apprehension of an older child trudges after the nimbleness of a conjurer. It is the greatest failure to take these little *gobe-mouches* to a good conjurer. His successes leave them cold, for they had not yet understood what it was the good man meant to surprise them withal. The amateur it is who really astonishes them. They cannot come up even with your amateur beginner, performing at close quarters; whereas the master of his craft on a platform runs quite away at the outset from the lagging senses of his honest audience.

You may rob a child of his dearest plate at table, almost from under his ingenuous eyes, send him off in chase of it, and have it in its place and off again ten times before the little breathless boy has begun to perceive in what direction his sweets have been snatched.

Teachers of young children should therefore teach themselves a habit of awaiting, should surround themselves with pauses of patience. The simple little processes of logic that arrange the grammar of a common sentence are too quick for these young blunderers, who cannot use two pronouns but they must confuse them. I never found that a young child—one of something under nine years—was able to say, "I send them my love" at the first attempt. It will be "I send me my love," "I send them their love," "They send me my love"; not, of course, through any confusion of understanding, but because of the tardy setting of words in order with the thoughts. The child visibly grapples with the difficulty, and is beaten.

It is no doubt this unreadiness that causes little children to like twice-told tales and foregone conclusions in their games. They are not eager, for a year or two yet to come, for surprises. If you hide and they cannot see you hiding, their joy in finding you is comparatively small; but let them know perfectly well what cupboard you are in, and they will find you with shouts of discovery. The better the hiding-place is understood between you the more lively the drama. They make a convention of art for their play. The younger the children the more dramatic; and when the house is filled with outcries of laughter from the breathless breast of a child, it is that he is pretending to be surprised at finding his mother where he bade her pretend to hide. This is the comedy that never tires. Let the elder who cannot understand its charm beware how he tries to put a more intelligible form of delight in the place of it; for, if not, he will find that children also have a manner of substitution, and that they will put half-hearted laughter in the place of their natural impetuous clamours. It is certain that very young children like to play upon their own imaginations, and enjoy their own short game.

There is something so purely childlike in the delays of a child that any exercise asking for the swift apprehension of later life, for the flashes of understanding and action, from the mind and members of childhood, is no pleasure to see. The piano, for instance, as experts understand it, and even as the moderately-trained may play it, claims all the immediate action, the instantaneousness, most unnatural to childhood. There may possibly be feats of skill to which young children could be trained without this specific violence directed upon the thing characteristic of their age—their unreadiness—but virtuosity at the piano cannot be one of them. It is no delight, indeed, to see the shyness of children, or anything that is theirs, conquered and beaten; but their poor little slowness is so distinctively their own, and must needs be physiologically so proper to their years, so much a natural condition of the age of their brain, that of all childishnesses it is the one that the world should have the intelligence to understand, the patience to attend upon, and the humanity to foster.

It is true that the movements of young children are quick, but a very little attention would prove how many apparent disconnexions there are between the lively motion and the first impulse; it is not the brain that is quick. If, on a voyage in space, electricity takes thus much time, and light thus much, and sound thus much, there is one little jogging traveller that would arrive after the others had forgotten their journey, and this is the perception of a child. Surely our own memories might serve to remind us how in our childhood we inevitably missed the principal point in any procession or pageant intended by our elders to furnish us with a historical remembrance for the future. It was not our mere vagueness of understanding, it was the unwieldiness of our senses, of our reply to the suddenness of the grown up. We lived through the important moments of the passing of an Emperor at a different rate from theirs; we stared long in the wake of his Majesty, and of anything else of interest; every flash of movement, that got telegraphic answers from our parents' eyes, left us stragglers. We fell out of all ranks. Among the sights proposed for our instruction, that which befitted us best was an eclipse of the moon, done at leisure. In good time we found the moon in the sky, in good time the eclipse set in and made reasonable progress; we kept up with everything.

It is too often required of children that they should adjust themselves to the world, practised and alert. But it would be more to the purpose that the world should adjust itself to children in all its dealings with them. Those who run and keep together have to run at the pace of the tardiest. But we are apt to command instant obedience, stripped of the little pauses that a child, while very young, cannot act without. It is not a child of ten or twelve that needs them so; it is the young creature who has but lately ceased to be a baby, slow to be startled.

We have but to consider all that it implies of the loitering of senses and of an unprepared consciousness—this capacity for receiving a great shock from a noise and this perception of the shock after two or three appreciable moments—if we would know anything of the moments of a baby.

Even as we must learn that our time, when it is long, is too long for children, so must we learn that our time, when it is short, is too short for them. When it is exceedingly short they cannot, without an unnatural effort, have any perception of it. When children do not see the jokes of the elderly, and disappoint expectation in other ways, only less intimate, the reason is almost always there. The child cannot turn in mid-career; he goes fast, but the impetus took place moments ago.

THE JULY GRASS
Richard Jefferies

A JULY FLY went sideways over the long grass. His wings made a burr about him like a net, beating so fast they wrapped him round with a cloud. Every now and then, as he flew over the trees of grass, a taller one than common stopped him, and there he clung, and then the eye had time to see the scarlet spots—the loveliest colour—on his wings. The wind swung the burnet and loosened his hold, and away he went again over the grasses, and not one jot did he care if they were *Poa* or *Festuca,* or *Bromus* or *Hordeum,* or any other name. Names were nothing to him; all he had to do was to whirl his scarlet spots about in the brilliant sun, rest when he liked, and go on again. I wonder whether it is a joy to have bright scarlet spots, and to be clad in the purple and gold of life; is the colour felt by the creature that wears it? The rose, restful of a dewy morn before the sunbeams have topped the garden wall, must feel a joy in its own fragrance, and know the exquisite hue of its stained petals. The rose sleeps in its beauty.

The fly whirls his scarlet-spotted wings about and splashes himself with sunlight, like the children on the sands. He thinks not of the grass and sun; he does not heed them at all—and that is why he is so happy—any more than the barefoot children ask why the sea is there, or why it does not quite dry up when it ebbs. He is unconscious; he lives without thinking about living; and if the sunshine were a hundred hours long, still it would not be long enough. No, never enough of sun and sliding shadows that come like a hand over the table to lovingly reach our shoulder, never enough of the grass that smells sweet as a flower, not if we could live years and years equal in number to the tides that have ebbed and flowed counting backwards four years to every day and night, backward still till we found out which came first, the night or the day. The scarlet-dotted fly knows nothing of the names of the grasses that grow here where the sward nears the sea, and thinking of him I have decided not to wilfully seek to learn any more of their names either. My big grass book I have left at home, and the dust is settling on the gold of the bind-ing. I have picked a handful this morning of which I know nothing. I will sit here on the turf and the scarlet-dotted flies shall pass over me, as if I too were but a grass. I will not think, I will be unconscious, I will live.

Listen! that was the low sound of a summer wavelet striking the uncovered rock over there beneath in the green sea. All things that are beautiful are found by chance, like everything that is good. Here by me is a praying-rug, just wide enough to kneel on, of the richest gold inwo-ven with crimson. All the Sultans of the East never had such beauty as that to kneel on. It is, indeed, too beautiful to kneel on, for the life in these golden flowers must not be broken down even for that purpose. They must not be defaced, not a stem bent; it is more reverent not to kneel on them, for this carpet prays itself. I will sit by it and let it pray for me. It is so common, the bird's-foot lotus, it grows everywhere; yet if I purposely searched for days I should not have found a plot like this, so rich, so golden, so glowing with sunshine. You might pass by it in one stride, yet it is worthy to be thought of for a week and remembered for a year. Slender grasses, branched round about with slenderer boughs, each tipped with pollen and rising in tiers cone-shaped—too delicate to grow tall—cluster at the base of the mound. They dare not grow tall or the wind would snap them. A great grass, stout and thick, rises three feet by the hedge, with a head another foot nearly, very green and strong and bold, lifting itself right up to you; you must say, "What a fine grass!" Grasses whose awns succeed each other alternately; grasses whose tops seem flattened; others drooping over the shorter blades beneath; some that you can only find by parting the heavier growth around them; hun-dreds and hundreds, thousands and thousands. The kingly poppies on the dry summit of the mound take no heed of these, the populace, their sub-jects so numerous they cannot be numbered. A barren race they are, the proud poppies, lords of the July field, taking no deep root, but raising up a brilliant blazon of scarlet heraldry out of nothing. They are useless, they are bitter, they are allied to sleep and poison and everlasting night; yet they are forgiven because they are not commonplace. Nothing, no abun-dance of them, can ever make the poppies commonplace. There is genius in them, the genius of colour, and they are saved. Even when they take the room of the corn we must admire them. The mighty multitude of nations, the millions and millions of the grass stretching away in inter-tangled ranks, through pasture and mead from shore to shore, have no kinship with these their lords. The ruler is always a foreigner. From England to China the native born is no king; the poppies are the Normans of the field. One of these on the mound is very beautiful, a width of petal, a clear silkiness of colour three shades higher than the rest—it is almost dark with scarlet. I wish I could do something more than gaze at all this scarlet and gold and crimson and green, something more than see it, not exactly to drink it or inhale it, but in some way to make it part of me that I might live it.

The July grasses must be looked for in corners and out-of-the-way places, and not in the broad acres—the scythe has taken them there. By the wayside on the banks of the lane, near the gateway—look, too, in uninteresting places behind incomplete buildings on the mounds cast up from abandoned foundations where speculation has been and gone. There weeds that would not have found resting-place elsewhere grow unchecked, and uncommon species and unusually large growths appear. Like everything else that is looked for, they are found under unlikely conditions. At the back of ponds, just inside the enclosure of woods, angles of corn-fields, old quarries, that is where to find grasses, or by the sea in the brackish marsh. Some of the finest of them grow by the mere road-side; you may look for others up the lanes in the deep ruts, look too inside the hollow trees by the stream. In a morning you may easily garner together a great sheaf of this harvest. Cut the larger stems aslant, like the reeds imitated deep in old green glass. You must consider as you gather them the height and slenderness of the stems, the droop and degree of curve, the shape and colour of the panicle, the dusting of the pollen, the motion and sway in the wind. The sheaf you may take home with you, but the wind that was among it stays without.

BOOK-BUYING
Augustine Birrell

THE MOST distinguished of living Englishmen, who, great as he is in many directions, is perhaps inherently more a man of letters than anything else, has been overheard mournfully to declare that there were more booksellers' shops in his native town sixty years ago when he was a boy in it than are to-day to be found within its boundaries. And yet the place "all unabashed" now boasts its bookless self a city!

Mr. Gladstone was, of course, referring to second-hand bookshops. Neither he nor any other sensible man puts himself out about new books. When a new book is published, read an old one, was the advice of a sound though surly critic. It is one of the boasts of letters to have glorified the term "second-hand," which other crafts have "soiled to all ignoble use." But why it has been able to do this is obvious. All the best books are necessarily second-hand. The writers of to-day need not grumble. Let them "bide a wee." If their books are worth anything they too one day will be second-hand. If their books are not worth anything there are ancient trades still in full operation amongst us—the pastry-cooks and the trunk-makers—who must have paper.

But is there any substance in the plaint that nobody now buys books, meaning thereby second-hand books? The late Mark Pattison, who had 16,000 volumes, and whose lightest word has therefore weight, once stated that he had been informed, and verily believed, that there were men of his own University of Oxford who, being in uncontrolled possession of annual incomes of not less than £500, thought they were doing the thing handsomely if they expended £50 a year upon their libraries. But we are not bound to believe this unless we like. There was a touch of morosity about the late Rector of Lincoln which led him to take gloomy views of men, particularly Oxford men.

No doubt arguments *à priori* may readily be found to support the contention that the habit of book-buying is on the decline. I confess to knowing one or two men, not Oxford men either, but Cambridge men (and the passion of Cambridge for literature is a by-word), who, on the plea of being pressed with business, or because they were going to a funeral, have passed a bookshop in a strange town without so much as stepping inside "just to see whether the fellow had anything." But painful as facts of this sort necessarily are, any damaging inference we might feel disposed to draw from them is dispelled by a comparison of price-lists. Compare a bookseller's catalogue of 1862 with one of the present year, and your pessimism is washed away by the tears which unrestrainedly flow as you see what *bonnes fortunes* you have lost. A young book-buyer might well turn out upon Primrose Hill and bemoan his youth, after comparing old catalogues with new.

Nothing but American competition, grumble some old stagers.

Well! why not? This new battle for the books is a free fight, not a private one, and Columbia has "joined in." Lower prices are not to be looked for. The book-buyer of 1900 will be glad to buy at to-day's prices. I take pleasure in thinking he will not be able to do so. Good finds grow scarcer and scarcer. True it is that but a few short weeks ago I picked up (such is the happy phrase, most apt to describe what was indeed a "street casualty") a copy of the original edition of *Endymion* (Keats's poem—O subscriber to Mudie's!—not Lord Beaconsfield's novel) for the easy equivalent of half-a-crown—but then that was one of my lucky days. The enormous increase of booksellers' catalogues and their wide circulation amongst the trade has already produced a hateful uniformity of prices. Go where you will it is all the same to the odd sixpence. Time was when you could map out the country for yourself with some hopefulness of plunder. There were districts where the Elizabethan dramatists were but slenderly protected. A raid into the "bonnie North Countrie" sent you home again cheered with chapbooks and weighted with old pamphlets of curious interest; whilst the West of England seldom failed to yield a crop of novels. I remember getting a complete set of the Brontë books in the original issues at Torquay, I may say, for nothing. Those days are over. Your country bookseller is, in fact, more likely, such tales does he hear of London auctions, and such catalogues does he receive by every post, to exaggerate the value of his wares than to part with them pleasantly, and as a country bookseller should, "just to clear my shelves, you know, and give me a bit of room." The only compensation for this is the catalogues themselves. You get *them,* at least, for nothing, and it cannot be denied that they make mighty pretty reading.

These high prices tell their own tale, and force upon us the conviction that there never were so many private libraries in course of growth as there are to-day.

Libraries are not made; they grow. Your first two thousand volumes present no difficulty, and cost astonishingly little money. Given £400 and five years, and an ordinary man can in the ordinary course, without any undue haste or putting any pressure upon his taste, surround himself with this number of books, all in his own language, and thenceforward have at least one place in the world in which it is possible to be happy. But pride is still out of the question. To be proud of having two thousand books would be absurd. You might as well be proud of having two top-coats. After your first two thousand difficulty begins, but until you have ten thousand volumes the less you say about your library the better. *Then* you may begin to speak.

It is no doubt a pleasant thing to have a library left you. The present writer will disclaim no such legacy, but here undertakes to accept it, however dusty. But, good as it is to inherit a library, it is better to collect one. Each volume then, however lightly a stranger's eye may roam from shelf to shelf, has its own individuality, a history of its own. You remember where you got it, and how much you gave for it; and your word may safely be taken for the first of these facts, but not for the second.

The man who has a library of his own collection is able to contemplate himself objectively, and is justified in believing in his own existence. No other man but he would have made precisely such a combination as his. Had he been in any single respect different from what he is, his library, as it exists, never would have existed. Therefore, surely he may exclaim, as in the gloaming he contemplates the backs of his loved ones, "They are mine, and I am theirs."

But the eternal note of sadness will find its way even through the key-hole of a library. You turn some familiar page, of Shakspeare it may be, and his "infinite variety," his "multitudinous mind," suggests some new thought, and as you are wondering over it, you think of Lycidas, your friend, and promise yourself the pleasure of having his opinion of your discovery the very next time when by the fire you two "help waste a sullen day." Or it is, perhaps, some quainter, tenderer fancy that engages your solitary attention, something in Sir Philip Sidney or Henry Vaughan, and then you turn to look for Phyillis, ever the best interpreter of love, human or divine. Alas! the printed page grows hazy beneath a filmy eye as you suddenly remember that Lycidas is dead—"dead ere his prime,"—and that the pale cheek of Phyllis will never again be relumined by the white light of her pure enthusiasm. And then you fall to thinking of the inevitable, and perhaps, in your present mood, not unwelcome hour, when the "ancient peace" of your old friends will be disturbed, when rude hands will dislodge them from their accustomed nooks and break up their goodly company.

> Death bursts amongst them like a shell,
> And strews them over half the town.

They will form new combinations, lighten other men's toil, and soothe another's sorrow. Fool that I was to call anything *mine!*

NOTES ON THE MOVEMENTS
OF YOUNG CHILDREN
Robert Louis Stevenson

I WISH TO direct the reader's attention to a certain quality in the movements of children when young, which is somehow lovable in them, although it would be even unpleasant in any grown person. Their movements are not graceful, but they fall short of grace by something so sweetly humorous that we only admire them the more. The imperfection is so pretty and pathetic, and it gives so great a promise of something different in the future, that it attracts us more than many forms of beauty. They have something of the merit of a rough sketch by a master, in which we pardon what is wanting or excessive for the sake of the very bluntness and directness of the thing. It gives us pleasure to see the beginning of gracious impulses and the springs of harmonious movement laid bare to us with innocent simplicity.

One night some ladies formed a sort of impromptu dancing-school in the drawing-room of an hotel in France. One of the ladies led the ring, and I can recall her as a model of accomplished, cultured movement. Two little girls, about eight years old, were the pupils; that is an age of great interest in girls, when natural grace comes to its consummation of justice and purity, with little admixture of that other grace of forethought and discipline that will shortly supersede it altogether. In these two, particularly, the rhythm was sometimes broken by an excess of energy, as though the pleasure of the music in their light bodies could endure no longer the restraint of regulated dance. So that, between these and the lady, there was not only some beginning of the very contrast I wish to insist upon, but matter enough to set one thinking a long while on the beauty of motion. I do not know that, here in England, we have any good opportunity of seeing what that is; the generation of British dancing men and women are certainly more remarkable for other qualities than for grace: they are, many of them, very conscientious artists, and give quite a serious regard to the technical parts of their performance; but the spectacle, somehow, is not often beautiful, and strikes no note of pleasure. If I had seen no more, therefore, this evening might have remained in my memory as a rare experience. But the best part of it was yet to come. For after the others had desisted, the musician still continued to play, and a little button between two and three years old came out into the cleared space and began to figure before us as the music prompted. I had an opportunity of seeing her, not on this night only, but on many subsequent nights; and the wonder and comical admiration she inspired was only deepened as time went on. She had an admirable musical ear; and each new melody, as it struck in her a new humour, suggested wonderful combinations and variations of movement. Now it would be a dance with which she would suit the music, now rather an appropriate pantomime, and now a mere string of disconnected attitudes. But whatever she did, she did it with the same verve and gusto. The spirit of the air seemed to have entered into her, and to possess her like a passion; and you could see her struggling to find expression for the beauty that was in her against the inefficacy of the dull, half-formed body. Though her footing was uneven, and her gestures often ludicrously helpless, still the spectacle was not merely amusing; and though subtle inspirations of movement miscarried in tottering travesty, you could still see that they had been inspirations; you could still see that she had set her heart on realising something just and beautiful, and that, by the discipline of these abortive efforts, she was making for herself in the future a quick, supple, and obedient body. It was grace in the making. She was not to be daunted by any merriment of people looking on critically; the music said something to her, and her whole spirit was intent on what the music said: she must carry out its suggestions, she must do her best to translate its language into that other dialect of the modulated body into which it can be translated most easily and fully.

Just the other day I was witness to a second scene, in which the motive was something similar; only this time with quite common children, and in the familiar neighbourhood of Hampstead. A little congregation had formed itself in the lane underneath my window, and was busy over a skipping-rope. There were two sisters, from seven to nine perhaps, with dark faces and dark hair, and slim, lithe little figures clad in lilac frocks. The elder of these two was mistress of the art of skipping. She was just and adroit in every movement; the rope passed over her black head and under her scarlet-stockinged legs with a precision and regularity that was like machinery; but there was nothing mechanical in the infinite variety and sweetness of her inclinations, and the spontaneous agile flexure of her lean waist and hips. There was one variation favourite with her, in which she crossed her hands before her with a motion not unlike that of weaving, which was admirably intricate and complete. And when the two took the rope together and whirled in and out with occasional interruptions, there was something Italian in the type of both—in the length of nose, in the slimness and accuracy of the shapes—and something gay and harmonious in the double movement, that added to the whole scene a Southern element, and took me over sea and land into distant and beautiful places. Nor was this impression lessened when the elder girl took in her arms a fair-haired baby, and while the others held the rope for her, turned and gyrated, and went in and out over it lightly, with a quiet regularity that seemed as if it might go on for ever. Somehow, incongruous as was the occupation, she reminded me of Italian Madonnas. And now, as before in the hotel drawing-room, the humorous element was to be introduced; only this time it was in broad farce. The funniest little girl, with a mottled complexion and a big, damaged nose, and looking for all the world like any dirty, broken-nosed doll in a nursery lumber-room, came forward to take her turn. While the others swung the rope for her as gently as it could be done—a mere mockery of movement—and playfully taunted her timidity, she passaged backwards and forwards in a pretty flutter of indecision, putting up her shoulders and laughing with the embarrassed laughter of children by the water's edge, eager to bathe and yet fearful. There never was anything at once so droll and so pathetic. One did not know whether to laugh or cry. And when at last she had made an end of all her deprecations and drawings back, and summoned up heart enough to straddle over the rope, one leg at a time, it was a sight to see her ruffle herself up like a peacock and go away down the lane with her damaged nose, seeming to think discretion the better part of valour, and rather uneasy lest they should ask her to repeat the exploit. Much as I had enjoyed the grace of the older girls, it was now just as it had been before in France, and the clumsiness of the child seemed to have a significance and a sort of beauty of its own, quite above this grace of the others in power to affect the heart. I had looked on with a certain sense of balance and completion at the silent, rapid, masterly evolutions of the eldest; I had been pleased by these in the way of satisfaction. But when little broken-nose began her pantomime of indecision I grew excited. There was something quite fresh and poignant in the delight I took in her imperfect movements. I remember, for instance, that I moved my own shoulders, as if to imitate her; really, I suppose, with an inarticulate wish to help her out.

Now, there are many reasons why this gracelessness of young children should be pretty and sympathetic to us. And, first, there is an interest as of battle. It is in travail and laughable *fiasco* that the young school their bodies to beautiful expression, as they school their minds. We seem, in watching them, to divine antagonists pitted one against the other; and, as in other wars, so in this war of the intelligence against the unwilling body, we do not wish to see even the cause of progress triumph without some honourable toil; and we are so sure of the ultimate result, that it pleases us to linger in pathetic sympathy over these reverses of the early campaign, just as we do over the troubles that environ the heroine of a novel on her way to the happy ending. Again, people are very ready to disown the pleasure they take in a thing merely because it is big, as an Alp, or merely because it is little, as a little child; and yet this pleasure is surely as legitimate as another. There is much of it here; we have an irrational indulgence for small folk; we ask but little where there is so little to ask it of; we cannot overcome our astonishment that they should be able to move at all, and are interested in their movements somewhat as we are interested in the movements of a puppet. And again, there is a prolongation of expectancy when, as in these movements of children, we are kept continually on the very point of attainment and ever turned away and tantalised by some humourous imperfection. This is altogether absent in the secure and accomplished movements of persons more fully grown. The tight-rope walker does not walk so freely or so well as any one else can walk upon a good road; and yet we like to watch him for the mere sake of the difficulty; we like to see his vacillations; we like this last so much even, that I am told a really artistic tight-rope walker must feign to be troubled in his balance, even if he is not so really. And again, we have in these baby efforts an assurance of spontaneity that we do not have often. We know this at least certainly, that the child tries to dance for its own pleasure, and not for any by-end of ostentation and conformity. If we did not know it we should see it. There is a sincerity, a directness, an impulsive truth, about their free gestures that shows throughout all imperfection, and it is to us as a reminiscence of primitive festivals and the Golden Age. Lastly, there is in the sentiment much of a simple human compassion for creatures more helpless than ourselves. One nearly ready to die is pathetic; and so is one scarcely ready to live. In view of their future, our heart is softened to these clumsy little ones. They will be more adroit when they are not so happy.

Unfortunately, then, this character that so much delights us is not one that can be preserved by any plastic art. It turns, as we have seen, upon consideration not really æsthetic. Art may deal with the slim freedom of a few years later; but with this fettered impulse, with these stammering motions, she is powerless to do more than stereotype what is ungraceful, and, in the doing of it, lose all pathos and humanity. So these humorous little ones must go away into the limbo of beautiful things that are not beautiful for art, there to wait a more perfect age before they sit for their portraits.

ON PLEASURE BENT
George Bernard Shaw

[November 20, 1897.]

UP TO a certain point, I have never flinched from martyrdom. By far the heaviest demand ever made upon me by the public weal is that which nearly three years ago devoted my nights to the theatres and my days to writing about them. If I had known how exceedingly trying the experience would be, I am not sure that I should not have seen the public weal further before making this supreme sacrifice to it. But I had been so seldom to the theatre in the previous years that I did not realize its horrors. I firmly believe that the trials upon which I then entered have injured my brain. At all events matters reached a crisis after the critical activities of last week. I felt that I must have a real experience of some kind, under conditions, especially as regards fresh air, as unlike those of the stalls as possible. After some consideration it occurred to me that if I went into the country, selected a dangerous hill, and rode down it on a bicycle at full speed in the darkest part of the night, some novel and convincing piece of realism might result. It did.

Probably no man has ever misunderstood another so completely as the doctor misunderstood me when he apologized for the sensation produced by the point of his needle as he corrected the excessive openness of my countenance after the adventure. To him who has endured points made by actors for nearly three years, the point of a surgeon's darning needle comes as a delicious relief. I did not like to ask him to put in a few more stitches merely to amuse me, as I had already, through pure self-indulgence, cut into his Sunday rest to an extent of which his kindness made me ashamed; but I doubt if I shall ever see a play again without longing for the comparative luxury of that quiet country surgery, with the stillness without broken only by the distant song and throbbing drumbeat of some remote Salvation Army corps, and the needle, with its delicate realism, touching my sensibilities, stitch, stitch, stitch, with

181

absolute sincerity in the hands of an artist who had actually learned his business and knew how to do it.

To complete the comparison it would be necessary to go into economics of it by measuring the doctor's fee against the price of a stall in a West End theatre. But here I am baffled by the fact that the highest art revolts from an equation between its infinite value and a finite pile of coin. It so happened that my voice, which is an Irish voice, won for me the sympathy of the doctor. This circumstance must appear amazing almost beyond credibility in the light of the fact that he was himself an Irishman; but so it was. He rightly felt that sympathy is beyond price, and declined to make it the subject of a commercial transaction. Thereby he made it impossible for me to mention his name without black ingratitude; for I know no more effectual way of ruining a man in this country than by making public the smallest propensity on his part to adopt a benevolent attitude towards necessitous strangers. Here the West End manager will perhaps whisper reproachfully, "Well; and do *I* ever make you pay for your stall?" To which I cannot but reply, "Is that also due to the sympathy my voice awakens in you when it is raised every Saturday?" I trust I am not ungrateful for my invitations; but to expect me to feel towards the manager who lacerates my nerves, enfeebles my mind, and destroys my character, as I did towards the physician who healed my body, refreshed my soul, and flattered my vocal accomplishments when I was no more to him than an untimely stranger with an unheard-of black eye, is to dethrone justice and repudiate salvation. Besides, he said it was a mercy I was not killed. Would any manager have been of that opinion?

Perhaps the most delightful thing about this village was that its sense of the relative importance of things was so rightly adjusted that it had no theatrical gossip; for this doctor actually did not know who I was. With a cynicism for which his charity afterwards made me blush, I sought to reassure him as to the pecuniary competence of his muddy, torn, ensanguined and facially spoiled visitor by saying "My name is G. B. S.," as who should say "My name is Cecil Rhodes, or Henry Irving, or William of Germany." Without turning a hair, he sweetly humoured my egotistic garrulity by replying, in perfect lightness of heart, "Mine's F——: *what are you?*" Breathing at last an atmosphere in which it mattered so little who and what G. B. S. was, that nobody knew either one or the other, I almost sobbed with relief whilst he threaded his needle with a nice white horsehair, tactfully pretending to listen to my evasive murmur that I was a "sort of writer," an explanation meant to convey to him that I earned a blameless living by inscribing names in letters of gold over shop windows and on perforated wire blinds. To have brought the taint of my factitious little vogue into the unperverted consciousness of his benevolent and sensible life would have been the act of a serpent.

On the whole, the success of my experiment left nothing to be desired; and I recommend it confidently for imitation. My nerves completely recovered their tone and my temper its natural sweetness. I have been peaceful, happy and affectionate ever since, to a degree which amazes my associates. It is true that my appearance leaves something to be desired; but I believe that when my eye becomes again visible, the softness of its expression will more than compensate for the surrounding devastation.

However, a man is something more than an omelette; and no extremity of battery can tame my spirit to the point of submitting to the sophistry by which Mr. Beerbohm Tree has attempted to shift the guilt of "Katherine and Petruchio" from his shoulders and Garrick's to those of Shakespeare. I have never hesitated to give our immortal William as much of what he deserves as is possible considering how far his enormities transcend my powers of invective; but even William is entitled to fair play. Mr. Tree contends that as Shakespeare wrote the scenes which Garrick tore away from their context, they form a genuine Shakespearean play; and he outdares even this audacity by further contending that since the play was performed for the entertainment of Christopher Sly the tinker, the more it is debauched the more appropriate it is. This line of argument is so breath-bereaving that I can but gasp out an inquiry as to what Mr. Tree understands by the one really eloquent and heartfelt line uttered by Sly:—"'T is a very excellent piece of work: would 't were done!"

This stroke, to which the whole Sly interlude is but as the handle to the dagger, appears to me to reduce Mr. Tree's identification of the tastes of his audiences at Her Majesty's with those of a drunken tinker to a condition distinctly inferior to that of my left eye at present. The other argument is more seriously meant, and may even impose upon the simplicity of the Cockney playgoer. Let us test its principle by varying its application. Certain anti-Christian propagandists, both here and in America, have extracted from the Bible all those passages which are unsuited for family reading, and have presented a string of them to the public as a representative sample of Holy Writ. Some of our orthodox writers, though intensely indignant at this controversial ruse, have nevertheless not scrupled to do virtually the same thing with the Koran. Will Mr. Tree claim for these collections the full authority, dignity, and inspiration of the authors from whom they are culled? If not, how does he distinguish Garrick's procedure from theirs? Garrick took from a play of Shakespeare's all the passages which served his baser purpose, and suppressed the rest. Had his object been to discredit Shakespeare in the honest belief that Shakespearolatry was a damnable error, we might have respected "Katherine and Petruchio" even whilst deploring it. But he had no such conviction: in fact, he was a professed Shakespearolater, and no doubt a sincere one, as far as his wretched powers of appreciation went. He debased "The Taming of the Shrew" solely to make money out of the vulgarity of the taste of his time. Such a transaction can be defended on commercial grounds: to defend it on any other seems to me to be either an artistic misdemeanor or a profession of Philistinism. If Mr. Tree were to declare boldly that he thinks "Katherine and Petruchio" a better play than "The Taming of the Shrew," and that Garrick, as an actor-manager, knew his business better than a mere poet, he would be within his rights. He would not even strain our credulity; for a long dynasty of actor-managers, from Cibber to Sir Henry Irving, have been unquestionably sincere in preferring their own acting versions to the unmutilated masterpieces of the genius on whom they have lavished lip-honor. But Mr. Tree pretends to no such preference: on the contrary, he openly stigmatizes the Garrick version as tinker's fare, and throws the responsibility on Shakespeare because the materials were stolen from him.

I do not wish to pose academically at Mr. Tree. My object is a practical one: I want to intimidate him into a thorough mistrust of his own judgment where Shakespeare is concerned. He is about to produce one of Shakespeare's great plays, "Julius Cæsar"; and he is just as likely as not to cut it to ribbons. The man who would revive "Katherine and Petruchio" at this time of day would do anything un-Shakespearean. I do not blame him for this: it is a perfectly natural consequence of the fact that, like most actors and managers, he does not like Shakespeare and does not know him, although he conforms without conscious insincerity to the convention as to the Swan's greatness. I am far from setting up my own Shakespearean partialities and intimacies, acquired in my childhood, as in any way superior to Mr. Tree's mature distaste or indifference. But I may reasonably assume—though I admit that the assumption is unusual and indeed unprecedented—that Shakespeare's plays are produced for the satisfaction of those who like Shakespeare, and not as a tedious rite to celebrate the reputation of the author and enhance that of the actor. Therefore I hope Mr. Tree, in such cutting of "Julius Cæsar" as the limits of time may force upon him, will carefully retain all the passages which he dislikes and cut out those which seem to him sufficiently popular to meet the views of Christopher Sly. He will not, in any case, produce an acting version as good as Mr. Forbes Robertson's "Hamlet," because Mr. Forbes Robertson seems to have liked "Hamlet"; nor as good as Mr. George Alexander's "As You Like It," because Mr. Alexander apparently considers Shakespeare as good a judge of a play as himself; but we shall at least escape a positively anti-Shakespearean "Julius Cæsar." If Mr. Tree had suffered as much as I have from seeing

Shakespeare butchered to make a cockney's holiday, he would sympathize with my nervousness on the subject.

As I write—or rather as I dictate—comes the remarkable news that the London managers have presented the Vice-Chamberlain with 500 ounces of silver. One cannot but be refreshed by the frank publicity of the proceeding. When the builders in my parish proffer ounces of silver to the sanitary inspector, they do so by stealth, and blush to find it fame. But the Vice-Chamberlain, it appears, may take presents from those over whom he is set as an inspector and judge without a breath of scandal. It seems to me, however, that the transaction involves a grave injustice to Mr. Redford. Why is he to have nothing? A well-known Irish landlord once replied to a threatening letter by saying, "If you expect to intimidate me by shooting my agent, you will be disappointed." One can imagine Mr. Redford saying to the managers in a similar spirit, "If you expect to bribe me by presenting 500 ounces of silver to my vice-principal, you will be disappointed." I do not suppose that Sir Spencer Ponsonby-Fane has dreamt of giving any serious thought to this aspect of what I shall permit myself to describe as a ludicrously improper proceeding; for the Censorial functions of his department will not bear serious thought. His action is certainly according to precedent. Sir Henry Herbert, who, as Master of the Revels to Charles I, did much to establish the traditions of the Censorship, has left us his grateful testimony to the civility of a contemporary actor-manager who tactfully presented his wife with a handsome pair of gloves. Still, that actor-manager did not invite the Press to report the speech he made on the occasion, nor did he bring a large public deputation of his brother managers with him. I suggest that his example in this respect should be followed in future rather than that of Tuesday last. I shall be told, no doubt, that Sir Spencer Ponsonby-Fane has nothing to do with the licensing of plays. And I shall immediately retort, "What then have the London managers to do with Sir Spencer Ponsonby-Fane?"

A DEFENCE OF SKELETONS

G. K. Chesterton

SOME LITTLE time ago I stood among immemorial English trees that seemed to take hold upon the stars like a brood of Yggdrasils. As I walked among these living pillars I became gradually aware that the rustics who lived and died in their shadow adopted a very curious conversational tone. They seemed to be constantly apologizing for the trees, as if they were a very poor show. After elaborate investigation, I discovered that their gloomy and penitent tone was traceable to the fact that it was winter and all the trees were bare. I assured them that I did not resent the fact that it was winter, that I knew the thing had happened before, and that no forethought on their part could have averted this blow of destiny. But I could not in any way reconcile them to the fact that it *was* winter. There was evidently a general feeling that I had caught the trees in a kind of disgraceful deshabille, and that they ought not to be seen until, like the first human sinners, they had covered themselves with leaves. So it is quite clear that, while very few people appear to know anything of how trees look in winter, the actual foresters know less than any one. So far from the line of the tree when it is bare appearing harsh and severe, it is luxuriantly indefinable to an unusual degree; the fringe of the forest melts away like a vignette. The tops of two or three high trees when they are leafless are so soft that they seem like the gigantic brooms of that fabulous lady who was sweeping the cobwebs off the sky. The outline of a leafy forest is in comparison hard, gross and blotchy; the clouds of night do not more certainly obscure the moon than those green and monstrous clouds obscure the tree; the actual sight of the little wood, with its grey and silver sea of life, is entirely a winter vision. So dim and delicate is the heart of the winter woods, a kind of glittering gloaming, that a figure stepping towards us in the chequered twilight seems as if he were breaking through unfathomable depths of spiders' webs.

But surely the idea that its leaves are the chief grace of a tree is a vulgar one, on a par with the idea that his hair is the chief grace of a pianist. When winter, that healthy ascetic, carries his gigantic razor over hill and valley, and shaves all the trees like monks, we feel surely that they are all the more like trees if they are shorn, just as so many painters and musicians would be all the more like men if they were less like mops. But it does appear to be a deep and essential difficulty that men have an abiding terror of their own structure, or of the structure of things they love. This is felt dimly in the skeleton of the tree: it is felt profoundly in the skeleton of the man.

The importance of the human skeleton is very great, and the horror with which it is commonly regarded is somewhat mysterious. Without claiming for the human skeleton a wholly conventional beauty, we may assert that he is certainly not uglier than a bull-dog, whose popularity never wanes, and that he has a vastly more cheerful and ingratiating expression. But just as man is mysteriously ashamed of the skeletons of the trees in winter, so he is mysteriously ashamed of the skeleton of himself in death. It is a singular thing altogether, this horror of the architecture of things. One would think it would be most unwise in a man to be afraid of a skeleton, since Nature has set curious and quite insuperable obstacles to his running away from it.

One ground exists for this terror: a strange idea has infected humanity that the skeleton is typical of death. A man might as well say that a factory chimney was typical of bankruptcy. The factory may be left naked after ruin, the skeleton may be left naked after bodily dissolution; but both of them have had a lively and workmanlike life of their own, all the pulleys creaking, all the wheels turning, in the House of Livelihood as in the House of Life. There is no reason why this creature (new, as I fancy, to art), the living skeleton, should not become the essential symbol of life.

The truth is that man's horror of the skeleton is not horror of death at all. It is man's eccentric glory that he has not, generally speaking, any objection to being dead, but has a very serious objection to being undignified. And the fundamental matter which troubles him in the skeleton is the reminder that the ground-plan of his appearance is shamelessly grotesque. I do not know why he should object to this. He contentedly takes his place in a world that does not pretend to be genteel—a laughing, working, jeering world. He sees millions of animals carrying, with quite a dandified levity, the most monstrous shapes and appendages, the most preposterous horns, wings, and legs, when they are necessary to utility. He sees the good temper of the frog, the unaccountable happiness of the hippopotamus. He sees a whole universe which is ridiculous, from the animalcule, with a head too big for its body, up to the comet, with a tail too big for its head. But when it comes to the delightful oddity of his own inside, his sense of humour rather abruptly deserts him.

In the Middle Ages and in the Renaissance (which was, in certain times and respects, a much gloomier period) this idea of the skeleton had a vast influence in freezing the pride out of all earthly pomps and the fragrance out of all fleeting pleasures. But it was not, surely, the mere dread of death that did this, for these were ages in which men went to meet death singing; it was the idea of the degradation of man in the grinning ugliness of his structure that withered the juvenile insolence of beauty and pride. And in this it almost assuredly did more good than harm. There is nothing so cold or so pitiless as youth, and youth in aristocratic stations and ages tended to an impeccable dignity, an endless summer of success which needed to be very sharply reminded of the scorn of the stars. It was well that such flamboyant prigs should be convinced that one practical joke, at least, would bowl them over, that they would fall into one grinning man-trap, and not rise again. That the whole structure of their existence was as wholesomely ridiculous as that of a pig or a parrot they could not be expected to realize; that birth was humorous, coming of age humorous, drinking and fighting humorous, they were far too young and solemn to know. But at least they were taught that death was humorous.

There is a peculiar idea abroad that the value and fascination of what we call Nature lie in her beauty. But the fact that Nature is beautiful in the sense that a dado or a Liberty curtain is beautiful is only one of her charms, and almost an accidental one. The highest and most valuable quality in Nature is not her beauty, but her generous and defiant ugliness. A hundred instances might be taken. The croaking noise of the rooks is, in itself, as hideous as the whole hell of sounds in a London railway tunnel. Yet it uplifts us like a trumpet with its coarse kindliness and honesty, and the lover in *Maud* could actually persuade himself that this abominable noise resembled his lady-love's name. Has the poet, for whom Nature means only roses and lilies, ever heard a pig grunting? It is a noise that does a man good—a strong, snorting, imprisoned noise, breaking its way out of unfathomable dungeons through every possible outlet and organ. It might be the voice of the earth itself, snoring in its mighty sleep. This is the deepest, the oldest, the most wholesome and religious sense of the value of Nature—the value which comes from her immense babyishness. She is as top-heavy, as grotesque, as solemn, and as happy as a child. The mood does come when we see all her shapes like shapes that a baby scrawls upon a slate—simple, rudimentary, a million years older and stronger than the whole disease that is called art. The objects of earth and heaven seem to combine into a nursery tale, and our relation to things seems for a moment so simple that a dancing lunatic would be needed to do justice to its lucidity and levity. The tree above my head is flapping like some gigantic bird standing on one leg; the moon is like the eye of a Cyclops. And, however much my face clouds with sombre vanity, or vulgar vengeance, or contemptible contempt, the bones of my skull beneath it are laughing for ever.

A DEFENCE OF NONSENSE

G. K. Chesterton

THERE ARE two equal and eternal ways of looking at this twilight world of ours: we may see it as the twilight of evening or the twilight of morning; we may think of anything, down to a fallen acorn, as a descendant or as an ancestor. There are times when we are almost crushed, not so much with the load of the evil as with the load of the goodness of humanity, when we feel that we are nothing but the inheritors of a humiliating splendour. But there are other times when everything seems primitive, when the ancient stars are only sparks blown from a boy's bonfire, when the whole earth seems so young and experimental that even the white hair of the aged, in the fine biblical phrase, is like almond-trees that blossom, like the white hawthorn grown in May. That it is good for a man to realize that he is "the heir of all the ages" is pretty commonly admitted; it is a less popular but equally important point that it is good for him sometimes to realize that he is not only an ancestor, but an ancestor of primal antiquity; it is good for him to wonder whether he is not a hero, and to experience ennobling doubts as to whether he is not a solar myth.

The matters which most thoroughly evoke this sense of the abiding childhood of the world are those which are really fresh, abrupt and inventive in any age; and if we were asked what was the best proof of this adventurous youth in the nineteenth century we should say, with all respect to its portentous sciences and philosophies, that it was to be found in the rhymes of Mr. Edward Lear and in the literature of nonsense. "The Dong with the Luminous Nose," at least, is original, as the first ship and the first plough were original.

It is true in a certain sense that some of the greatest writers the world has seen—Aristophanes, Rabelais and Sterne—have written nonsense; but unless we are mistaken, it is in a widely different sense. The nonsense of these men was satiric—that is to say, symbolic; it was a kind of exuberant capering round a discovered truth. There is all the difference in the world between the instinct of satire, which, seeing in the Kaiser's moustaches something typical of him, draws them continually larger and larger; and the instinct of nonsense which, for no reason whatever, imagines what those moustaches would look like on the present Archbishop of Canterbury if he grew them in a fit of absence of mind. We incline to think that no age except our own could have understood that the Quangle-Wangle meant absolutely nothing, and the Lands of the Jumblies were absolutely nowhere. We fancy that if the account of the knave's trial in *Alice in Wonderland* had been published in the seventeenth century it would have been bracketed with Bunyan's "Trial of Faithful" as a parody on the State prosecutions of the time. We fancy that if "The Dong with the Luminous Nose" had appeared in the same period everyone would have called it a dull satire on Oliver Cromwell.

It is altogether advisedly that we quote chiefly from Mr. Lear's *Nonsense Rhymes.* To our mind he is both chronologically and essentially the father of nonsense; we think him superior to Lewis Carroll. In one sense, indeed, Lewis Carroll has a great advantage. We know what Lewis Carroll was in daily life: he was a singularly serious and conventional don, universally respected, but very much of a pedant and something of a Philistine. Thus his strange double life in earth and in dreamland emphasizes the idea that lies at the back of nonsense—the idea of *escape,* of escape into a world where things are not fixed horribly in an eternal appropriateness, where apples grow on pear-trees, and any odd man you meet may have three legs. Lewis Carroll, living one life in which he would have thundered morally against any one who walked on the wrong plot of grass, and another life in which he would cheerfully call the sun green and the moon blue, was, by his very divided nature, his one foot on both worlds, a perfect type of the position of modern nonsense. His Wonderland is a country populated by insane mathematicians. We feel the whole is an escape into a world of masquerade; we feel that if we could pierce their disguises, we might discover that Humpty Dumpty and the March Hare were Professors and Doctors of Divinity enjoying a mental holiday. This sense of escape is certainly less emphatic in Edward Lear, because of the completeness of his citizenship in the world of unreason. We do not know his prosaic biography as we know Lewis Carroll's. We accept him as a purely fabulous figure, on his own description of himself:

> "His body is perfectly spherical,
> He weareth a runcible hat."

While Lewis Carroll's Wonderland is purely intellectual, Lear introduces quite another element—the element of the poetical and even emotional.

Carroll works by the pure reason, but this is not so strong a contrast; for, after all, mankind in the main has always regarded reason as a bit of a joke. Lear introduces his unmeaning words and his amorphous creatures not with the pomp of reason, but with the romantic prelude of rich hues and haunting rhythms.

> "Far and few, far and few,
>   Are the lands where the Jumblies live,"

is an entirely different type of poetry to that exhibited in "Jabberwocky." Carroll, with a sense of mathematical neatness, makes his whole poem a mosaic of new and mysterious words. But Edward Lear, with more subtle and placid effrontery, is always introducing scraps of his own elvish dialect into the middle of simple and rational statements, until we are almost stunned into admitting that we know what they mean. There is a genial ring of commonsense about such lines as,

> "For his aunt Jobiska said 'Every one knows
>   That a Pobble is better without his toes,'"

which is beyond the reach of Carroll. The poet seems so easy on the matter that we are almost driven to pretend that we see his meaning, that we know the peculiar difficulties of a Pobble, that we are as old travellers in the 'Gromboolian Plain' as he is.

Our claim that nonsense is a new literature (we might almost say a new sense) would be quite indefensible if nonsense were nothing more than a mere aesthetic fancy. Nothing sublimely artistic has ever arisen out of mere art, any more than anything essentially reasonable has ever arisen out of the pure reason. There must always be a rich moral soil for any great aesthetic growth. The principle of *art for art's sake* is a very good principle if it means that there is a vital distinction between the earth and the tree that has its roots in the earth; but it is a very bad principle if it means that the tree could grow just as well with its roots in the air. Every great literature has always been allegorical—allegorical of some view of the whole universe. The *Iliad* is only great because all life is a battle, the *Odyssey* because all life is a journey, the Book of Job because all life is a riddle. There is one attitude in which we think that all existence is summed up in the word "ghosts"; another, and somewhat better one, in which we think it is summed up in the words *A Midsummer Night's Dream*. Even the vulgarest melodrama or detective story can be good if it expresses something of the delight in sinister possibilities—the healthy lust for darkness and terror which may come on us any night in walking down a dark lane. If, therefore, nonsense is really to be the literature of the future, it must have its own version of the Cosmos to offer; the world must not only be the tragic, romantic, and religious, it must be nonsensical also. And here we fancy that nonsense will, in a very unexpected way, come to the aid of the spiritual view of things. Religion has for centuries been trying to make men exult in the "wonders" of creation, but it has forgotten that a thing cannot be completely wonderful so long as it remains sensible. So long as we regard a tree as an obvious thing, naturally and reasonably created for a giraffe to eat, we cannot properly wonder at it. It is when we consider it as a prodigious wave of the living soil sprawling up to the skies for no reason in particular that we take off our hats, to the astonishment of the park-keeper. Everything has in fact another side to it, like the moon, the patroness of nonsense. Viewed from that other side, a bird is a blossom broken loose from its chain of stalk, a man a quadruped begging on its hind legs, a house a gigantesque hat to cover a man from the sun, a chair an apparatus of four wooden legs for a cripple with only two.

This is the side of things which tends most truly to spiritual wonder. It is significant that in the greatest religious poem existent, the Book of Job, the argument which convinces the infidel is not (as has been represented by the merely rational religionism of the eighteenth century) a picture of the ordered beneficence of the Creation; but, on the contrary, a picture of the huge and undecipherable unreason of it. "Hast Thou sent the rain upon the desert where no man is?" This simple sense of wonder at the shapes of things, and at their exuberant independence of our intellectual standards and our trivial definitions, is the basis of spirituality as it is the basis of nonsense. Nonsense and faith (strange as the conjunction may seem) are the two supreme symbolic assertions of the truth that to draw out the soul of things with a syllogism is as impossible as to draw out Leviathan with a hook. The well-meaning person who, by merely studying the logical side of things, has decided that "faith is nonsense," does not know how truly he speaks; later it may come back to him in the form that nonsense is faith.

TWELVE MEN

G. K. Chesterton

THE OTHER day, while I was meditating on morality and Mr. H. Pitt, I was, so to speak, snatched up and put into a jury box to try people. The snatching took some weeks, but to me it seemed something sudden and arbitrary. I was put into this box because I lived in Battersea, and my name began with a C. Looking round me, I saw that there were also summoned and in attendance in the court whole crowds and processions of men, all of whom lived in Battersea, and all of whose names began with a C.

It seems that they always summon jurymen in this sweeping alphabetical way. At one official blow, so to speak, Battersea is denuded of all its C's, and left to get on as best it can with the rest of the alphabet. A Cumberpatch is missing from one street—a Chizzolpop from another—three Chucksterfields from Chucksterfield House; the children are crying out for an absent Cadgerboy; the woman at the street corner is weeping for her Coffintop, and will not be comforted. We settle down with a rollicking ease into our seats (for we are a bold, devil-may-care race, the C's of Battersea), and an oath is administered to us in a totally inaudible manner by an individual resembling an Army surgeon in his second childhood. We understand, however, that we are to well and truly try the case between our sovereign lord the King and the prisoner at the bar, neither of whom has put in an appearance as yet.

Just when I was wondering whether the King and the prisoner were, perhaps, coming to an amicable understanding in some adjoining public-house, the prisoner's head appears above the barrier of the dock; he is accused of stealing bicycles, and he is the living image of a great friend of mine. We go into the matter of the stealing of the bicycles. We do well and truly try the case between the King and the prisoner in the affair of the bicycles. And we come to the conclusion, after a brief but reasonable discussion, that the King is not in any way implicated. Then we pass on to a woman who neglected her children, and who looks as if somebody or something had neglected her. And I am one of those who fancy that something had.

All the time that the eye took in these light appearances and the brain passed these light criticisms, there was in the heart a barbaric pity and fear which men have never been able to utter from the beginning, but which is the power behind half the poems of the world. The mood cannot even inadequately be suggested, except faintly by this statement that tragedy is the highest expression of the infinite value of human life. Never had I stood so close to pain; and never so far away from pessimism. Ordinarily, I should not have spoken of these dark emotions at all, for speech about them is too difficult; but I mention them now for a specific and particular reason to the statement of which I will proceed at once. I speak these feelings because out of the furnace of them there came a curious realization of a political or social truth. I saw with a queer and indescribable kind of clearness what a jury really is, and why we must never let it go.

The trend of our epoch up to this time has been consistently towards specialism and professionalism. We tend to have trained soldiers because they fight better, trained singers because they sing better, trained dancers because they dance better, specially instructed laughers because they laugh better, and so on and so on. The principle has been applied to law and politics by innumerable modern writers. Many Fabians have insisted that a greater part of our political work should be performed by experts. Many legalists have declared that the untrained jury should be altogether supplanted by the trained judge. Now, if this world of ours were really what is called reasonable, I do not know that there would be any fault to find with this. But the true result of all experience and the true foundation of all religion is this. That the four or five things that it is most practically essential that a man should know, are all of them what people call paradoxes. That is to say, that though we all find them in life to be mere plain truths, yet we cannot easily state them in words without being guilty of seeming verbal contradictions. One of them, for instance, is the unimpeachable platitude that the man who finds most pleasure for himself is often the man who least hunts for it. Another is the paradox of courage; the fact that the way to avoid death is not to have too much aversion to it. Whoever is careless enough of his bones to climb some hopeless cliff above the tide may save his bones by that carelessness. Whoever will lose his life, the same shall save it; an entirely practical and prosaic statement.

Now, one of these four or five paradoxes which should be taught to every infant prattling at his mother's knee is the following: That the more a man looks at a thing, the less he can see it, and the more a man learns a thing the less he knows it. The Fabian argument of the expert, that the man who is trained should be the man who is trusted would be absolutely unanswerable if it were really true that a man who studied a thing and practised it every day went on seeing more and more of its significance. But he does not. He goes on seeing less and less of its significance. In the same way, alas! we all go on every day, unless we are continually goading ourselves into gratitude and humility, seeing less and less of the significance of the sky or the stones.

It is a terrible business to mark a man out for the vengeance of men. But it is a thing to which a man can grow accustomed, as he can to other terrible things; he can even grow accustomed to the sun. And the horrible thing about all legal officials, even the best, about all judges, magistrates, barristers, detectives, and policemen, is not that they are wicked (some of them are good), not that they are stupid (several of them are quite intelligent), it is simply that they have got used to it. Strictly they do not see the prisoner in the dock; all they see is the usual man in the usual place. They do not see the awful court of judgment; they only see their own workshop. Therefore, the instinct of Christian civilization has most wisely declared that into their judgments there shall upon every occasion be infused fresh blood and fresh thoughts from the streets. Men shall come in who can see the court and the crowd, and coarse faces of the policeman and the professional criminals, the wasted faces of the wastrels, the unreal faces of the gesticulating counsel, and see it all as one sees a new picture or a play hitherto unvisited.

Our civilization has decided, and very justly decided, that determining the guilt or innocence of men is a thing too important to be trusted to trained men. It wishes for light upon that awful matter, it asks men who know no more law than I know, but who can feel the things that I felt in the jury box. When it wants a library catalogued, or the solar system discovered, or any trifle of that kind, it uses up its specialists. But when it wishes anything done which is really serious, it collects twelve of the ordinary men standing round. The same thing was done, if I remember right, by the Founder of Christianity.

HOURS IN A LIBRARY
Virginia Woolf

LET US begin by clearing up the old confusion between the man who loves learning and the man who loves reading, and point out that there is no connexion whatever between the two. A learned man is a sedentary, concentrated, solitary enthusiast, who searches through books to discover some particular grain of truth upon which he has set his heart. If the passion for reading conquers him, his gains dwindle and vanish between his fingers. A reader, on the other hand, must check the desire for learning at the outset; if knowledge sticks to him well and good, but to go in pursuit of it, to read on a system, to become a specialist or an authority, is very apt to kill what it suits us to consider the more humane passion for pure and disinterested reading.

In spite of all this, we can easily conjure up a picture which does service for the bookish man and raises a smile at his expense. We conceive a pale, attenuated figure in a dressing-gown, lost in speculation, unable to lift a kettle from the hob, or address a lady without blushing, ignorant of the daily news, though versed in the catalogues of the secondhand booksellers, in whose dark premises he spends the hours of sunlight—a delightful character, no doubt, in his crabbed simplicity, but not in the least resembling that other to whom we would direct attention. For the true reader is essentially young. He is a man of intense curiosity; of ideas; open-minded and communicative, to whom reading is more of the nature of brisk exercise in the open air than of sheltered study; he trudges the high road, he climbs higher and higher upon the hills until the atmosphere is almost too fine to breathe in; to him it is not a sedentary pursuit at all.

But, apart from general statements, it would not be hard to prove by an assembly of facts that the great season for reading is the season between the ages of eighteen and twenty-four. The bare list of what is read then fills the heart of older people with despair. It is not only that we read so many books, but that we had such books to read. If we wish to refresh our memories, let us take down one of those old notebooks which we have all, at one time or another, had a passion for beginning. Most of the pages are blank, it is true; but at the beginning we shall find a certain number very beautifully covered with a strikingly legible handwriting. Here we have written down the names of great writers in their order of merit; here we have copied out fine passages from the classics; here are lists of books to be read; and here, most interesting of all, lists of books that have actually been read, as the reader testifies with some youthful vanity by a dash of red ink. We will quote a list of the books that someone read in a past January at the age of twenty, most of them probably for the first time. 1. *Rhoda Fleming*. 2. *The Shaving of Shagpat*. 3. *Tom Jones*. 4. *The Laodicean*. 5. Dewey's *Psychology*. 6. *The Book of Job*. 7. Webbe's *Discourse of Poesie*. 8. *The Duchess of Malfi*. 9. *The Revenger's Tragedy*. And so he goes on from month to month, until, as such lists will, it suddenly stops in the month of June. But if we follow the reader through his months it is clear that he can have done practically nothing but read. Elizabethan literature is gone through with some thoroughness; he read a great deal of Webster, Browning, Shelley, Spenser, and Congreve; Peacock he read from start to finish; and most of Jane Austen's novels two or three times over. He read the whole of Meredith, the whole of Ibsen, and a little of Bernard Shaw. We may be fairly certain, too, that the time not spent in reading was spent in some stupendous argument in which the Greeks were pitted against the moderns, romance against realism, Racine against Shakespeare, until the lights were seen to have grown pale in the dawn.

The old lists are there to make us smile and perhaps sigh a little, but we would give much to recall also the mood in which this orgy of reading was done. Happily, this reader was no prodigy, and with a little thought we can most of us recall the stages at least of our own initiation. The books we read in childhood, having purloined them from some shelf supposed to be inaccessible, have something of the unreality and awfulness of a stolen sight of the dawn coming over quiet fields when the household is asleep. Peeping between the curtains we see strange shapes of misty trees which we hardly recognize, though we may remember them all our lives; for children have a strange premonition of what is to come. But the later reading of which the above list is an example is quite a different matter. For the first time, perhaps, all restrictions have been removed, we can read what we like; libraries are at our command, and, best of all, friends who find themselves in the same position. For days upon end we do nothing but read. It is a time of extraordinary excitement and exaltation. We seem to rush about recognizing heroes. There is a sort of wonderment in our minds that we ourselves are really doing this, and mixed with it an absurd arrogance and desire to show our familiarity with the greatest human beings who have ever lived in the world. The passion for knowledge is then at its keenest, or at least most confident, and we have, too, an intense singleness of mind which the great writers gratify by making it appear that they are at one with us in their estimate of what is good in life. And as it is necessary to hold one's own against someone who has adopted Pope, let us say, instead of Sir Thomas Browne, for a hero, we conceive a deep affection for these men, and feel that we know them not as other people know them, but privately by ourselves. We are fighting under their leadership, and almost in the light of their eyes. So we haunt the old bookshops and drag home folios and quartos, Euripides in wooden boards, and Voltaire in eighty-nine volumes octavo.

But these lists are curious documents, in that they seem to include scarcely any of the contemporary writers. Meredith and Hardy and Henry James were of course alive when this reader came to them, but they were already accepted among the classics. There is no man of his own generation who influences him as Carlyle, or Tennyson, or Ruskin influenced the young of their day. And this we believe to be very characteristic of youth, for unless there is some admitted giant he will have nothing to do with the smaller men, although they deal with the world he lives in. He will rather go back to the classics, and consort entirely with minds of the very first order. For the time being he holds himself aloof from all the activities of men, and, looking at them from a distance, judges them with superb severity.

Indeed, one of the signs of passing youth is the birth of a sense of fellowship with other human beings as we take our place among them. We should like to think that we keep our standard as high as ever; but we certainly take more interest in the writings of our contemporaries and pardon their lack of inspiration for the sake of something that brings them nearer to us. It is even arguable that we get actually more from the living, although they may be much inferior, than from the dead. In the first place there can be no secret vanity in reading our contemporaries, and the kind of admiration which they inspire is extremely warm and genuine because in order to give way to our belief in them we have often to sacrifice some very respectable prejudice which does us credit. We have also to find our own reasons for what we like and dislike, which acts as a spur to our attention, and is the best way of proving that we have read the classics with understanding.

Thus to stand in a great bookshop crammed with books so new that their pages almost stick together, and the gilt on their backs is still fresh, has an excitement no less delightful than the old excitement of the secondhand bookstall. It is not perhaps so exalted. But the old hunger to know what the immortals thought has given place to a far more tolerant curiosity to know what our own generation is thinking. What do living men and women feel, what are their houses like and what clothes do they wear, what money have they and what food do they eat, what do they love and hate, what do they see of the surrounding world, and what is the dream that fills the spaces of their active lives? They tell us all these things in their books. In them we can see as much both of the mind and of the body of our time as we have eyes for seeing.

When such a spirit of curiosity has fully taken hold of us, the dust will soon lie thick upon the classics unless some necessity forces us to read them. For the living voices are, after all, the ones we understand the best. We can treat them as we treat our equals; they are guessing our riddles, and, what is perhaps more important, we understand their jokes. And we soon develop another taste, unsatisfied by the great—not a valuable taste, perhaps, but certainly a very pleasant possession—the taste for bad books. Without committing the indiscretion of naming names we know which authors can be trusted to produce yearly (for happily they are prolific) a novel, a book of poems or essays, which affords us indescribable pleasure. We owe a great deal to bad books; indeed, we come to count their authors and their heroes among those figures who play so large a part in our silent life. Something of the same sort happens in the case of the memoir writers and autobiographers, who have created almost a fresh branch of literature in our age. They are not all of them important people, but strangely enough, only the most important, the dukes and the statesmen, are ever really dull. The men and women who set out, with no excuse except perhaps that they saw the Duke of Wellington once, to confide to us their opinions, their quarrels, their aspirations and their diseases, generally end by becoming, for the time at least, actors in those private dramas with which we beguile our solitary walks and our sleepless hours. Refine all this out of our consciousness and we should be poor indeed. And then there are the books of facts and history, books about bees and wasps and industries and gold mines and Empresses and diplomatic intrigues, about rivers and savages, trade unions, and Acts of Parliament, which we always read and always, alas! forget. Perhaps we are not making out a good case for a bookshop when we have to confess that it gratifies so many desires which have apparently nothing to do with literature. But let us remember that here we have a literature in the making. From these new books our children will select the one or two by which we shall be known for ever. Here, if we could recognize it, lies some poem, or novel, or history which will stand up and speak with other ages about our age when we lie prone and silent as the crowd of Shakespeare's day is silent and lives for us only in the pages of his poetry.

This we believe to be true; and yet it is oddly difficult in the case of new books to know which are the real books and what it is that they are telling us, and which are the stuffed books which will come to pieces when they have lain about for a year or two. We can see that there are many books, and we are frequently told that every one can write nowadays. That may be true; yet we do not doubt that at the heart of this immense volubility, this flood and foam of language, this irreticence and vulgarity and triviality, there lies the heat of some great passion which only needs the accident of a brain more happily turned than the rest to issue in a shape which will last from age to age. It should be our delight to watch this turmoil, to do battle with the ideas and visions of our own time, to seize what we can use, to kill what we consider worthless, and above all to realize that we must be generous to the people who are giving shape as best they can to the ideas within them. No age of literature is so little submissive to authority as ours, so free from the dominion of the great; none seems so wayward with its gift of reverence, or so volatile in its experiments. It may well seem, even to the attentive, that there is no trace of school or aim in the work of our poets and novelists. But the pessimist is inevitable, and he shall not persuade us that our literature is dead, or prevent us from feeling how true and vivid a beauty flashes out as the young writers draw together to form their new vision, the ancient words of the most beautiful of living languages. Whatever we may have learnt from reading the classics we need now in order to judge the work of our contemporaries, for whenever there is life in them they will be casting their net out over some unknown abyss to snare new shapes, and we must throw our imaginations after them if we are to accept with understanding the strange gifts they bring back to us.

But if we need all our knowledge of the old writers in order to follow what the new writers are attempting, it is certainly true that we come from adventuring among new books with a far keener eye for the old. It seems that we should now be able to surprise their secrets; to look deep down into their work and see the parts come together, because we have watched the making of new books, and with eyes clear of prejudice can judge more truly what it is that they are doing, and what is good and what bad. We shall find, probably, that some of the great are less venerable than we thought them. Indeed, they are not so accomplished or so profound as some of our own time. But if in one or two cases this seems to be true, a kind of humiliation mixed with joy overcomes us in front of others. Take Shakespeare, or Milton, or Sir Thomas Browne. Our little knowledge of how things are done does not avail us much here, but it does lend an added zest to our enjoyment. Did we ever in our youngest days feel such amazement at their achievement as that which fills us now that we have sifted myriads of words and gone along uncharted ways in search of new forms for our new sensations? New books may be more stimulating and in some ways more suggestive than the old, but they do not give us that absolute certainty of delight which breathes through us when we come back again to *Comus,* or "Lycidas," "Urn Burial," or *Antony and Cleopatra*. Far be it from us to hazard any theory as to the nature of art. It may be that we shall never know more about it than we know by nature, and our longer experience of it teaches us this only— that of all our pleasures those we get from the great artists are indisputably among the best; and more we may not know. But, advancing no theory, we shall find one or two qualities in such works as these which we can hardly expect to find in books made within the span of our lifetime. Age itself may have an alchemy of its own. But this is true: you can read them as often as you will without finding that they have yielded any virtue and left a meaningless husk of words; and there is a complete finality about them. No cloud of suggestions hangs about them teasing us with a multitude of irrelevant ideas. But all our faculties are summoned to the task, as in the great moments of our own experience; and some consecration descends upon us from their hands which we return to life, feeling it more keenly and understanding it more deeply than before.

ADOLF

D. H. Lawrence

WHEN WE were children our father often worked on the night-shift. Once it was spring-time, and he used to arrive home, black and tired, just as we were downstairs in our night-dresses. Then night met morning face to face, and the contact was not always happy. Perhaps it was painful to my father to see us gaily entering upon the day into which he dragged himself soiled and weary. He didn't like going to bed in the spring morning sunshine.

But sometimes he was happy, because of his long walk through the dewy fields in the first daybreak. He loved the open morning, the crystal and the space, after a night down pit. He watched every bird, every stir in the trembling grass, answered the whinneying of the pee-wits and tweeted to the wrens. If he could, he also would have whinnied and tweeted and whistled, in a native language that was not human. He liked non-human things best.

One sunny morning we were all sitting at table when we heard his heavy slurring walk up the entry. We became uneasy. His was always a disturbing presence, trammeling. He passed the window darkly, and we heard him go into the scullery and put down his tin bottle. But directly he came into the kitchen. We felt at once that he had something to communicate. No one spoke. We watched his black face for a second.

"Give me a drink," he said.

My mother hastily poured out his tea. He went to pour it out into the saucer. But instead of drinking, he suddenly put something on the table, among the tea-cups. A tiny brown rabbit! A small rabbit, a mere morsel, sitting against the bread as still as if it were a made thing.

"A rabbit! A young one! Who gave it you, father?"

But he laughed enigmatically, with a sliding motion of his yellow-grey eyes, and went to take off his coat. We pounced on the rabbit.

"Is it alive? Can you feel its heart beat?"

My father came back and sat down heavily in his arm-chair. He

202

dragged his saucer to him, and blew his tea, pushing out his red lips under his black moustache.

"Where did you get it, father?"

"I picked it up," he said, wiping his naked forearm over his mouth and beard.

"Where?"

"Is it a wild one?" came my mother's quick voice.

"Yes, it is."

"Then why did you bring it?" cried my mother.

"Oh, we wanted it," came our cry.

"Yes, I've no doubt you did—" retorted my mother. But she was drowned in our clamour of questions.

On the field path, my father had found a dead mother rabbit and three dead little ones—this one alive, but unmoving.

"But what had killed them, Daddy?"

"I couldn't say, my child. I s'd think she'd eaten something."

"Why did you bring it!" again my mother's voice of condemnation. "You know what it will be."

My father made no answer, but we were loud in protest.

"He must bring it. It's not big enough to live by itself. It would die," we shouted.

"Yes, and it will die now. And then there'll be another outcry."

My mother set her face against the tragedy of dead pets. Our hearts sank.

"It won't die, father, will it? Why will it? It won't."

"I s'd think not," said my father.

"You know well enough it will. Haven't we had it all before—!" said my mother.

"They dunna always pine," replied my father testily.

But my mother reminded him of other little wild animals he had brought, which had sulked and refused to live, and brought storms of tears and trouble in our house of lunatics.

Trouble fell on us. The little rabbit sat on our lap, unmoving, its eye wide and dark. We brought it milk, warm milk, and held it to its nose. It sat as still as if it was far away, retreated down some deep burrow, hidden, oblivious. We wetted its mouth and whiskers with drops of milk. It gave no sign, did not even shake off the wet white drops. Somebody began to shed a few secret tears.

"What did I say?" cried my mother. "Take it and put it down the field."

Her command was in vain. We were driven to get dressed for school. There sat the rabbit. It was like a tiny obscure cloud. Watching it, the emotions died out of our breast. Useless to love it, to yearn over it. Its little feelings were all ambushed. They must be circumvented. Love and affection were a trespass upon it. A little wild thing, it became more mute and asphyxiated still in its own arrest, when we approached with love. We must not love it. We must circumvent it, for its own existence.

So I passed the order to my sister and my mother. The rabbit was not to be spoken to, nor even looked at. Wrapping it in a piece of flannel, I put it in an obscure corner of the cold parlour, and put a saucer of milk before its nose. My mother was forbidden to enter the parlour whilst we were at school.

"As if I should take any notice of your nonsense," she cried, affronted. Yet I doubt if she ventured into that parlour.

At midday, after school, creeping into the front room, there we saw the rabbit still and unmoving in the piece of flannel. Strange grey-brown neutralization of life, still living! It was a sore problem to us.

"Why won't it drink its milk, mother?" we whispered. Our father was asleep.

"It prefers to sulk its life away, silly little thing." A profound problem. Prefers to sulk its life away! We put young dandelion leaves to its nose. The sphinx was not more oblivious.

At tea-time, however, it had hopped a few inches, out of its flannel, and there is sat again, uncovered, a little solid cloud of muteness, brown, with unmoving whiskers. Only its side palpitated slightly with life.

Darkness came, my father set off to work. The rabbit was still unmoving. Dumb despair was coming over the sisters, a threat of tears before bed-time. Clouds of my mother's anger gathered, as she muttered against my father's wantonness.

Once more the rabbit was wrapped in the old pit-singlet. But now it was carried into the scullery and put under the copper fireplace, that it might think itself inside a burrow. The saucers were placed about, four or five, here and there on the floor, so that if the little creature should chance to hop abroad, it could not fail to come upon some food. After this my mother was allowed to take from the scullery what she wanted and then she was forbidden to open the door.

When morning came, and it was light, I went downstairs. Opening the scullery door I heard a slight scuffle. Then I saw dabbles of milk all over the floor and tiny rabbit-droppings in the saucers. And there the miscreant, the tips of his ears showing behind a pair of boots. I peeped at him. He sat bright-eyed and askance, twitching his nose and looking at me while not looking at me.

He was alive—very much alive. But still we were afraid to trespass much on his confidence.

"Father!" My father was arrested at the door. "Father, the rabbit's alive!"

"Back your life it is," said my father.

"Mind how you go in."

By evening, however, the little creature was tame, quite tame. He was christened Adolf. We were enchanted by him. We couldn't really love him, because he was wild and loveless to the end. But he was an unmixed delight.

We decided he was too small to live in a hutch—he must live at large in the house. My mother protested, but in vain. He was so tiny. So we had him upstairs, and he dropped his tiny pills on the bed and we were enchanted.

Adolf made himself instantly at home. He had the run of the house, and was perfectly happy, with his tunnels and his holes behind the furniture.

We loved him to take meals with us. He would sit on the table humping his back, sipping his milk, shaking his whiskers and his tender ears, hopping off and hobbling back to his saucer, with an air of supreme unconcern. Suddenly he was alert. He hobbled a few tiny paces, and reared himself up inquisitively at the sugar-basin. He fluttered his tiny fore-paws, and then reached and laid them on the edge of the basin, whilst he craned his thin neck and peeped in. He trembled his whiskers at the sugar, then did his best to lift down a lump.

"Do you think I will have it! Animals in the sugar pot!" cried my mother, with a rap of her hand on the table.

Which so delighted the electric Adolf that he flung his hind-quarters and knocked over a cup.

"It's your own fault, mother. If you left him alone—"

He continued to take tea with us. He rather liked warm tea. And he loved sugar. Having nibbled a lump, he would turn to the butter. There he was shooed off by our parent. He soon learned to treat her shooing with indifference. Still, she hated him to put his nose in the food. And he loved to do it. And so one day between them they overturned the cream-jug. Adolf deluged his little chest, bounced back in terror, was seized by his little ears by my mother and bounced down on the hearth-rug. There he shivered in momentary discomfort, and suddenly set off in a wild flight to the parlour.

This last was his happy hunting ground. He had cultivated the bad habit of pensively nibbling certain bits of cloth in the hearth-rug. When chased from this pasture, he would retreat under the sofa. There he would twinkle in Buddhist meditation until suddenly, no one knew why, he would go off like an alarm clock. With a sudden bumping scuffle he would whirl out of the room, going through the doorway with his little ears flying. Then we would hear his thunder-bolt hurtling in the parlour, but before we could follow, the wild streak of Adolf would flash past us, on an electric wind that swept him round the scullery and carried him back, a little mad thing, flying possessed like a ball round the parlour. After which ebullition he would sit in a corner composed and distant, twitching his whiskers in abstract meditation. And it was in vain we questioned him about his outbursts. He just went off like a gun, and was as calm after it as a gun that smokes placidly.

Alas, he grew up rapidly. It was almost impossible to keep him from the outer door.

One day, as we were playing by the stile, I saw his brown shadow loiter across the road and pass into the field that faced the houses. Instantly a cry of "Adolf!" a cry he knew full well. And instantly a wind swept him away down the sloping meadow, his tail twinkling and zig-zagging through the grass. After him we pelted. It was a strange sight to see him, ears back, his little loins so powerful, flinging the world behind him. We ran ourselves out of breath, but could not catch him. Then somebody headed him off, and he sat with sudden unconcern, twitching his nose under a bunch of nettles.

His wanderings cost him a shock. One Sunday morning my father had just been quarreling with a pedlar, and we were hearing the aftermath indoors, when there came a sudden unearthly scream from the yard. We flew out. There sat Adolf cowering under a bench, whilst a great black and white cat glowered intently at him, a few yards away. Sight not to be forgotten. Adolf rolling back his eyes and parting his strange muzzle in another scream, the cat stretching forward in a slow elongation.

Ha, how we hated that cat! How we pursued him over the chapel wall and across the neighbours' gardens. Adolf was still only half grown.

"Cats!" said my mother. "Hideous detestable animals, why do people harbour them!"

But Adolf was becoming too much for her. He dropped too many pills. And suddenly to hear him clumping downstairs when she was alone in the house was startling. And to keep him from the door was impossible. Cats prowled outside. It was worse than having a child to look after.

Yet we would not have him shut up. He became more lusty, more callous than ever. He was a strong kicker, and many a scratch on face and arms did we owe to him. But he brought his own doom on himself. The lace curtains in the parlour—my mother was rather proud of them—fell on to the floor very full. One of Adolf's joys was to scuffle wildly through them as though through some foamy undergrowth. He had already torn rents in them.

One day he entangled himself altogether. He kicked, he whirled round in a mad nebulous inferno. He screamed—and brought down the curtain-rod with a smash, right on the best beloved pelargonium, just as my mother rushed in. She extricated him, but she never forgave him. And he never forgave either. A heartless wildness had come over him.

Even we understand that he must go. It was decided; after a long delib-
eration, that my father should carry him back to the wildwoods. Once
again he was stowed into the great pocket of the pit-jacket.

"Best pop him i' th' pot," said my father, who enjoyed raising the
wind of indignation.

And so, next day, our father said that Adolf, set down on the edge of
the coppice, had hopped away with utmost indifference, neither elated
nor moved. We heard it and believed. But many, many were the heart
searchings. How would the other rabbits receive him? Would they smell
his tameness, his humanized degradation, and rend him? My mother
pooh-poohed the extravagant idea.

However, he was gone, and we were rather relieved. My father kept an
eye open for him. He declared that several times, passing the coppice in
the early morning, he had seen Adolf peeping through the nettlestalks.
He had called him, in an odd, high-voiced, cajoling fashion. But Adolf
had not responded. Wildness gains so soon upon its creatures. And they
become so contemptuous then of our tame presence. So it seemed to me.
I myself would go to the edge of the coppice, and call softly. I myself
would imagine bright eyes between the nettle-stalks, flash of a white,
scornful tail past the bracken. That insolent white tail, as Adolf turned
his flank on us! It reminded me always of a certain rude gesture, and a
certain unprintable phrase, which may not even be suggested.

But when naturalists discuss the meaning of the white rabbit's tail, that
rude gesture and still rude phrase always come to my mind. Naturalists
say that the rabbit shows his white tail in order to guide his young safely
after him, as a nurse-maid's flying strings are the signal to her toddling
charges to follow on. How nice and naïve! I only know that my Adolf
wasn't naïve. He used to whisk his flank at me, push his white feather in
my eye, and say *Merde!* It's a rude word—but one which Adolf was always
semophoring at me, flag-wagging it with all the derision of his narrow
haunches.

That's a rabbit all over—insolence, and the white flag of spiteful derision. Yes, and he keeps his flag flying to the bitter end, sporting, insolent
little devil that he is. See him running for his life. Oh, how his soul is
fanned to an ecstasy of fright, a fugitive whirlwind of panic. Gone mad,
he throws the world behind him, with astonishing hind legs. He puts
back his head and lays his ears on his sides and rolls the white of his eyes
in sheer ecstatic agony of speed. He knows the awful approach behind
him: bullet or stoat. He knows! He knows, his eyes are turned back
almost into his head. It is agony. But it is also ecstasy. Ecstasy! See the
insolent white flag bobbing. He whirls on the magic wind of terror. All
his pent-up soul rushes into agonized electric emotion of fear. He flings
himself on, like a falling star swooping into extinction. White heat of the

agony of fear. And at the same time, bob! bob! bob! goes the white tail, *merde! merde! merde!* it says to the pursuer. The rabbit can't help it. In his utmost extremity he still flings the insult at the pursuer. He is the inconquerable fugitive, the indomitible meek. No wonder the stoat becomes vindictive.

And if he escapes, this precious rabbit! Don't you see him sitting there, in his earthly nook, a little ball of silence and rabbit-triumph? Don't you see the glint on his black eye? Don't you see, in his very immobility, how the whole world is *merde* to him? No conceit like the conceit of the meek. And if the avenging angel in the shape of the ghostly ferret steals down on him, there comes a shriek of terror out of that little hump of self-satisfaction sitting motionless in a corner. Falls the fugitive. But even fallen, his white feather floats. Even in death it seems to say: "I am the meek, I am the righteous, I am the rabbit. All you rest, you are evil-doers, and you shall be *bien emmerdé.*"

DOVER·THRIFT·EDITIONS

NONFICTION

NARRATIVE OF THE LIFE OF FREDERICK DOUGLASS, Frederick Douglass. 96pp. 28499-9

SELF-RELIANCE AND OTHER ESSAYS, Ralph Waldo Emerson. 128pp. 27790-9

THE LIFE OF OLAUDAH EQUIANO, OR GUSTAVUS VASSA, THE AFRICAN, Olaudah Equiano. 192pp. 40661-X

THE AUTOBIOGRAPHY OF BENJAMIN FRANKLIN, Benjamin Franklin. 144pp. 29073-5

TOTEM AND TABOO, Sigmund Freud. 176pp. (Not available in Europe or United Kingdom.) 40434-X

LOVE: A Book of Quotations, Herb Galewitz (ed.). 64pp. 40004-2

PRAGMATISM, William James. 128pp. 28270-8

THE STORY OF MY LIFE, Helen Keller. 80pp. 29249-5

TAO TE CHING, Lao Tze. 112pp. 29792-6

GREAT SPEECHES, Abraham Lincoln. 112pp. 26872-1

THE PRINCE, Niccolò Machiavelli. 80pp. 27274-5

THE SUBJECTION OF WOMEN, John Stuart Mill. 112pp. 29601-6

SELECTED ESSAYS, Michel de Montaigne. 96pp. 29109-X

UTOPIA, Sir Thomas More. 96pp. 29583-4

BEYOND GOOD AND EVIL: Prelude to a Philosophy of the Future, Friedrich Nietzsche. 176pp. 29868-X

THE BIRTH OF TRAGEDY, Friedrich Nietzsche. 96pp. 28515-4

COMMON SENSE, Thomas Paine. 64pp. 29602-4

SYMPOSIUM AND PHAEDRUS, Plato. 96pp. 27798-4

THE TRIAL AND DEATH OF SOCRATES: Four Dialogues, Plato. 128pp. 27066-1

A MODEST PROPOSAL AND OTHER SATIRICAL WORKS, Jonathan Swift. 64pp. 28759-9

CIVIL DISOBEDIENCE AND OTHER ESSAYS, Henry David Thoreau. 96pp. 27563-9

SELECTIONS FROM THE JOURNALS (Edited by Walter Harding), Henry David Thoreau. 96pp. 28760-2

WALDEN; OR, LIFE IN THE WOODS, Henry David Thoreau. 224pp. 28495-6

NARRATIVE OF SOJOURNER TRUTH, Sojourner Truth. 80pp. 29899-X

THE THEORY OF THE LEISURE CLASS, Thorstein Veblen. 256pp. 28062-4

DE PROFUNDIS, Oscar Wilde. 64pp. 29308-4

OSCAR WILDE'S WIT AND WISDOM: A Book of Quotations, Oscar Wilde. 64pp. 40146-4

UP FROM SLAVERY, Booker T. Washington. 160pp. 28738-6

A VINDICATION OF THE RIGHTS OF WOMAN, Mary Wollstonecraft. 224pp. 29036-0